FACTUAL TELEVISION

FACTUAL TELEVISION

by

NORMAN SWALLOW

COMMUNICATION ARTS BOOKS

Hastings House, Publishers
New York

Library of Congress Catalog Card Number 65-29186

Printed 1966 in Great Britain by Billing and Sons Ltd., Guildford and London

CONTENTS

5

To the Memory
of
Cecil McGivern

PREFACE

THIS book has been written during moments snatched from the life of a practising television producer. Whether I am too close to the trees to be able to survey the forest, whether an active practitioner is indeed the proper person to attempt such an essay as this, whether the advantages of being in constant touch with its subject-matter outweigh my inability to be totally objective—these are questions which the reader will himself be able to answer. I can only say that I have found in the writing of it not only an excuse to reconsider very seriously my own attitudes to factual television, but also an opportunity to discuss the subject with many friends and colleagues at a length which had hitherto been denied either by my own laziness or the limitations imposed upon people who are normally too busy to consider anything beyond the problems of the moment.

The only claim which I can honestly make for this book is that it fairly represents the approach to the techniques and purpose of factual television of someone who has himself worked in it as a writer, producer, and director for sixteen years. I have quoted at length from the written or spoken words of other writers, producers, and television executives, but I have deliberately excluded the views of those who have written much about television without having themselves adopted it as a profession—critics, students, and those who have found in it a subject for serious academic study. To have included the opinions of such people would have shifted the book's perspective and introduced moments of objectivity into a work whose only merit must be that it was written out of the experience of men who devote their working lives to the making of television programmes.

The definitive book about factual television has yet to appear, though Dr A. William Bluem's *Documentary in American Tele-*

vision is a splendid example of what can be done in a deliberately limited field. When it comes to be written it will no doubt be the work of someone who has either devoted many years to the study of television or else has himself retired from it after a lifetime of hard experience. My own modest offering is merely an interim report from a corner of the battlefield.

I do not claim to have seen even the majority of factual programmes produced by the television organisations of my own country, though I have always tried to see those which can reasonably claim to be 'important'. One of the frustrations of making programmes yourself is that you get precious little time to watch the work of your colleagues, but I have done my best. If a programme of significance has been omitted from these pages it is because, for one reason or another, I have not seen it. Moreover I calculate that some five thousand British factual programmes have been transmitted between the moment when I wrote the first word of this book and the day when the completed book was made available to the public. The author of an essay on the cinema or the theatre does not suffer from this particular problem. Moreover, because I regard it as exceedingly immoral to discuss what I have never seen, I have made reference only to those programmes with which I am familiar. Now and then I have taken the liberty of referring to my own work, not because it has any particular merit but because it has occasionally seemed relevant to a specific point which I have wanted to make.

Because of television's enormous output this book was in a sense out of date even before it was completed. Indeed by an unhappy chance its completion coincided with the withdrawal from British screens of several 'regular' programmes which had long been part of the established pattern of things, and which I have felt obliged to discuss at length in these pages: *World in Action*, *Gallery*, *Tonight* and *Monitor*. It is too soon, as I write these words, to comment on their successors, and therefore I must ask my readers to accept this book as an analysis of factual television as it was in the summer of 1965.

Many friends have generously spared precious time to help me. Among them are *Kenneth Adam, David Attenborough, James Bredin, Richard Cawston, Geoffrey Cox, Robin Day, Donald Edwards, Kenneth Fawdrey, Denis Forman, Paul Fox, Grace Wyndham Goldie, Helmut Hammerschmidt, Barrie*

12

Heads, Tim Hewat, Jeremy Isaacs, Paul Johnstone, Ronald Kelly, Alex Kendrick, Ludovic Kennedy, William K. McClure, Denis Mitchell, Peter Morley, Jeremy Murray-Brown, John Ormond, Michael Reddington, Robert Reid, and Professor Richard Titmuss. I owe my grateful thanks to all these and many others, as well as to those television organisations and individuals who have so kindly provided me with access to whatever facts I chanced to seek. I would also like to put on record my thanks to the *Society of Film and Television Arts* for its goodwill and its practical assistance.

I need hardly say that the opinions in this book are my own, and no one else should be held responsible for them. Finally I must express my gratitude to *Maureen Kerr*, not only for so capably finding her way through a diffuse and sometimes incoherent manuscript, but also for insisting, with a charmingly firm tact, that I kept to my timetable.

There is one name which I could not bring myself to mention within the pages of this book, for fear of distorting, however slightly and unintentionally, his opinion. He was the man who brought me into television, whose leadership, wisdom, and humanity were always a profound inspiration, and to whom every television producer in Europe—and indirectly throughout the whole world—owes a profound debt which may not always be as conscious as it is to those of us who were privileged to work with him so closely. I have taken the liberty of dedicating this tentative essay to his memory, in the hope that although there must be much in it with which he would have argued fiercely, there may here and there be distant echoes of the attitudes which he tried to instil in those who served under him.

NORMAN SWALLOW

TELEVISION AND WORLD AFFAIRS

" *D URING today"*, writes Donald Edwards. editor of news and current affairs at the BBC, *"well over twenty million people will listen to at least one radio news bulletin. Television news bulletins, either BBC or ITN, will have been seen by more than thirty million. The news audience exceeds the circulations of all daily newspapers in London and the provinces put together."*

A recent survey asked people, "How do you mainly get the news—from newspapers or from television?" Two-thirds said they got it from television.

Sir William Haley, the present editor of *The Times* (London), and a former director-general of the BBC, once wrote :

"It has been the primary conception of British broadcasting ever since it decided to speak to peoples beyond its borders, that it would pour through the world, hour by hour, day by day, and year by year, an unending, undeviating, irrigating flow of truthful news as objectively and impartially as British professional men and women could make it."

Those quotations are a fair summary of the main characteristics of television news as currently presented in the United Kingdom. It has a larger audience than either newspapers or sound-radio, and it strives to achieve complete impartiality. The size of its audience makes it powerful, and its power demands, in a responsible society, that it should be impartial.

The Impartiality of Television News

Every television-producing country has its news programmes. The world's 'newscasters' are the personal friends of the world's families, the men and women on whom we rely increasingly for our information on national and international affairs. Those whose faces appear on our domestic screens to describe, with as many accompanying pictures as their employers' resources and talents allow, the events of the past hours are certainly as familiar and possibly as important as the images of monarchs, presidents, and prime ministers.

This apparent reliability—in truth it is, of course, a relative thing, varying from place to place and reflecting the honesty or otherwise of the local system of government—is one of the reasons for the startling success of television's invasion of the Fourth Estate.

Television news, always and everywhere, *seems* to be much more honest than the national press; indeed it *is* more honest in countries where both media enjoy freedom from the interference of governments.

In Britain both the BBC and the ITA are independent organisations, and national news on the ITA has always been produced by Independent Television News. In the USA, as in the provincial bulletins of Independent Television in Britain, commercial programme companies have always been careful to preserve a similar objectivity in their news programmes. In what is sometimes known, mysteriously, as 'the free world', news, next to education, is the most honourable and the least corrupt form of television, apparently uninfluenced by the pressures of advertisers and the glances of governments.

The Influence of Television Comment

Facts are sacred, we are told, but comment is free, and television has its programmes of comment, as well as its programmes of 'straight' news: *CBS Reports, NBC's White Paper, Meet the Press, Eyewitness to History, Twentieth Century, Cinq Colonnes à la Une, Panorama* (one in Britain and one in Germany), *Tonight, This Week, Enquiry, Gallery, World in Action, Report, The Four Corners, Division*. The success of these programmes can be measured by the size of their audiences, which in its turn is a fair measure of their social and political impact. The average audience of *CBS Reports* in 1964, for example, was ten million. *Cinq Colonnes*, transmitted on the last Friday of each month, also had an audience of ten million. *Report*, a co-production of Stuttgart, Munich, and Cologne, claimed eight million viewers a week in 1964; in Britain *Panorama* was seen by ten million people every Monday, *This Week* by eleven million, and *World in Action* by ten million.[1] The equivalent of these programmes in the field of written journalism would be the *New Statesman* or the *Spectator*; the British circulation of the former is 90,000 and of the latter about 50,000.

Not only do television current affairs programmes have a big audience, very often at peak hours, but they have an influence which cannot be assessed by a mere mathematical calculation. They help to form public opinion, they ventilate matters of social and political concern, and occasionally, if we are to believe what has sometimes been written of them, they appear to threaten the very fabric of politics by assuming the functions of Parliament.

When Britain was threatened with a national rail strike in the autumn of 1962 the Minister of Transport confronted the General Secretary of the National Union of Railwaymen in *Panorama* before they had officially met one another in the more usual atmosphere of a conference chamber, Richard Dimbleby, who chaired their argument, was later accused of assuming the duties of the Minister of Labour.

Edward R. Murrow's brave exposure of McCarthy in *See it Now* in 1954 proved for the first time that the Senator from Wisconsin was vulnerable after all, and set an example that other liberals, as honest as Murrow but not apparently so courageous, wasted no time in copying.

Report's item on the *Der Spiegel* affair was one of the most courageous examples of frank journalism in any medium within the past few years. In 1961 *CBS Reports* transmitted its *Biography of a Bookie Joint*, a 'revelation of the operations of an illegal gambling establishment in Boston, filmed from the inside as well as the outside', and the immediate consequence was an official investigation into gambling in Boston.

It was a fearless 'live' interview by John Freeman which began the chain of enquiries that finally resulted in the public exposure of Communist infiltration into the Executive Committee of the Electrical Trades Union. On more than one occasion the producers of *Cinq Colonnes*, assuming that they too were citizens of the 'free world', have expressed a most righteous indignation at the powers of censorship used by de Gaulle's Minister

---

[1] There are no comparative figures which are accepted both by the BBC and ITV. These estimates are based on what I hope is a fair reading of the BBC's Audience Research and TAM.

of Information—proof, at least, that television journalism is powerful enough to be politically embarrassing.

Because of the size of its audience, because of its access to the world's leading figures (who these days appear to be queueing up to tell the public what is going on in their policies and their minds), and because of the flexibility of its technical resources, television has in the past decade taken over from the press, the radio, and the cinema, the role of the principal mass-informer; and this phenomenon alone would justify its claim to be the most powerful single contributor to the culture of the twentieth century.

The Dictates of Policy

In Britain, North America, and most of Western continental Europe, television organisations are either asked or obliged to pursue a policy of objectivity in their news programmes and impartiality in their programmes of comment. They cannot express an editorial line of their own, and it is their duty to preserve a balance of opposing forces. The British Government's standing directions to the BBC contain these words: "The Postmaster General . . . relies upon the Corporation to carry on its existing policy of treating controversial subjects with complete impartiality." Not only the BBC: when Granada chose to make in its *World in Action* series a programme which the Defence Correspondent of the *Guardian* called "an indignant description of the waste of vast sums or the apparent waste of vast sums on defence" the ITA refused to sanction its transmission, and to this day it has not been seen in its entirety.

The position is similar in the United States, where the Television Code of the National Association of Radio and Television Broadcasters laid down this broad directive on the handling of "controversial public issues":

"Television provides a valuable forum for the expression of responsible views on public issues of a controversial nature. In keeping therewith the television broadcaster should seek out and develop with accountable individuals, groups, and organisations, programmes relating to controversial public issues of import to its fellow citizens; and to give fair representation to opposing sides of issues which materially affect the life or welfare of a substantial segment of the public."

18

CBS could boldly transmit Ed Murrow's indictment of Senator McCarthy, but they allowed the Senator the right of reply, at equal length, in a later programme. During the Suez Crisis of 1956 both the BBC and the ITA had to tread with skill the tightrope between the policy of the Eden government and the fierce opposition of the Labour Party and at least half the nation.

Impartiality might seem a dull and restrictive policy, a great deal less exciting than the biased junketings of newspapers, which can wear their allegiance openly on their sleeves. Yet it is difficult to see how any other policy could possibly be acceptable to television organisations that are free of party loyalties and have in their hands the most powerful weapon of communication that the world has so far invented. The impartiality must be endured, in the knowledge that any other attitude would be altogether too dangerous.

It can even be made into a social virtue, and the positive side of impartiality as a policy is well expressed by Donald Edwards:

"If broadcasting is to reflect the nation we must include matters in dispute. We must communicate the views of others, however distasteful or embarrassing it may be to some. This is our duty as honest reporters. The public is entitled to the truth as interpreted by all sides—and so, on behalf of the public, we put probing, searching questions to Cabinet Ministers, railway chiefs, industrial bosses—all 'them who push us around'. The public have not the opportunity of putting the questions themselves. We do it for them. Of course it is wrong to interview aggressively, to behave like prosecuting counsel hectoring a witness. But we have the right, on behalf of the public, to probe the evasive and expose the misleading."

Aspects of Impartiality

Impartiality, therefore, need be far from dull. But it is also, in the strictest sense, impossible. Indeed there are many spheres of public and social life in which the television services of the western world have cheerfully, if discreetly, abandoned it, and no one has apparently complained. A foreign visitor to Britain or the USA, who for a few months regularly watched television's coverage of public affairs, might justifiably conclude that their combined television organisations shared a common and positive viewpoint on many of the major issues of the day. They are

19

apparently anti-Fascist, anti-Communist, opposed to racial intolerance and violent crime, highly critical of the governments of the USSR, Communist China, Cuba, Spain, Portugal, South Africa, and Eastern Europe, Christian (especially in Britain) but tolerant of agnostics, friendly towards surviving monarchies, hostile to most social and political cranks, suspicious of professional politicians (but nevertheless enticing them into their studios as often as possible), and supporters of 'the wind of change' as long as it never reaches gale force.

It is the ambition of many, perhaps most, current affairs producers on both sides of the Atlantic to widen even farther the territory where partiality is permitted, for the best current affairs producer is probably a radical—which means that he can be a Conservative just as easily as a Socialist—and he is certainly a man who himself holds firm political convictions. If he has no convictions of this sort it means that he cares little for the material prosperity of mankind; and if he cares little about that, then he will be a bad producer and should turn his attention to matters that require less personal involvement, such as horticulture.

It is one of the ironies of television that its current affairs producers should at the same time be men and women with strong personal convictions, and also be able to resist the constant temptation to parade those convictions in public. They have in truth been remarkably successful in combining an involvement in the social and political struggles of the day with a lack of bias in the way they handle them, with the result that in those countries which are democracies in practice as well as in theory current affairs programmes are generally regarded as fairer and more honest than the daily newspaper or the weekly magazine.

Television has set new standards in journalistic integrity, and it has made hysteria seem ludicrous. It has also performed a valuable service in preventing the suppression of news. Geoffrey Cox, Editor of Independent Television News, says:

"Television, because of its objectivity and impartiality, has no excuse for suppressing any news item which is important or in the public interest. And once television has covered a story it is impossible for a newspaper to suppress it. To take a specific instance; a few years ago, at the Conservative Conference at

Blackpool, there was a fight which followed the interruptions of the League of Empire Loyalists. This was kept dark by some of the newspapers the next day. But we, and the BBC, showed it as recorded by our cameras in the hall. After that, the papers which had neglected it began to write of it. I think this is one way in which television has improved the quality of news reporting."

Impartiality, in television, like chastity in fiancées, is much admired but hard to sustain. It is constantly subjected to the pressures of those for whom the objective truth is a thing to be concealed at all costs. The pressures of the sponsor, in those places where direct sponsorship is the accepted method of financing programmes, is something to be expected. Within the terms of reference set by western capitalist society it is perfectly fair, indeed open and honourable. When the Aluminium Corporation of America withdrew its sponsorship of *See it Now* there were a few voices raised in anger, but none in surprise.

Moreover, it is due to the demands of sponsors that so many public affairs programmes in the United States are placed at 'off peak' viewing times. Indeed on several occasions programmes of a strictly 'informational' sort have been withdrawn altogether because of the failure to find a sponsor. There was, for example, the much-quoted CBS series *The Search*, which visited colleges and research establishments, cost over half a million dollars, and was taken off after twenty-six weeks because a sponsor was never found for it. Yet it is too easy, especially for someone writing in Britain where the hazards of sponsorship are unknown, to regard the American system as altogether restrictive—a naïve attitude that is in any case amply disproved by the record of NBC and CBS in the field of controversial programmes.

Fred W. Friendly, formerly the executive producer of *CBS Reports*, writes very firmly that

"No sponsor ever sees CBS Reports before it is broadcast, or has any voice in its content. The fact that such important businesses as the Travellers Insurance Company encourage and underwrite our editorial integrity is, I believe, an eloquent testimonial to the health of the television system this country enjoys."

Far more dangerous than the attitude of the sponsor, because they are also devious and hidden, are the pressures which every television producer of current affairs programmes has to face every day of his life from organisations and individuals who have no official relationship with television, but who stand to gain or lose a great deal by what they would call, or pretend to call (for it is sometimes difficult to distinguish what they say from what they mean), the 'bias' of his programmes.

We live in the age of the public relations officer, and the path of the television producer in his innocent search for facts is littered by highly trained gentlemen whose concern is to sell the interests of their masters, and to prevent, by whatever means occur to them, the transmission of any fact or idea that seems to contradict those interests. Political parties have their PROs and so do commercial empires. Government departments, filled with permanent civil servants and therefore apparently as immortal as they are theoretically objective, prefer the phrase 'information officer'. There are PROs (or IOs) of religions, trade unions, business empires, educational establishments, armies and navies, museums and art galleries, football teams, local authorities, and the Police.

Television organisations also have PROs, and sometimes even more sinister IOs, so that getting the truth from a television company is almost as hard a task as it is for the television company to find the truth about anything else.

Every Government, of course, has its own 'information' service, and is constantly concerned that its doings are presented to the watching world in a favourable light. When its assistance is sought by television organisations, as it frequently must be, it uses every opportunity, quietly and courteously, to direct the producer into the 'proper' channels, to introduce him to the 'best informed people', and generally to indulge in some gentle brain-washing (the producer knows this, of course, and the game that results from their mutual knowledge of each other's intentions has its delicious moments for both parties, quite apart from resulting in the amiable consumption of much food and drink).

When a television programme is shown which is not to a Government's liking, that Government will be quick, through its IOs, to make its protests known. The London office of the South African Government did so when the BBC announced its intention of showing the CBS programme *Sabotage in South Africa*. British *Panorama* items have been the cause of publicly expressed protests from the Governments of India, Portugal, and the United Arab Republic.

When a Government concerned feels itself to be slighted beyond endurance it can resort to the ultimate weapon—refusal to allow the personnel of the offending programme to enter its boundaries in the future, and this has happened, to my personal knowledge, in the case of India, the UAR, Spain, and East Germany. The television producer has his own answer to this, which is to smuggle his reporter and his technicians into the protesting country in the guise of tourists, for a 16 mm camera is fortunately an accepted part of the normal tourist's baggage in the mid-twentieth century.

I am making this point at length because I believe it to be a fundamental part of any discussion on the policy background to television current affairs. Granted that impartiality is the only acceptable policy that a television organisation can fairly adopt in a democracy, how can it be achieved in the face of so many powerful pressure groups for whom the complete truth is an unpleasantness which should be concealed? The answer to that question is the known record of the best regular current affairs programmes in those countries which still believe in granting freedom to their media of information.

I have already mentioned several splendid examples of outspoken television journalism, and to those I would now add a few more; NBC's 'White Paper' on segregation, called *Sit-in*, and the CBS report on the same theme, *Who Speaks for Birmingham?*; from Britain, Granada's series *World in Action* has included courageous programmes on Spain, the *Lakonia* disaster, and Moral Rearmament; *Panorama* can boast a fearless examination of the problem of London's homeless, a quite brilliant report by James Mossman from the Yemen, an interview with Georges Bidault in London at a time when the British Home Office denied that he was in the country, a brave exposé by David Dimbleby of the Ku Klux Klan, and several frank expeditions to South Africa, Eastern Europe, Algeria, Cuba, and Asia. It was *This Week* which first exposed the somewhat peculiar ways in which British troops were spending their time in Ger-

23

many, and it was *CBS Reports* which openly reminded the nation of the state of its migratory farm workers in *Harvest of Shame* (a programme which the US Government vainly tried to dissuade the BBC from screening in Britain).

Comparing the Records

Any discussion of the policy background to television news and current affairs should concern itself not only with the attitude of television organisations to programme content—their acceptance of objectivity in news and impartiality in controversy—but also with the degree of importance that they attach to such programmes, as measured by the number of transmissions, the amount of money spent on them, and the times of day or night when they are shown. To take an extreme and fortunately fictitious example, a company that paid lip-service to the value of current affairs television, and openly accepted the 'impartiality' doctrine, could hardly be described as having a serious policy in this field if it produced only one public affairs programme a month, spent £200 on it, and showed it for ten minutes at eleven o'clock at night. What, in fact, is the position?[1]

In Britain the BBC in the spring of 1965, presented on its first network a weekly average of four hours of news and six hours and twenty minutes of comment and controversy. Its main daily news bulletin ran for ten minutes and was shown at 9.15 pm. It had three regular 'magazine' programmes of comment: *Panorama*, for fifty minutes each Monday from 8.25 pm, *Gallery* every Thursday during those weeks when Parliament was sitting, lasting thirty minutes and starting at varying times between 10 pm and 10.30 pm; and *Tonight*, every evening from Monday to Friday from 6.55 to 7.30 pm. BBC-2 had a fortnightly series called *Enquiry*, which ran for thirty minutes from 8 pm; a weekly series of public affairs 'interviews', *Encounter*, for half an hour at 7.30 pm each Thursday; and a twenty-five minute parliamentary report, *Westminster at Work*, towards the end of each Friday evening. The same channel's *Newsroom*, every night, was at varying times and of varying lengths, though it was always both later and longer than the main bulletin on

---

[1] Television programme schedules change rapidly. My analysis was made in the spring of 1965. *World in Action* has now ceased, *Tonight* has been renamed *24 Hours* and is later in the evening, and there is no *Gallery*.

24

BBC-1. In addition each 'region' of the BBC presented its own news magazine programme at 6.10 pm on weekdays.

There were also regional variations in the output of the ITA, but the viewer to Channel Nine in London could see some two and three-quarter hours of 'straight' news every week, and nearly three hours of public affairs other than news. The main nightly news programme ran for fifteen minutes from 8.55 pm during every weekday and, like the BBC's principal bulletin, tended to be later and shorter at weekends. The most important programmes of comment were *Dateline*, running late at night for ten minutes from Monday to Friday, and produced by Independent Television News; *World in Action* (Granada) for thirty minutes at 10.05 pm for thirty-six Tuesdays in the year; *This Week* (Rediffusion) every Thursday between 9.10 pm and 9.40 pm; *ITN Reports* which 'surveys the big news stories of the week in depth' for half an hour towards the end of every Thursday evening; *What the Papers Say* (Granada) for a quarter of an hour at about 10.35 pm on Thursdays and *Division* (Rediffusion), a weekly report on "politics and people", for half an hour towards the end of each Tuesday.

My broad conclusion is not at all unexpected. It is that the best record in the field of current affairs is held by the independent public corporation. The BBC not only produces more regular current affairs programmes than any other single organisation but, significantly, it shows them at a more popular time. If one assumes (though I admit that such assumptions are personal) that the 'peak' viewing hours are between seven and ten o'clock in the evening, it appeared that the BBC presented on its first channel three and three-quarter hours of public affairs programmes (other than news) at times which in a commercial organisation would be the most valuable, and which can be relied upon to attract the largest audience; and this record becomes even more impressive when one considers the additional output of the BBC's second channel. The record of the British commercial network was less glorious; *This Week*, lasting thirty minutes, was the only regular programme of comment placed during the 'peak' period, though *World in Action* missed it by only five minutes. In the USA the position was as bad; of the three main national networks only one, CBS, allowed a major public affairs series to be seen at peak times. *CBS Reports* was accurately described in 1964 by its producers as "network television's only regularly scheduled public affairs programme in prime evening time".

The BBC does not perhaps deserve too much praise for its position of eminence, for after all it is the job of a public corporation to behave in this way. Nor do I wish to imply that individual producers in the BBC are men of greater public spirit than their colleagues elsewhere. Such an assumption would be false, for—as anyone knows who has worked himself in this field—many of the finest current affairs producers in the world are working for commercial companies. The truth is that whereas the BBC has an obligation to behave as it does, the attitude of commercial companies to what has always been regarded (though not quite accurately) as 'minority material' depends entirely on the outcome of the conflict between their respect for their public consciences and their fascination with their bank accounts. Some companies have a better record than others.

For the BBC, Donald Edwards has written:

"I am sometimes asked: Should the BBC give the public what it wants or what it ought to have? I cannot better the answer of our first Director-General, now Lord Reith. He said, 'Few know what they want and very few what they need.'

"We try to achieve a balance between what the public wants and what the maturer members of the public need. We are both people's television and public service television. We think of majorities but we think also of minorities. We try to be ahead of public taste. Not too far ahead or the public will not listen. Just enough ahead to tempt them on to higher and wider interests.

"If we had planned our programmes only for a mass audience there would never have been a Panorama. When we first put it on, we deliberately sacrificed mass ratings. But little by little we stimulated public interest, and now over ten million watch it."

This is surely an important point. It is not only, as Donald Edwards implies, that audiences can be 'trained' to enjoy serious programmes, but also that a new generation is growing up which actively *wants* such programmes. Current affairs television, like so much else in the world of entertainment, has sometimes suffered from the impresario's tendency to underrate his audience, to play safe until the point where the public has

26

not only caught up with him but is way ahead of him. Geoffrey Cox puts it this way:

"There was a time, quite recently, when many of the people running television used to describe it as 'Show business with a tiny bit of journalism'. Today they call it 'Show business and journalism'. Soon they'll have to admit that it's become 'journalism and show business'. There's a real sense in which television has become increasingly like a twenty-odd page newspaper, in which information on what is going on in the world comes first, and comment and feature pieces second, with the pure entertainment programmes taking the place of the short story, the gossip page, and the strip cartoon."

It is because of this development, which nobody can stop however hard they try, that news and current affairs is today almost certainly television's main programme function, just as for a long time past it has been its principal social obligation.

Television matters, because in the confused, dangerous, and exciting world in which we live, real information matters. As Fred Friendly writes:

"Every day there is more for the people of the world to know; and every day, what we don't know can kill us."

TELEVISION NEWS

THE most curious thing about television news in Britain is that it came so late. Before the second world war the BBC's television service relied for its news on the screening of newsreels made for the cinemas. After the war the hostility of the competitive film industry forced it to fulfil its own need, but for most of six more years its imagination was limited to a carbon copy of what the cinemas had traditionally provided. Most of the stories were shot with a silent film camera, all of them were on 35 mm film (as opposed to the cheaper and more portable 16 mm), and the backing to the unseen reader's voice was rarely anything better than canned mood music.[1] Those British television viewers who really cared about world events and wanted to know of the latest developments in political situations which could conceivably result in either the salvation or the destruction of mankind were obliged to switch off their television sets and turn to sound radio. Until July 1954 BBC news meant sound-radio news.

Taking Over from Sound

This odd state of affairs was bound to change. Indeed it could never have survived the day when the audiences for television exceeded those for radio—and certainly it could never have lived into the age of ITN. That it had lasted so long was presumably due in part to the fact that the BBC in terms of staffing, capital expenditure, and allocation of programme money, remained for many years after the end of the war a sound-radio organisation, and partly to the public's happy acceptance of the familiar newsreel format. When the change at last came, the BBC had this to say of it:

[1] I am being a little unfair, in my generalisation, to the work of Richard Cawston and Paul Fox, who, before the newsreel came off the air for ever, had begun to inject into it a new relevance, both in content and technique.

28

"News and Newsreel . . . *aims at giving the public in the United Kingdom as comprehensive an illustrated service of news as is possible within the limitations imposed by the existing sources of illustration and their availability. It is hoped that eventually this service will be the equal in scope of that which has been given in sound for many years.*

"The Corporation intends to secure world-wide sources of news in pictures, rather in the same way that it has secured sources in words. . . . Eventually, perhaps, there will be little more delay in receiving moving pictures of happenings in some parts of the world than there now is in getting words. The full potentialities of television in this field are only beginning to suggest themselves."

Yet when the change had taken place, and *News and Newsreel* (that second word died reluctantly and unmourned a year later) was on the air, there were spontaneous complaints from both critics and audiences that the new service was both amateur and dull, and nothing more than illustrated radio. The charge of amateurism was sometimes true, if scarcely surprising at that time, and the dullness of the visuals was one of the consequences of being up to the minute.

We have travelled far since the summer of 1954. Fourteen months later ITN began its life as the organisation which provides British independent television stations with their daily programmes of national and international news. Those stations —or some of them—presented their own local news, and so did the regional stations of the BBC. Today in Britain as in the United States and in many countries of Europe, the public relies on television for its basic information about national and international affairs. TV cameramen have taken over the old functions of the still photographer and the cameramen working for the cinema newsreels; they were on the spot in Suez in 1956, in the Congo in 1960, in Cuba in 1962, in Cyprus in 1964, in Viet-Nam in 1965. Whenever a public figure, politician or scientist or entertainer, arrives at an international airport he is immediately confronted by television reporters and television cameras.

The BBC today has fifty staff reporters, working both for radio and television, in places as far apart as Washington and New Delhi, Cape Town and Berlin, Nairobi and Aberdeen. In every continent there are teams of independent cameramen, all

29

earning a good living by feeding news stories into TV networks. The BBC has a permanent live studio at Westminster, within yards of the Houses of Parliament.

When President Kennedy was assassinated the world's television news resources converged on Dallas and on Washington in the largest single news-getting operation in the history of journalism. When the fight for the Heavyweight Championship of the World was fought in Florida between Clay and Liston it was shown live in Britain by relay satellite at six o'clock in the morning, and the British Electricity Authority registered an increased national load of 100,000 kilowatts, equal to the full output of a big power station.

Two things can be said with certainty of news by television: that its audience exceeds the readership of the national newspapers put together, and does so by a margin that, throughout the world, increases every year; and that it has brought the public into a closer contact with daily events and with the people who cause them than has so far been possible in any other medium.

In the course of its brief life television news has hammered out its own techniques. What are they, and how are they used?

Television News Presentation

There are five ways in which a story can be presented in a television news programme:

1. By a newscaster speaking in vision, and directly facing the studio camera.
2. By film, either shot for the purpose at the scene of the story, or else taken from the film library.
3. By recorded videotape.
4. By live cameras from the scene of the story.
5. By the use of stills in the studio. These stills may be photographs or diagrams or maps.

Each of these methods has its appropriate uses, and each deserves separate analysis.

The Newscaster

News on sound-radio, at least in the United Kingdom, has traditionally been read. Experienced readers have spoken from a written text, and they have departed from it at their peril.

They were voices rather than human beings, and their voices were sufficiently neutral for one to suspect now and then that they were creatures without either emotions or normal bodily functions. During the war they grew names—for security reasons—and after the war they lost them again. Today, and without doubt because of the humanising influence of television, they possess their names once more.

The public apparently accepted without complaint the old nameless voices, because their enunciation was always admirably clear, and because a voice that is without personality or emotion cannot possibly display anything as off-beat as a personal bias. The BBC's world-wide reputation for truth in its news bulletins rested to a considerable extent on the fact that the news was at no point allowed to be filtered by anything resembling a human being.

Things are different in television, and I believe the basic reason is that whereas a mere voice can be as mechanical as a computer, the addition of a face at once introduces an indestructible element of humanity. A news reader in television could never be as remote and impersonal as his colleague in sound broadcasting.

The newscaster is a compromise between the radio reader and the personal performer, possessing the objectivity of the former and the humanity of the latter. He is someone to be known as a friend, visiting one's sitting-room every night, and also someone who seemingly possesses the gift of being able to absorb all of the day's news, and then select those parts of it which are important. Television news, therefore, shares with sound-radio the merit of seeming to be honest and true, but it also adds an ingredient of humanity. The news reader is a machine; the newscaster is a man.

ITN, which from its conception has taken the lead in the development of the British newscaster, puts it this way:

"The news is presented not by readers but by newscasters—that is by men of personality and authority. But they are not just personalities. They are above all working journalists, whose authority stems from professional experience and skill, and who do their share of gathering and writing the news, as well as presenting it. This adds an invaluable element of strength and vitality to television news broadcasting."

31

Geoffrey Cox, himself a firm believer in the newscaster, says this:

"One of the basic problems about television news is that in a given period of time you can fit in only a few items—say twenty in ten minutes, at most. Radio can use more stories in the same number of minutes, and of course the newspaper can include more still. The newscaster is one good solution, psychologically, to the problem of giving impact to the spoken news. For the newscaster is a man who is well known to the audience, whose authority and integrity is respected by them. He is the man who appears on the screen, and seems to say 'Now from the dozens of news items that have come my way today, these are the ones that I believe are important.' In other words, he is a person who must be immediately trusted, not only to tell the truth, but to select those stories that are really important. Clearly it helps him to do this if he can write, or at least re-write, his own material, and it is an advantage if he is himself a practising journalist. For a newscaster is a man who is personally associated with the news he presents. He is not, and never can be, a depersonalised being, as it were, from outer space."

The newscaster is the man (and almost always, incidentally, a man, for the notion of a pretty young woman announcing a revolution or a sudden death is regarded as highly inappropriate) who holds the news programme together. His is almost always the first face seen on the screen, and invariably the last. To some extent, therefore, each individual programme assumes the style and 'image' of the newscaster on duty at the time, without of course allowing him to dominate it. The total time of a newscaster's appearance within a single programme will vary considerably. In a programme which carries its main stories in the form of film coverage shot overseas he will be seen and heard only rarely, but he will play a much bigger part in a bulletin which includes several stop press items that he alone can handle, together with a studio interview or two which he might himself conduct. The BBC, which even in its news still leans towards the news*reader*, allows him to speak the commentary behind some of the filmed stories, but ITN prefers to hand this job over to a second and unseen voice. Similarly the extent to which the newscaster is permitted an opinion of his own depends on an interpretation of the impartiality policy which varies from station to station. Newscasters seem to be allowed greater freedom in the USA than Britain, and rather more freedom in ITN than in the BBC. In their book, *Television and Radio News,*[1] three American newsmen, Bob Siller (ABC), Ted White (NBC), and Hal Terkel (CBS), make a pertinent comment on the work of NBC's two principal newscasters, Chet Huntley and David Brinkley:

"NBC News *allows its commentators a certain leeway that is comparatively new to network broadcasting. It does not permit outright editorialising, but commentator opinion is allowed. It must be pointed out, however, that* NBC News *hires only seasoned newsmen with substantial experience as its commentators. The commentators must identify all opinion as such, and may express it only when opinion is considered to be integral to coverage of a news story."*

The extent to which the anchor man in a news programme, whether he be called a newscaster, newsreader, or news commentator, shall be allowed to be anything more than a man who, however efficiently and with whatever personal style, merely tells us the important news of the day, is a fundamental argument that is never likely to be resolved to everybody's satisfaction. Too much depends on the local News Editor, on the broad policy of the station for which he works, and on the experience and reputation of the man himself. But almost all those who work in television news would agree that as long as the attitude of 'objectivity' is adequately sustained, it adds to the effectiveness of a programme if its newscaster seems to be personally involved in what he is saying. The less of an automaton he appears to be, the better his programme—bearing in mind that for the audience it is *his* choice and *his* own presentation that it is watching. There are those who believe that complete objectivity is in any case impossible; this is what Barrie Heads, executive producer of many of Granada's current affairs programmes, has to say:

"*A news service is staffed by human beings. Of course they can wish to be objective, to be intense in their search for infinite truth. But human beings assess things on the basis of their own characters, environment, upbringing, and training as human*

[1] Published by the Macmillan Company, New York (1960).

C

beings. They select what interests them. There is no accurate definition of truth in news.

"The quality of a news organisation depends upon the people it employs as well as on the facilities for news gathering which it has organised for itself. People who are accurate, honest, trained reporters will, of course, report the news from within their own subjectivity. They will at the same time maintain scrupulous standards of reporting fact, will attempt to provide their viewers with every facet of a controversy or argument— will indeed be good journalists.

"The great danger of a central organisation is that the quality of its news coverage must tend to be grey, flat, and uniform. The newspapers in this country which succeed and last as newspapers are those which have an attitude. This attitude should not, of course, be reflected in the selection of fact, in the 'loading' of a story. But a newspaper will always be idiosyncratic. It will at the same time separate its facts from its opinions as far as this is humanly possible."

So the debate goes on. News on television must always be objective, and yet it should also be exciting. It is not always possible to be both of those things, but each TV News organisation, in its own way, must try.

This is one of the two basic problems of the newscaster's part in the programme. The other is the extent to which he should appear—the total number of minutes and seconds when his face is seen or his voice heard. Here the issue is not one of policy, but an artistic problem arising from the aesthetic fact that the combination of a human face and a synchronised human voice is by no means the most imaginative combination of image and sound available to the television producer. A ten-minute bulletin which consisted entirely of a newscaster would probably be a very dull one indeed; more than that, it would seem to be a negation of creative television. Television news, by definition, is a method of presenting the day's happenings in the form of pictures, and to present them entirely, or even largely, in the form of spoken words is to opt out of its accepted responsibilities. On this assumption, the newscaster should appear only briefly, and the news stories that he himself presents should be those that are too immediate to be treated in any other way. He can always lead in to a film story, or he can conduct a studio interview, or he can sometimes be helped out by the use of still photographs or maps or diagrams. But, in theory, his function is limited to that of the man who ties the programme together, who leads us from one story to the next, who can sometimes be himself an interviewer (and indeed sometimes a reporter on the spot), and who is always available to tell the audience of the latest developments—including those which have occurred during the actual transmission of the programme itself. The two opposed dangers are that he should appear too briefly, thereby helping to create an impression of scrappiness, or that he should appear too often, thereby producing boredom. A news programme that is read almost entirely by a newscaster is not television at all : it is illustrated sound-radio.

News by Film

At present about 60 per cent of British TV news is on film, the bulk of which has been specially shot for television, either by the reporters and camera crews of the programme itself, or else by one of the agencies which nowadays service television networks with news coverage.

Film that has been shot on the scene of the news story is still the most vivid and effective means of presenting not only the facts of the news, but—and more importantly—the flavour and the smell of it. The point has been well made by Geoffrey Cox:

"Where the cameraman has been able to catch an event just as the page, if not of history at least of the day's news, was turning, it is possible to present the news on television with an impact and an economy unrivalled in any other medium. The classic cases of this in recent years were the scenes of the Hungarian uprising, and again the landing of the American troops in the Lebanon. The exultations of the shabbily dressed, bandoliered crowds when the Soviet star was toppled from the Communist headquarters in Budapest, or the spectacle of the American landing craft moving inshore, the ramps coming down, and the marines charging ashore past the incredulous lines of bathers and ice-cream vendors, gave the exact flavour of these events in a way which took columns of space in a newspaper. They provided not only their own story, but to a large degree their own interpretation. Only a minimum of

35

commentary was needed. Where natural sound of the event is available the impact is even more effective."[1]

Of the use of film within a television news bulletin, Stuart Hood (formerly editor of BBC television news) has this to say:

"First of all there comes the kind of story in which the picture is of supreme importance—is in fact the story told in the most vivid and economic terms. I have in mind a piece of film showing a naval plane plunging over the side of an aircraft carrier and the pilot struggling to release the escape hatch before the waves engulf him. The whole things runs to no more than 30 seconds. No other way of telling the story could have been so dramatic or terse. But this kind of film is understandably rare. It depends upon accident or coincidence—in this case a film photographer happened to be on a routine facility trip. Sometimes the man on the spot will not even be a professional cameraman but an amateur who has the presence of mind to press the button on his ciné-camera. The quality may be poor and the film may well be 8 mm, but the result is worth showing if it makes the news point dramatically. Sometimes, as in much good journalism, the story is captured because the cameraman exploits an accidental opening. Thus a BBC cameraman, by a combination of good fortune and initiative, found himself within a few feet of King Hussein on the day the Syrians tried to intercept the royal plane. The result was excellent shooting of the King, straight from the plane, addressing the crowd from the steps of the palace.

"A variant on this type of story is the filmed press conference or interview where the story lies in the exchange of question and answer, and the newspoint is the speaker's replies. There is in these cases no substitute for ipsissima verba. Here too there is clearly a fortuitous element, although the interviewer ought to have a clear idea in his mind of the kind of answer he wishes to elicit. The problem in terms of news gathering is that the interview is generally carried out under unfavourable conditions— the scrum at London Airport, for instance—which do not allow for the more sophisticated techniques we have learned to expect from Tonight *and* Panorama. *There is, of course, always the possibility that the subject of the interview may, as it were, be*

[1] *Journal of the Society of Film and Television Arts*, Spring 1960, page 7.

mute of malice. But when it does come off there is no better way of dealing with a certain type of story.

"There is, however, by the nature of things a great deal of news in which the picture plays a secondary role. There are the comings and goings of politicians—the familiar shots of the President of Atlantis coming sedately down the gangway of his aircraft, inspecting the guard of honour, clambering into his car and driving off surrounded by police motor-cyclists. It is a sequence of events which, unless the central character is one whom the viewer is particularly anxious to see, can hardly impinge much upon his consciousness. It is in the jargon of the trade 'moving wallpaper'—but it may be the only film which the bulletin editor has to put to an important political story. This is one of the occasions when he is at a disadvantage as compared to his counterpart in sound radio, who can wrap the whole thing up in a couple of lines in his sound bulletin. Perhaps the courageous thing to do is to cast the film out altogether or else, given the technical equipment, to run it by back projection behind the newsreader and to say in effect to the viewers: 'You need not look very carefully at this film—but we were there and this is the man the newsreader is talking about.' "[1]

The technical merit of ciné film in television news is the portability of its equipment. Before there was television, professional film-making meant the use of 35 mm cameras, with an optical sound track. The 16 mm gauge was regarded as amateur movies, the preserve of film societies and unpaid enthusiasts. Synchronised camera equipment which was small, light, and sturdy did not exist until the early 1950s, nor were the laboratories fitted with machines for fast and efficient processing. It was television which forced the professionals to accept 16 mm, that compelled the manufacturers of cameras and sound recorders to develop the new equipment that television demanded, and persuaded the laboratories that unless they took 16 mm work seriously they would shortly starve to death in an age when the bulk of the world's film was being shot for the small screen. The necessary technical revolution took place in the 1950s. New 16 mm cameras were developed, equipped to work with a sound track recorded by a magnetic stripe running down the edge of the film-stock, and simple

[1] *Journal of the Society of Film and Television Arts*, Spring 1960, page 2.

developing baths were manufactured, allowing a TV news editor to process his incoming film in a matter of minutes. Film editing equipment, already existing, was modified to suit the faster needs of television news, and improved telecine machines made it possible for high-quality pictures to be transmitted from a 16 mm negative.

Today the news camera team normally consists of three men. the reporter, the cameraman, and the sound recordist, and they can all travel in the same estate car, with one of them at the wheel. Where necessary they are joined by one or two lighting engineers—if, for example, they are filming an interview with a Cabinet Minister in his own office. But essentially and usually this is a three-man team, working at high speed and with equipment that is both light and reliable.

The weakness of film in television news is the time taken between the shooting of the story and its actual transmission. For film is a physical commodity, unlike a live television link; it has to be sent to a centre where it can be processed and viewed and perhaps edited, and where a commentary can be written that will precisely match its pictures. This means that by the traditional timetable of news gathering, television newsfilm is almost always out of date, whether by minutes or by hours. Some time ago a news cameraman of Westward Television (Plymouth) was in the camera room a few minutes before the regular evening bulletin was due to go on the air. Chancing to look out of the window he saw a huge fire, burning in an office block a street or so away, and at once picked up his camera and filmed the story. His exposed negative was processed immediately, and the bulletin was able to say, with honesty, that "at this moment" a fire is raging in such-and-such a street in Plymouth. On the other hand a film story shot in Asia is unlikely to be seen in Britain until the following day. Yet even here the extent of the delay should not be exaggerated. It is perfectly possible for a can of film to be placed on the daily midnight flight out of Bombay and to be shown on the television news programmes of any western European capital at lunch-time the next day. But the fact remains that news on TV is still showing material that is strictly out of date, a pictorial record of a story that the viewer has already heard on the radio and read about in the newspaper.

Extraordinarily, this rarely seems to matter. For years the
38

cinema-going public had seen newsreels that were anything up to a week out of date, and had never complained. Why should it now complain when its news stories are a mere twenty-four hours behind the clock? Television, indeed, has revolutionised the conventional attitude to the timing of a news story. It never pretends that the story is new, and it assumes on the contrary that its audience already has some knowledge of the bare facts of the story itself. To these essential facts its specially-shot news-film, with the words of its reporter or commentator, adds another dimension. How this happens in detail is so admirably described by Messrs. Siller, White, and Terkel in *Television and Radio News* that I make no apology for quoting it at length :

"In an extravagant mood of belligerency, following the refusal of the West, and especially the United States, to supply him funds for the Aswan Dam, Nasser made a speech. . . . Using language and gestures which seemed to spring from the vocabulary of demi-gods, he called down the wrath of vengeance on the United States, called its people blood-thirsty, said they would pay a million times over for the insults they had heaped upon Egypt's honour. The newspaper accounts printed the text of this speech, over which hung the explosive threat of war. The radio newscasters spoke of its implications. They turned the clock back and suggested that Nasser's language and mood were those of a tyrant. But to an extent inconceivable to its competing colleagues, television news brought the story to a new plane of focus. The film of Nasser making that speech arrived in New York two days after the event. In the consciousness of the world, and particularly here in the United States, the words were still before everyone who had read a newspaper. At the time, every day brought new developments in the uneasy Middle Eastern situation. That day's news was told live by the newscaster. There was no problem of getting into the film of Nasser and his speech. The only thing to do was to say 'The deep apprehension the world feels today over the growing sense of impending war was precipitated two days ago in Alexandria'.

"The face of the newscaster vanishes from the screen, and the scene is Alexandria. The newscaster's voice recites the bare facts. This enormous crowd wanted to hear Egypt's Nasser. He leaves the rest to the picture. The feeling it gives is powerful enough. A throng of Egyptians mills in the streets, advancing.

In the multitude there is all the wild frenzy of mass hysteria, faces alight with frank hero-worship; the scene recalls the crowds in the Piazza Venezia when Mussolini spoke. Over the heads of the Egyptians are pictures of Nasser. Looking at this scene now, one can easily imagine what a hold he has upon their imagination. The newscaster is not obliged to point it out. Then Nasser appears and he has all the arrogance of the dictator. The crowd roars forward to touch him; his smile suggests how extraordinarily pleased he is with himself at this moment. Again this is what you see. The newscaster need say nothing more than 'Here comes Nasser'. The adoring Egyptians close in around him. Pandemonium. The screen is filled with wide-eyed Egyptians pressing close to their leader. And as the eyes of the Egyptians rest upon him, so do ours, this figure with the moustache standing on a stage festooned with pictures of himself. His gaze turns towards them; he lifts his arms for silence. Then he speaks. There is no sound on this film. But the great importance of this moment is what he said.

"Here the newscaster says, 'This is what Nasser said'. The newscaster only repeats what Nasser said. We hear the dispassionate voice of the newscaster saying exactly what Nasser said. But as we hear the words we see on the screen the look and the emotion of Nasser as he spoke. His lips move, and it is almost as if we hear him, not the newscaster. Nasser's hate is there to see. We recognise the condition of a man with a sense of power. A certain section of a man's mind and purpose, filled with hate and destruction, is brought home to us in the expression he uses as he vilifies the Western world.

"This is a different kind of reporting, different from the newspaper and the radio. The programme itself has not commented editorially. The editorial staff exercised scrupulous care in the preparation of the lead-in to the film. The newscaster recited only the facts which told how many people were there, what time they had begun to gather, what time Nasser appeared; then he repeated the exact words Nasser spoke. All this had been done two days before by the newspapers and the radio. But now the entire story has a wider scope, for a new element has been introduced. We are driven to think for ourselves. We remember the past. Our view of what happened in Alexandria when Nasser spoke has been enlarged because for a few minutes we were among the crowd in the square.

"Previously, some viewers might not have quite believed that the situation was as tense as all that in Egypt. Now they can see and judge for themselves. Others might not have believed that the Egyptians were capable of hysteria for their leader. Because of what we have seen and heard, we now have vivid knowledge of the tense complications in the Middle East. TV has gone a long way towards explaining, at least in part, some of the elements of an important story. It has made comprehensive use of its facilities, which are fundamentally different from those of any other news medium. Placing new-found values upon film of that important speech, TV news got to the very centre of a news story's value and significance." [1]

That particular story is now nearly ten years old. Today Nasser's speech would not have been shot on silent film, and faster jet aircraft would cut down the delay between the shooting of the film and its screening in New York. But the essential values remain the same. Television news can afford to be late because it adds its own special quality to every story it handles on film.

There are occasions when the film in a news programme has not been shot for the purpose, but taken from a film library. The obituary of a famous man, for example, might well consist of a brief biography on film, showing the highlights of his career; an important speech on the anniversary of a battle or a revolution could be the excuse to repeat film shots that were taken on the original occasion; the publication of a Government report on education might be covered, in part, by showing existing film material which illustrates the points made in the report.

The use of old film in this way is never more than a minor technique in a form of television that by definition is always concerned with what is happening 'now'. But the fact that TV news cameramen are each day recording the events of our time produces, as a by-product, a fund of valuable material for the historians of the future, and the use of this material, either through television or by other means, has exciting possibilities that are strictly outside the scope of a book of this kind. Nevertheless, the point is worth noting; today's news is tomorrow's history.

[1] *Television and Radio News* (the Macmillan Company, New York, 1960).

41

Recorded Videotape

Film is one of the two main methods of recording images and sounds. The other is videotape. Film has to be carried from the camera to the laboratory, and then has to be processed. Videotape is recorded immediately, either on location or, by line or radio-link, at the headquarters of the news programme itself. No laboratory processing is necessary, and it can be shown within moments of being recorded. Because tape recording cuts out the delay of the film laboratory it is a fair guess that in time it will supersede the ciné-camera altogether, and TV news stories will as a routine be covered by men with small electronic cameras, recording picture and sound on to narrow magnetic tape, which can either be sent back at once to the news editor, or else fed into the programme from a source nearer to the scene of the story.[1]

The revolution that will see the end of film in television, and the conversion of all of its programmes to tape, cannot be far away; I have myself seen recording equipment which is a quarter the size of that in normal use at the present time, and although the quality of the picture was by no means equal to currently accepted tape standards, it was a great deal better than the normal quality of a news story shot hastily on 16 mm film and transmitted as a rapidly processed negative.

Meanwhile videotape is used only occasionally in news programmes, and then usually as an excerpt from a transmission that was seen live earlier in the day. The funeral of Sir Winston Churchill was thus recorded and repeated in a shorter version the same night. The Queen arriving at London Airport after a Commonwealth journey was shown in a live broadcast; live cameras have been at an important football match which ended a few minutes before the News bulletin began; the announcement of a Royal Birth outside the gates of Buckingham Palace might be an excuse to keep live cameras there throughout the day, and the moment of the actual announcement, with the cheers of the crowd outside, might be fed into the next news programme as a tape recording. In the United States the proceedings of several Senate investigating committees have been shown

[1] More mobile tape equipment has recently become available. The main problem, next year or the year after, will not be the shooting or recording of tape, but the editing of it.

as live broadcasts, and extracts from them have been used later on as news items.

To rig a full outside broadcast unit is usually too expensive a business for a news item that might run for a couple of minutes at the most. It is done sometimes, but rarely. It becomes worthwhile if, for example, the Prime Minister is making an important speech in a provincial city within half an hour or so of a main news programme. The whole of his speech might be recorded for the purpose, and key sections shown as recordings in the bulletin. On such an occasion film would be too late, and to have the newscaster read from a text of the speech, possibly with the help of a still photograph or two, is a dull and unimpressive way of handling it. A tape recording, however costly, at least allows the audience to see and hear the Prime Minister as he made his important speech 'a few minutes ago'.

But the extensive use of videotape in television news remains, at this moment, a hope for the future.

Live Cameras on the Spot

When Harold Macmillan returned to Britain from the tour of Africa which had included his important 'wind of change' speech, his address at London Airport was carried directly into ITN's early evening bulletin. When Pope John lay dying in Castel Gandolfo, BBC News used the Eurovision link for a shot of the dark palace with its single lighted window. When the first of the Soviet astronauts arrived at Moscow airport after his historical orbit of the earth, viewers in Britain watched the ceremony by live relay—not in fact in a normal news programme, for it was at the wrong time of day for that, but in a special programme that was arranged at a few hour's notice. The funeral of President Kennedy was seen live in Britain, relayed from Washington by satellite. The actual moment of the linking up of the Swiss and Italian teams tunnelling under the St. Bernard Pass was presented, again live, in ITN's main evening bulletin. It has already become a tradition for the returning officers in British elections to announce the result of the voting at one and the same time to the crowd of thousands outside the local Town Hall and to the unseen audience watching television at home.

This dramatic use of live TV cameras was perhaps what most people expected from television news when it first began, but so far it has happened only rarely. There are several simple reasons for this. A live outside broadcast is a costly operation; its equipment is still far less mobile than a ciné-camera; international links are not always available at the appropriate moment, and of course important news stories have a habit of occurring outside the normal times of a regular series of daily bulletins. Those occasions when a news story can be anticipated, and be guaranteed to happen at the precise time of a news programme, are rare and usually insignificant, such as a Bank Holiday traffic jam, or crowds milling at a main line station during a rail strike.

The technical fact is that at this moment the live coverage of news stories, not only from the country of origin but from anywhere in continental Europe and, since 'Early Bird', from across the Atlantic, is possible. Indeed a news programme that consisted entirely of live news items could begin today or tomorrow. But it would cost a great deal of money, and it would inevitably miss out most of the important stories of the day. It would become a magazine programme rather than a news programme.

Yet time is undoubtedly on the side of electronic television. The substitution of recorded tape for film, and eventually of live stories for tape, is a development that seems inevitable. How long it will take is anybody's guess, but the day when television news is really live and really news will be the day that every television journalist has prayed for. Meanwhile we live in a time of technical compromise, when the occasional live story is an unexpected luxury—and all the more exciting for that.

Using Studio 'Stills'

Television news frequently makes use of 'visual aids' in the studio. The announcement of a revolution in Venezuela may be accompanied by a map of Latin America, so that the European audience knows exactly where Venezuela is. An important public appointment will justify the screening of a still photograph of the man who has been appointed—always assuming that the film library has no shots of him. A Budget makes more sense to the layman if its main headlines are accompanied by a simple animated diagram that refers, item by item, to the changes in taxation.

There will always be a place for still or animated diagrams, but they will never be much more than a secondary method of illustration. A picture that moves is more exciting than one which does not, but a static picture is better than nothing at all.

Limitation of Television News

That television is today the most popular medium for the transmission of news is due partly to the fact that more people are watching television *of any kind* than listen to the radio or go to the cinema or read the whole of a newspaper, and partly to the immediate appeal of a pictorial digest. Television news contains moving pictures, and moving pictures are attractive and interesting. Its newscaster appears to select those items that are important, and to have one's news sifted in this way is a pleasant time-saver. What television news cannot claim, however, is to be the most *complete* of the news media. Its bulletins contain fewer stories than a radio bulletin of the same length, and far fewer than a newspaper. Some of the disadvantages of TV news have been listed by Donald Edwards:

"First, lack of space for words. Radio is difficult enough— 1,200 words in a ten-minute bulletin; but there are even fewer in a TV bulletin. There is no room for details, and many news items have to be killed. All the problems of selection are even greater in television. You can cut film, but you cannot summarize it. And you cannot summarize studio interviews or live outside broadcasts.

"We (the BBC) are aware that our television news is often shallow and unexplained. What else can it be in ten minutes? Explanation and thorough treatment, news in length—or news in depth, if you want to call it that—require more programme time. But this would be at the expense of other audience interests. . . .

"Second problem. Television news is slap in the middle of an evening's entertainment. You have to make concessions to the audience. Your bulletin has to be a programme, a show, which will retain the audience. Besides the significant and worthy news, there must also be something light and pictorially interesting. Views as well as news. As someone said, television has dragged journalists into show business. Well, no harm in that if we keep our eye on the main purpose—to give new information."

On a more detailed aspect of television's limitations as a new medium, Geoffrey Cox has this to say :

"Television is in no way a journal or record, to which people can turn back should they wish to study a picture or a story in detail. For this reason court cases are difficult to report on television, and so are Parliamentary debates. . . .

"Perhaps the biggest problem for a television news editor is the 'situationer', the task of bringing his viewers up to date on an ambling, shapeless, but important story like a disarmament conference. This is a story which the cameras cannot tell, and for which television is forced back on to what is virtually a radio report with the reporter in vision. A certain amount can be done by the use of the sound camera to give atmosphere and authenticity, so that the reporter delivers his report against the background of the place where the conference is being held, or by bringing up film underlays to illustrate his points. But even if this is done very skilfully the viewer's attention is liable to wander unless the report is kept short and pointed. Probably the most effective way with this type of story is to do these reports only at intervals, and then to give them a good spread of space, with the full complement of diagrams and maps. But certainly the daily political or diplomatic 'situationer' which the newspaper can carry has little space in a television bulletin. At best it amounts to no more than an extended headline."[1]

To remedy its most obvious defect—how to treat the main stories adequately in a medium that is slower than radio or print—television news programmes are becoming longer. The main bulletins of NBC and CBS have for some time run for a full half-hour, and the BBC's second channel has from the start included a regular nightly news programme of 25 minutes. But television news, however long or however ingenious, is only a part of TV's coverage of public affairs. It simply announces the news and, as far as possible, presents the scene and the flavour of it. This alone, however, is not enough. Television, because of its power and because of its self-confessed social purpose, needs also to analyse the news that it presents, and to ventilate the explosively controversial issues that lie behind almost every statement of public policy. To do this it has developed its own programmes of comment, prepared at a slower pace than the

[1] *Journal of the Society of Film and Television Arts*, Spring, 1960, page 8.

news bulletins, and with more space in which to handle matters that a news editor is obliged to cover in a minute or so.

These programmes tend to fall into two clear categories; the magazine programme (*Panorama, This Week, Cinq Colonnes, Report*), and the current affairs documentary (*CBS Reports, World in Action, Enquiry, White Paper*).

THE MAGAZINE PROGRAMME

"*I AM certain that without what we have come to know as the regular magazine programmes our coverage of current affairs would be quite inadequate. To deal effectively with the events of a world where every day is likely to offer three or four headlines which deserve serious comment and analysis, any responsible television service, so it seems to me, needs regular programmes which are longer than the News and more topical and more urgent than a considered documentary. They should be placed at a regular time, so that the audience knows exactly where to find them, they should have sufficient resources to handle stories from Tooting to Tokio, and their prestige should be as high as, and probably higher than, that of the most responsible newspapers and published journals.*"

The words are those of Paul Fox, formerly editor of the BBC's weekly magazine programme, *Panorama*, and now its Head of Public Affairs.

The magazine programme meets two essential conditions: it appears regularly at the same transmission time, just as a published magazine is sold on the same day each week or each month; and it consists, again like the printed magazine, of several separate items. A third condition, usually met though not perhaps essential, is its reliance upon a permanent team of visible contributors—men who supply a sense of continuity and provide the programme with its public image. No doubt it requires courage to mount a major current affairs programme, with its high production costs and considerable technical resources, but the gamble seems more likely than not to pay off. That *Panorama* and *This Week*, both of them placed at peak viewing times, have regular audiences of more than ten million each is not only a credit to the professionalism of the BBC and Rediffusion, but also a smack in the eye for those cynics who believe that although a democracy would seem to assume that all men are interested in politics, it cannot by any means suppose that they are sufficiently interested to watch a weekly programme whose sole subject-matter is current affairs.

The Role of the Reporter

It is hard to estimate the extent to which the success of the magazine programmes is due to the appeal of their constant contributors. They are, in show business terms, the stars of their programmes, and they receive the fan mail of stars. The freedom to comment (within the usual policy limits) gives them an enormous advantage over their news colleagues, and the fact that each of their reports might well run for fifteen or even thirty minutes gives them an envied elbow-room. To the television public these men *are* the programme. It is relevant that many of them came into television from the Press, for their job is still that of the traditional newspaper reporter, sending back their stories from the other end of the earth, or exposing some social scandal, or interviewing some public figure in a way that will display not only his views but also his motives. Although they are fairly expected to tackle every kind of story as it comes along, some of them have inevitably developed their own specialities. Robin Day, for instance, is particularly skilful at the high-level political interview, while James Mossman's best work has been the action report from the scene of revolution or violence—the Yemen, or Indo China. James Cameron shines because of his lively commentary writing, while John Morgan has vigorously exposed a series of social scandals.

I have said that the part played by these reporters is one of the main differences between the magazine programme and the straight news programme. What other differences are there? The most obvious one is time. A magazine programme is usually three or four times as long as a news bulletin and often considerably longer in preparation. There is time, therefore, to select, to reconsider, and if necessary to reject. Ten minutes in which to interview a Cabinet Minister instead of one or two. Twenty minutes in which to present a profile of the Chancellor of the Exchequer. Fifteen minutes in which to cover the main aspects and personalities of a national strike. Twelve minutes in which to run an international discussion, live from three or four different studios. Or, if necessary, a whole programme can be

D

devoted to the examination of a single topic. *Panorama*, for instance, has devoted complete programmes to Berlin, to Moscow, and to the United Nations. *This Week* has more than once allocated its full half-hour to interviews in depth with the leaders of the main political parties, and has frequently, especially in the past eighteen months, found room for filmed reports of equal length.

Power and Prestige

There is another difference between the magazine programme and the news, which is perhaps the most significant of all. I refer to the public status of programmes like *Panorama* and *This Week*, which with *World in Action* remained for years the "leading articles" of the two British networks. This gives them a power and a prestige greater than that of any current national newspaper.

This power and prestige are inevitably reduced to some extent by the need to be impartial, and one of the chronic problems of the editors of the magazine programmes is how to be stimulating without being biased. In practice, this conjuring trick is rather easier than it seems. As far as social subjects are concerned, it is generally accepted that a blatant evil can be attacked. When, for instance, John Morgan reported for *Panorama* about the squalid existence of the thousands of Londoners who were literally homeless, it was at no point suggested that he could take any other view than that this was, for whatever valid or invalid reasons, a social disgrace. There is also a sense in which a TV organisation, while expressing no opinion of its own, can permit its hired reporters to state judgments which are perfectly permissible as long as it is made clear that they are indeed the personal views of highly respected observers who have examined at first hand the facts upon which those views were formed. When Robin Day returned from the Congo at a particularly sticky time in the morbid relations between Katanga and the United Nations he expressed a personal view on the merits of their respective cases. It so happened that Day's judgment was rather kinder towards Katanga and rather more critical of the United Nations than either the programme's editor (Paul Fox) or its assistant editor (myself) would have liked. But he had been there and we had not. He is a conscientious reporter with liberal views. After considerable but amicable discussion it was agreed that he could say what he wanted to say, provided he made it clear that the views were his own, and that he spoke as a man who had just returned from the Congo, and whose judgment should be respected.

Such occasions are nevertheless exceptional. The normal practice is for the magazine programme to present the known facts on whatever subject it chooses to investigate, together with the personally expressed opinions of those concerned with it. It is then left to the viewing public to decide in their own minds who is right and who is wrong.

To achieve this delicate balance, to remain constantly exciting without being unfair, never to be out of date, to know in advance where in the world to send his reporters and camera teams, to persuade leading figures both at home and abroad to be interviewed without fear or favour (and certainly without a prearranged script), to book live international lines at the last moment, to find and train new reporters, to be willing to throw a prepared programme overboard at the last moment if the news of the day demands it—these are a few of the tasks of the editor of a television magazine programme. Sometimes, instead of following the news, he can create it—as *Panorama* created it by its interview with Georges Bidault. Now and then he can enjoy the satisfaction of knowing that his programme has acted forcefully as the voice of the public conscience. This can certainly be said of *This Week's* report on British troops in Germany, and of *Report's* enquiry into the *Der Spiegel* affair. On such splendid occasions the magazine programme is far removed in spirit and purpose from the routine news programme, and these are probably the moments when television journalism is at its very best.

It is of moments like these that Helmut Hammerschmidt, formerly the producer of *Report* (Stuttgart and Cologne) writes:

"We are proud to have made quite a number of accurate prophecies, and we are particularly pleased whenever official action follows our exposure of conditions which seem to us to demand criticism. In the same way there is a great deal of satisfaction in helping to eliminate popular but indefensible prejudices, or in explaining minority opinions, or in defending actions that seem to us to have been both necessary and misunderstood."

I would not wish to exaggerate the missionary element of television journalism, but it remains true that the programme editor who is merely an efficient technician is unlikely to be completely successful. A competent craftsman he must be, but unless he also cares deeply about the world and its ways he will never be more than that. Fred W. Friendly, whose large heart is as visible as his enormous professionalism, admits what others are sometimes too shy to shout about: *"We believe that our job is to try to cast a little light, create a little more understanding of what bothers people, what helps people, what can kill and what can save. Perhaps it is fair to say that we too, like so many other people, have 'fire in the belly'."*

Programme Content

Editors of television magazine programmes, like editors in any other media, cannot work to a fixed set of rules. The contents of each programme must depend on the news of the moment, the luck of knowing at the right time what is likely to happen in the future, the wisdom of researchers and contact men, and the ability to back an apparently illogical hunch. Nevertheless an examination of the main current affairs magazines does show enough of a consistent pattern to justify a few simple generalisations. In choosing them I hope I may be forgiven for limiting my examples to *Panorama* and *This Week*. I have selected these two British programmes (one BBC and one ITV) because I know more about them than I do about, say, *Report* or *Cinq Colonnes*; and I have preferred them to *Tonight* (which is not exclusively a current affairs programme) and *Gallery* (which is about the British political scene and therefore by definition contains few stories from overseas).[1]

The editor of a printed journal is restricted by the number of pages at his disposal, and the editor of a television magazine is restricted by the running time of his programme. *This Week* fills a thirty-minute space, and this means that its producer[2] has $26\frac{1}{2}$ minutes of screen time—the other $3\frac{1}{2}$ minutes being taken up with commercial advertisements. *Panorama* in the past few years has varied between 45 and 50 minutes, and because it is a BBC programme this is an actual length. Granted that few

[1] Since writing this chapter *Gallery* has died, and *Tonight* been transformed. My words are true of the summer of 1965.
[2] I have generally used the word 'editor', which the BBC prefers, but the man in charge of *This Week* has always been called its 'producer'.

52

stories can be adequately covered in less than ten minutes the producer of *This Week* probably has a harder assignment than his rival in *Panorama*. He can either have two stories of 13 minutes each (which is perhaps too long), or else two main stories of nine or ten minutes each, with a shorter and less important one which he would normally place at the end; or he can devote his whole programme to a single story.

The fifty minutes which *Panorama's* editor has at his disposal would seem to give him far greater flexibility. Not only can he have four stories without difficulty, but he can easily alter the length of each of them, thereby varying the pace of the programme as a whole. He is less frequently obliged, for reasons of running-time, to stretch an item for longer than it really needs. He can easily contain a twenty- or even thirty-minute story (a political profile, for instance, or an item that includes both a filmed report and a studio discussion at the end of it) without destroying the rest of his programme. On the other hand, there are those occasions when the news is dull, or the world mysteriously uneventful and at such times it is easier to be boring in 50 minutes than in $26\frac{1}{2}$.

Jeremy Isaacs, for two years producer of *This Week* and now editor of *Panorama*, believes that a running time of slightly less than half an hour is not without its advantages : *"Of course $26\frac{1}{2}$ minutes makes it virtually impossible for* This Week *to include within the same programme more than two stories of any weight. But on the other hand it is perfectly adequate for a couple of reports, each of about thirteen minutes—and I think that anything shorter than that would take us far too near to the length and technique of the news—and it is admirable for a long, single piece on a subject which deserves treatment in depth. This Week has increasingly devoted a whole programme to a single subject, from a studio discussion with the Prime Minister or the Leader of the Opposition to a filmed report on the state of Chile or Bolivia. Our running-time of $26\frac{1}{2}$ minutes would certainly be a disadvantage if we felt obliged to cover three or four subjects each week. But I believe this to be neither necessary or desirable."*

Each of these programmes is expected to cover the world, and each of them therefore has to keep a balance between home and foreign affairs. If *This Week* has two items, then one of them would normally be a story from Britain and one from abroad.

A story on horse racing at the beginning of the flat-racing season was followed by an assessment of de Gaulle. During the first three months of 1964, *This Week* had seven stories from overseas, and twelve from Britain. During the same period *Panorama* had thirty-six foreign stories, and twenty-eight from Britain. In any week of the year it is a safe assumption that at least one reporter from each of these programmes will be overseas with a camera crew.

Foreign assignments are almost invariably, for technical reasons, covered by film cameras, and are therefore visually much more interesting than a studio discussion or a straight interview. This suggests another factor for the editor to consider when he plans the contents of his programme; not only will he balance his home stories with his foreign ones, but he will try to follow a static studio item with a lively pictorial one. If the news of the day demands that his lead story must be an interview with a Cabinet Minister, then he will try to follow this with a filmed report from another country and another continent. He will possibly try to improve the look of his studio interview by prefacing it with a short piece of film.

The interview with Georges Bidault, for instance, was preceded by a two-minute film which summed up his public career and showed him in the days when he was one of the leading actors on the world's stage. Not only did this add point to the rather sad interview which followed it, but it gave pace and variety to the programme itself. For an edition of *Panorama* which consisted entirely of studio talk would be a very dull one indeed, and an edition which consisted of one film story after another would be monotonous.

Shaping the Programme

Building up the shape of a magazine programme introduces some of the familiar problems of the dramatist or the novelist: how to vary the pace and the mood, how to balance those sections that appeal to the head with those which appeal to the heart, how to begin effectively, how to build up to a third act or a last chapter. Choosing a lead story is clearly important, and although sometimes it selects itself (a strike on the morning of the programme, the publication of an important report, the outbreak of a revolution) there are many occasions when the editor finds himself with a choice of any one of three or four.

A lead story needs urgency and punch, and must always be on a major subject of national or international importance. Except in unusual circumstances it is probably a mistake to lead with a studio interview, but it would be equally mistaken to lead with a pleasant film story of an undramatic sort.

The choice of a final item introduces a different consideration, that of timing. It should be possible for the editor to extend his live stories if they are going well. Nothing is more irritating to the audience (not to mention the participants) if an important interview or discussion is arbitrarily chopped off at the moment when it is reaching its peak of excitement. To allow himself this flexibility the editor might well either choose as his last item a story which can be shortened or extended without losing its value, or else have two or three filmed stories of different lengths from which he will make his final choice when the programme is on the air. Once again this is easier to plan when he has 50 minutes than when he has only $26\frac{1}{2}$.

Above all, the magazine editor must be willing to throw out at the last moment not only one or two of his prepared stories, but if necessary the whole of his programme. This is a costly decision to take, but occasionally it must be taken and I can give a precise instance of this from my own experience.

In the middle of the week of January 28th, 1963, we had worked out a tentative list of contents for the *Panorama* of the following Monday. There were one or two gaps to be filled, and there was the usual possibility of an important story breaking over the weekend. But we had the rough shape of the programme in our minds. Then, in the middle of that week the Prime Minister made a TV broadcast. The following night the acting Leader of the Opposition, George Brown, also spoke on television. Despite their differences of view, they both echoed a similar sentiment. Harold Macmillan issued a challenge: "We must be ready to accept change, to modernise, to adapt, to get rid of obsolete plant, and perhaps more important, obsolete ideas." To which Mr. Brown added: "We simply cannot afford any longer to hang about. We must take decisive action, and take it now."

Both men were concerned with the mood of Britain, and expressed the same fear that in some ways we, as a country, might be in danger of dragging our heels. By the Friday, three days before our transmission, this theme was the subject of leading articles in the national press, and was indeed a constant topic of conversation wherever people got together to pass the time of day. Clearly it demanded a place in *Panorama*. But how should we treat it? We thought of discussions, and interviews, and debates. We made lists of public figures who might be asked to take part. But the more we argued among ourselves the clearer it became that what we were really talking about was, quite literally, the 'state of the nation', and this was surely a theme that could scarcely be adequately covered in ten or fifteen minutes.

We decided therefore to scrap our half-prepared programme and devote the whole of *Panorama* to this newly topical theme. We would take a critical look at Britain, her achievements, her shortcomings and, above all, her mood. So, in the middle of Friday afternoon, the decision was taken. The cutting rooms were emptied of their half-completed stories, and the BBC's film library was combed for whatever material might be of value to us. A live outside broadcast unit was sent to one of the biggest steelworks in South Wales, for we had decided to open the programme there, and to catch, live, the frank opinions of a group of steel-workers. At the same time we began to select a team of distinguished national figures who might debate the issue in the studio on the Monday night.

Cutting rooms and dubbing theatres worked throughout the weekend, producing what in the end became a twenty-minute pictorial survey of Britain, placed in the context of those statements by Harold Macmillan and George Brown. John Morgan, as the reporter assigned to this part of the programme, also spent his weekend in the cutting-rooms. On the Monday morning he wrote the whole of his commentary, and in the afternoon and early evening he recorded it. The job was finished within minutes of the programme going on the air.

Looking at the *Panorama* diary for that day I see that the live OB from South Wales ran for $9\frac{1}{2}$ minutes, and that the studio discussion—including Sir George Pollock (Director of the British Employers' Confederation), George Woodcock (General Secretary of the TUC), the Rt. Hon. Harold Watkinson (former Minister of Defence), Denis Healey, MP, and Mark Bonham-Carter—ran for over 15 minutes. This was Monday evening, and not a single minute of this final programme was even thought of before the previous Friday afternoon.

This is no doubt an exceptional instance. But although it is rare for a complete edition of a magazine programme to be cast aside in that way, it is very common for individual items to be thrown away on the day of the programme itself. Indeed it has long been a principle in *Panorama* to leave the list of contents open on the preceding Friday evening.

Looking back again at the diary, I see that we once mounted a whole item of fifteen minutes on a threatened electricity strike during the day of the programme itself, that we dispatched a reporter and a camera crew to Libya following an earthquake on Friday, February 22nd, 1963, and that during the weekend of January 19th, 1963, we prepared a completely new programme on the subject of the future of the Labour Party after the death of Hugh Gaitskell.

In a random list of twenty consecutive programmes in 1962-3 I see that the actual list of contents was changed as late as the Monday afternoon on no fewer than fifteen occasions. To make decisions as important as this, to stick to them, and if necessary to defend them afterwards, is something that a magazine programme's editor must always be prepared to do.

How all these considerations affect the make-up of a magazine programme in practice can best be seen by listing the contents of *Panorama* and *This Week* during a sample period. I have therefore taken the first three months of 1964 as an example, without pretending to claim that it was a particularly 'typical' time. I have chosen it purely at random, a period when troubles in Cyprus provided a running story in the field of world affairs, and when British politics were plunged into the moodiness of an election year:

SAMPLE PROGRAMME CONTENT

Date	'Panorama'	Date	'This Week'
Jan 6th:	Cyprus Safety At Sea The Pope in the Holy Land Date of British Election	Jan 2nd:	Death on the Roads
Jan 13th:	Jordan Waters Dispute Interview with W. German Foreign Minister Automation in Britain Smoking and Lung Cancer	Jan 9th:	The Army's Commitments Unemployment in the South-West

Date	'Panorama'	Date	'This Week'
Jan 20th:	Tanganyika: Independence Retail Price Maintenance Port Talbot Steel Strike The Clergy in Britain	Jan 16th:	Interview with Harold Wilson
Jan 27th:	Army Troubles in E. Africa Deployment of British Troops Nehru's Successor British Law and Law Reform (interview with Lord Devlin) First Ladies (the wives U.S. Presidents)	Jan 23rd:	The Corsican 'Leukaemia Cure' The Borneo War
Feb 3rd:	U.S. Republican Contenders Anglo-Soviet Relations Interview with Tanganyikan Foreign Minister Hospital Beds	Jan 30th:	The Future of Africa
Feb 10th:	Tribute to Harold Macmillan Dutch Royal Crisis Congo: film of police brutality The Johnson Administration Angry Young Men (writers) Chou En Lai's African tour	Feb 6th:	Princess Irene of the Netherlands Nuclear War by Mistake A Future for the Cunarders?
Feb 17th:	Interview with Prime Minister The Trial of Jack Ruby Cyprus The Watutsi Tribe Over - population in India	Feb 13th:	Poverty in the USA
Feb 24th:	Interviews with Chancellor of Exchequer and his 'Shadow' Kurdistan Bobby Baker Turkey (after attempted assassination of her Prime Minister) Indian Film Industry	Feb 20th:	Interview with Prime Minister

58

Date	'Panorama'	Date	'This Week'
March 2nd:	Air Safety Death of King of Greece Southern Rhodesia The Police Pakistan Langarone, 5 months after the dam disaster	Feb 27th:	*Fanny Hill* and the Law
March 9th:	Interview with Harold Wilson Ladakh Greece The (American) A II Cyprus Royal Babies	March 5th:	Television and Politics
March 16th:	Extract from President Johnson's TV Interview Trial of Jack Ruby Population Explosion in SE of England Cyprus (studio discussion) Electronic Eavesdropping The Auschwitz Trial	March 12th:	Interview with Rt. Hon. Jo Grimond, MP Meths Drinkers
March 23rd:	Profile of Sir Hugh Foot The Electricity Dispute The Position of the General Practitioner The Manufacture of Busts of Shakespeare	March 19th:	How Straight is British Racing? Assessment of de Gaulle
March 30th:	Spain (25 years after the end of the Civil War) Clacton Hooligans The Boston Strangler Profile of Brian Epstein The Singing Nun	March 26:	Society and the Psychopath

Against that background, what have those in charge of these two programmes to say about the function of a television current affairs magazine? First, Paul Fox:

"Obviously one of the main jobs of a programme like Panorama is to add comment and analysis to whatever may be 'in the news' at the time. There is no point in repeating a news story; it must add to what the audience has already seen or read about. What it can add is depth of comment, because it has (usually) more time in preparation and (always) more time on the screen. If a story is worth ten minutes, it will have ten minutes, but if it needs forty or fifty minutes then it can have forty or fifty. To this extent it is usually possible to guess in advance what some of the contents of the next Panorama will be, for there are always one or two stories which the programme must tackle if it is not to default on its responsibilities. There is nothing wrong with this, but I would be worried if the public found itself able to anticipate all the contents of a particular week's programme.

"I have always believed that the success of Panorama can be judged partly by the reaction of the audience and the critics, but more importantly by the extent to which it is mentioned in the news columns of the next morning's papers. This frequently happens, for instance, whenever a senior Cabinet Minister or a national leader from overseas makes an exclusive appearance in the programme. Or it happens when the programme itself starts an investigation which is later taken up by the whole of the national press—a good example of this was our report into London's homeless citizens. Similarly we made headline news when Ernest Marples and Sidney Greene clashed in Panorama on the eve of a potential railway strike—and this, by the way, was live television, which is always more dramatic than anything which is filmed or recorded on tape. We also made our own news when we interviewed Georges Bidault.

"Of course it is much easier to follow the news than to anticipate it, though the two are not necessarily mutually exclusive; we can follow the news of a major national strike, for instance, by presenting a story which might end with a confrontation in our studio between the leaders of both sides in the dispute. But the very fact of this confrontation is itself a piece of new news, and is almost certain to be quoted on the front page of the next morning's papers.

"Beyond this we have to remember that an enormous public relies upon us for serious and responsible reporting, and for influential comment. We are therefore more concerned, except

60

in weeks when the world is abnormally subdued, with issues of national and international importance than with what is merely trivial and amusing. Above all the job of a programme like Panorama cannot be considered in isolation; it is just one part, though a vitally important part, of the BBC's coverage of news and public affairs. The role and therefore the contents of a magazine programme in any television network will depend on whatever coverage that network has to offer in their fields."

The producer of *This Week* in 1964 was Jeremy Isaacs:

"The job of a programme like This Week *is to explain the headlines. But I myself don't see why those headlines need necessarily be today's or even yesterday's. A programme which appears for half an hour every week would dodge its responsibilities if it felt obliged to be as topical as that; it is a waste of those precious $26\frac{1}{2}$ minutes to fill them with stories which are in effect no more than slightly longer versions of what the audience has already seen, not only once but over and over again.*

"Any major issue (the Cyprus crisis is a good example) is nowadays treated day after day in the news and in programmes like Dateline *or ITN Reports. There was a period in 1964 when* This Week, *if it had merely been concerned with the week's news, would presumably have sent a reporter to Cyprus over and over again,[1] thereby filling its half-hour with material which would inevitably have been essentially the same as the daily reports of the news—though they would probably, though not inevitably, have been a little longer. This would have been absurd. A weekly programme, as I see it, has an obligation to do what is not being done otherwise; it can concern itself with a much broader interpretation of the word news and it has more time in which to cover a subject in depth.*

"I do not believe that This Week *should necessarily be concerned with the news of the day. It is probably more valuable for it to tackle subjects which are of interest and concern over a period of weeks or months (or even years) than those stories which are strictly topical. I believe it was perfectly valid for* This Week *to devote the whole of three programmes in the summer of 1964 to a group of the Latin American nations, though only one of them was headline news in the conventional*

[1] In fact there was no story from Cyprus in *This Week* during the first six months of 1964.

sense. Similarly we filled another complete programme with a report on the problem and treatment of mental illness within the community in Britain; the subject is important, is never far from the news, and deserves a longer and more considered coverage than the traditional ten or twelve minutes.

"Of course subjects of this sort, if we handle them badly, are open to the comment, 'It wasn't well done, and it wasn't even in the news at the time.' But if we do them effectively, then they at once become their own justification, and the very fact that they are unexpected gives them an extra excitement. If This Week confined itself to stories which are currently in the headlines, not only would its audience be inflicted with a great deal of material which is already familiar, but it would be denied the chance of watching subject-matter which in the long run might be even more important.

"To restrict a programme to the news of the day is to exclude nine-tenths of human activity and human experience. Of course it is always possible to scrap (or more likely to postpone) a prepared programme at the last minute if the immediate news is so vitally important that to ignore it would be to opt out of our clear responsibilities. But this happens infrequently."

Presentation

The presentation techniques of the magazine programme are similar to those of a news bulletin. *Panorama* is introduced, and its stories are linked by Richard Dimbleby, himself an experienced reporter in newspapers, radio, and TV. There can be few men in television anywhere who can equal his skill in handling the unexpected, or in retaining a magisterial calm in moments of crisis. Himself a fluent and fast writer, a superb reader of 'off the cuff' commentaries, and a first-class interviewer, he has all the merits that his job demands.

Just as the audience tends to regard the newscaster as the man who has personally chosen the items in his own bulletin, so Richard Dimbleby is publicly considered to be the man who is wholly responsible for the contents of *Panorama*. It is his image which has attached itself to the programme, one of calmness, knowledge, reliability, humanity, and the complete absence of fuss. Like the best of the newscasters he writes his own material, and although he is not in reality the 'boss' his influence on both content and presentation is considerable. Unlike the newscaster, on the other hand, his activities are not restricted to the mere presentation of fact; he frequently chairs a studio discussion, and occasionally expresses his own views on matters of moment.

The technique of a visible 'anchor man', attacked in some places as old-fashioned and slow, is stoutly defended by Paul Fox:

"Firstly, it makes for flexibility in presentation. Some people say that to have Richard Dimbleby in the studio, always in vision at the beginning of the programme, is a rigid arrangement which somehow puts the programme into a strait-jacket. In fact the opposite is the truth. With such a man available on camera at any point in the programme it is always possible to go, through him, to anything or anywhere. He could, if necessary, stop the arranged programme altogether and lead us somewhere else. He can introduce relevant news items which have come in during the transmission of the programme. He can extend or contract his own part of it, making it easier for the editor to vary the running times of particular stories even when they are on the air. In the (increasingly unlikely) event of technical trouble he can cover up.

"But although this flexibility is one of the reasons why I personally believe in the institution of the 'anchor man', it isn't the main one. More important, I think, is the family atmosphere in which a programme like Panorama is viewed every Monday. This is not a printed magazine, to be read in the morning train or in occasional minutes snatched from a coffee break. It is a programme which must be seen as it is transmitted (or not at all), and it is seen by families or parts of families in their own homes at the same time every Monday night. Under such conditions I am sure that the personal contact between the programme and its audience is vital, and I am equally sure that the best way to establish the proper kind of contact is by means of a visible personality, someone who has down the years become something of a family friend, a regular visitor to the sitting room, a man whose words are respected and whose very presence has become (and I doubt if I rate it too highly) a guarantee of integrity and common sense.

"In a world of increasing confusion and violence, in which so many versions of the 'truth' are readily available, here, it

63

seems, is a man who every Monday can help to shed a ray of light. There is something very reassuring about his appearance on the screen which seems to remove at once any suggestion of bias or propaganda or cheap emotionalising.

"Let me give just one example of the quite extraordinary relationship which Richard Dimbleby has built up with his unseen audience. During the Cuba crisis in the autumn of 1962 we presented a Panorama Special *at very short notice. This, let us remember, was during a week when the world seemed to be hovering on the brink of nuclear war. Tension was high, fear was just round the corner, and truth—as is always the case on such occasions—was hard to come by. Our programme was introduced and linked as always by Richard Dimbleby. During and immediately after it there were 'phone calls from dozens of viewers who tried, as they often do, to have a word with him. One of these calls was put through to me personally, and it was from a woman who told me, very simply, that she had a young family, and that her two sons would certainly not be going to school in the morning unless Richard Dimbleby himself assured them that it was quite safe to do so.*

"Trivial, perhaps; but not, I think, essentially so. I prefer to see it as proof that in Richard Dimbleby and in our use of him we have managed to build up a highly personal relationship between the programme and the public. To take him away would be to destroy that relationship, and with it, or so I believe, much of the respect which Panorama has for so long held in the minds and hearts of its vast audience. It is silly to talk of a technique being out of date (or conversely being 'with it'); techniques either succeed or they fail, and success and failure are determined by the measure of respect and affection which the programme commands."

For many years *This Week* also employed its own 'anchor man'—a position held by Brian Connell longer than by anyone else. But in the autumn of 1963 it changed its method of presentation. Brian Connell left the programme, and the present technique is to let each individual reporter introduce his own story, handing on at the end of it to the next man and the next story. Inevitably this is a faster method—*This Week* gets into its lead story much faster than *Panorama* does—but to some extent it destroys the programme's personality. *This Week* is slicker than

64

Panorama, but less homely, and possibly less friendly. Yet its technique is arguably more in keeping with the mood of the times (*Panorama* has kept the same basic shape for nearly ten years), and this is what Jeremy Isaacs says about it:

"*I have never believed that a programme like* This Week *needs to be introduced by someone in vision. This is a device which adds nothing to the programme, and merely steals precious time. Whatever is said by this visible chairman can be said more dramatically and effectively within the content of whatever reports the programme has to offer. We solve the problem of continuity by having each reporter, at the end of his own story, handing on to the next one. This way the whole programme flows more easily, without the need to jump back to the studio and out again every now and then.*"

Technique

Magazine programmes employ the same basic techniques as news. I would say that the editor of a current affairs magazine programme can expect the following facilities:

1. A live studio large enough to contain a group of twenty or thirty people, and capable of holding, for example, cars or scientific equipment or models.

2. The use of still and moving back projection.

3. A film unit large enough to handle at least one foreign and one home story every week, with access to further film facilities in an emergency.

4. Access at request to outside broadcast facilities. In an organisation as large as the BBC, these permanent facilities are considerable. The editor of the magazine programme can always ask for them; whether or not he is granted them will depend on the force of his argument as well as the existing technical commitments.

5. Access to international relays, whenever desirable. This, of course, is more complicated, and lines may well not be available at a convenient time. But my own experience with *Panorama* was that links between European cities was almost always possible, though sometimes the item concerned had to be pre-recorded an hour or two before our own transmission time. Relays from North America by satellite are more difficult to arrange, and certainly more costly, but they too have been included on several occasions in the past couple of years.

E

6. Access to tape-recording facilities, especially in the afternoon and early evening of the transmission day.

7. Access to a permanent staff large enough to supply all these programme needs.

A Critical Look at the Set-up

I would make two further points about magazine programmes, and the first of them is organisational. It is my belief that the British habit of separating administratively news from current affairs is absurd, confusing, and uneconomic. Yet the BBC's tradition in this respect was copied by Independent Television in 1955. In the BBC, news has always been one department, or set of departments, and current affairs another. It was so in sound broadcasting, and it has remained so in television. In British commercial television the same division remains; national news is a monopoly of Independent Television News, and programmes like *This Week* and *The World Tonight* are made by separate programme companies. Philosophically this division is presumably justified by the assumed distinction between news and comment, by the sacredness of the former and the possible irresponsibility of the latter. News must always be honest and true, and invariably beyond controversy, and this happy state of affairs can only be guaranteed if its practitioners work together in their own organisation, free from the tainting influence of those with points of view.

The resulting confusion is unsatisfactory from everybody's standpoint. For one thing, it causes expensive and illogical duplication. Robin Day, sent to the Congo by *Panorama*, finds that a colleague from BBC News is already there (this is by no means an isolated example, nor is it confined to the BBC). There are also those occasions, when the main news story in the evening bulletin is also the lead story in *Panorama* on the same night, and the audience sees what are sometimes literally the same pictures twice within the space of an hour.

It may, perhaps, be argued that this does not matter, that the relationship between a news programme and a magazine programme is like that between the front page and the leader page of a newspaper; both can and should be contained within the same publication.

This, I think, is to make a merit of what is a minor anarchy. For although the newspaper certainly comments in its leading
66

articles on the major events of its own front page, it does at least have the same editor, whereas the editor of ITN is not employed by the same organisation as the producer of *This Week*, and although communication between the editor of BBC Television News and the editor of *Panorama* is no doubt frequent, it is sometimes fortuitous and almost always by telephone (for their offices are a dozen miles apart). It is true that the BBC possesses an 'Editor, News and Current Affairs', but what is needed is formal collaboration at the level of tactics as well as of strategy.

My own personal view is that the present confusion neither can nor should continue much longer. I hope that what I have written about news and current affairs is sufficient evidence for the view that each is an inseparable part of the same public service. The reflection of comment and controversy on important items of the day is as essential to television as the accurate reporting of those items in the first place. There is a fundamental absurdity in having the mere facts of the news in one programme, and the analysis of those facts scattered through several other programmes on three channels. The combination of news and of comment within the same programme is, I believe, what the audience needs, and what it will eventually get. The main nightly news programme will be extended to half-an-hour,[1] and will thus inevitably contain stories that in length and in technique are closer to the present *Panorama* and *This Week* than to the brief item in a ten-minute bulletin. Once this happens, the dividing line between the two sorts of programmes will become so blurred as to be meaningless even to television executives, and eventually it will disappear.

The first of my general points about the television magazine programme, therefore, is to suggest that its days are numbered, and that its present function will be taken over by a longer news-cum-comment programme on the one hand and by an increased number of news documentaries (what NBC has called 'instant news specials') on the other. I am also arguing that a development of this kind will demand, at least in Britain, a reorganisation of the present administrative method in both BBC and ITV. The organisational separation of news and current affairs will no longer be possible.

[1] It is significant that when BBC-2 began in 1964 it included a nightly programme called *Newsroom*, running for 25 minutes.

My second point is a slight contradiction of my first. For, although I believe that the magazine programme may soon be out of date in terms of national networks, I suspect that it might find itself a new future in international television. A magazine item of ten minutes or so is potentially a very saleable commodity, and stories from *Panorama* and *This Week* have frequently been sold throughout the world. When I was myself working on *Panorama* we often made use of stories shot by similar programmes overseas, and notably from the French *Cinq Colonnes* and the German *Report*.

The notion of an international magazine programme was canvassed for many years, and a number of tentative experiments have already taken place. It is over a decade since Paul Rotha, then Head of Documentaries for the BBC, persuaded the many film units in the British Commonwealth to co-operate in *Commonwealth Magazine*, until apathy and shortage of good material forced it to close down. In the autumn of 1963 a more ambitious, though so far only occasional programme called *European Journal* was started, making use of specially-shot stories from several television networks. The idea behind *European Journal* is that it shall be shown at approximately the same time by those TV organisations that have contributed to its production.

A parallel though more restricted experiment is taking place between the production teams of television magazines in South Germany, Italy, French Canada, and Belgium, and this is described by Helmut Hammerschmidt :

"The directors of these magazines have established a joint office which operates as a base for the exchange of information on each other's plans. This office is in Brussels. The idea behind the scheme is to help us to make more ambitious and therefore more costly stories, and we believe that we can do this more frequently and more effectively together than we could separately. Each station, in rotation, sends out a technical crew with a director, and this team is joined by directors from the other stations. Each station thus shares the film coverage with the others, but has the advantage of its own script, and if it wishes, its own sequences. The cost of production is shared mutually."

68

There is of course an essential difference between the co-operation of Mr. Hammerschmidt and his colleagues, and *European Journal*. The former is nothing more than a convenient technical collaboration, which avoids duplication and saves money. What it does not do is ask the contributing countries to accept the absolute control of a man from one of those countries. Each national network retains its authority in matters of editorial policy, and it guarantees this by providing its own director and its own commentary. *European Journal* is both more important and more ambitious. For although each contributing country is largely responsible for choosing its own stories, the principle behind the experiment is that the same edition of *European Journal*, with the same contributions, shall be shown by all the national networks involved in it.

This voluntary surrender of authority to a team of television practitioners who are probably not one's own nationals has always been hard to achieve, and international collaboration in the field of controversial television has usually proved as hazardous as in the world of international politics. One's hope is that *European Journal* will succeed, that it will hammer out its own style and image, and that it will cease to be merely occasional. But a taste of the problems that it can expect was experienced as early as its second edition, when the *New Statesman* carried this story in its London Diary:

"The firm grip which General de Gaulle has on French radio and television is no joke to the French, but occasionally his use of RTF as a government propaganda station has its faintly comic moments. This week the principal European television networks, among them the BBC, transmitted a Journal *composed of internationally compiled film reports. Nation speaking unto nation, as it were. The German contribution was a study of Gaston Deferre, the Mayor of Marseilles and the General's socialist opponent. It was a cool enough look at Monsieur X. The French, however, refused to show it. The General does not believe that his opponents should be heard speaking on his television station. In place of M. Deferre the French network showed a film about Napoleon on St. Helena."*

This piece of somewhat sardonic comedy shows clearly enough how far we are from having an internationally accepted policy for television current affairs. *European Journal*, alas, is a programme created by a committee. Although the western European television networks have greeted it with varying degrees of enthusiasm or apathy, and many of them have at any rate contributed stories to it, their national pride has so far prevented them from abandoning their own editorial control. The programme still lacks what it essentially needs—an editor, of whatever nationality, who has as much authority over content and policy as the editor of *Panorama*. Without such a person, and also without the permanent staff that goes with him, *European Journal* seems likely to remain a noble experiment, too infrequent to have a big impact, and too diffuse to have its own style and point of view.

Nevertheless I am enough of an optimist to believe that the battle will eventually be won—if only because the creative men in factual television, regardless of nationality, have a splendid habit of agreeing with one another whenever good and exciting television is being debated. Many of them are thinking along similar lines and are using similar techniques. They are in constant contact with one another, by personal visits, by post, and by telephone, and already a great deal of know-how is exchanged, internationally if informally. All that is needed is the will of the parochially-minded to remember that we are in the middle of the twentieth century, that parish-pump attitudes are singularly pointless in this day and age, and that quality and truth are virtues which deserve more from us all than mere lip-service.

I believe that eventually this will happen, and that the television magazine programme, out of date though I believe it to be in purely national terms, will assume a new vigour in the world of international television.

THE CURRENT AFFAIRS
DOCUMENTARY

BY 'current affairs documentary' I mean a long programme, so far almost always on film, which deals in depth with a subject of topical importance. News programmes in 1964 dealt with the latest developments in Cyprus in stories which lasted a couple of minutes; *Panorama* gave then ten or fifteen minutes; but *World in Action* could give Cyprus half an hour. At the height of the Algerian crisis the News programmes had reporters permanently in Algiers, sending back filmed stories of the usual length; *Panorama* from time to time sent its own reporters to Algiers or to Paris; but *CBS Reports*, in May 1961, analysed the background of the Franco-Algerian conflict in an hour-long film. In the past few years News programmes on both sides of the Atlantic have reflected the immediate moments of crisis in the battle for Negro rights. Magazine programmes have frequently sent reporters and camera-teams to the scenes of the latest disturbances, but NBC devoted the whole of a *White Paper* programme, lasting an hour, to a detailed examination of a particular incident, and *CBS Reports* made a film of similar length—*Who Speaks for Birmingham?*—an account of day-to-day life in an industrial city torn with racial tension. When the Greek cruise-liner *Lakonia* caught fire in the Atlantic causing the deaths of three hundred holiday-makers, it received the usual coverage in news and magazine programmes; but *World in Action* produced a forty-minute film which reconstructed the chain of events in the words, and with the faces, of those who survived the disaster.

The current affairs documentary is a form of television which is now some fifteen years old. The BBC had a series called *Foreign Correspondent* as long ago as 1949. Produced by Grace Wyndham Goldie, it featured such established radio reporters as Edward Ward and the late Chester Wilmot. Alas, the primitive facilities of those days compelled it to be firmly based in a live studio, with maps and interviews, plus fifteen minutes or so of specially shot film, all of it on 35 mm, and most of it silent. The same producer was responsible for *World Survey* (1951) in which Christopher Mayhew and Graham Hutton alternately surveyed the scene overseas and at home, using the same technique.

Those early programmes suffered in impact by being necessarily studio-bound, but nevertheless they succeeded in their main purpose of casting light on the important issues of the day, and undoubtedly they generated an impressive sense of responsible authority. Their limitations were, of course, partly technical, springing from the shortage of studio space, the lack of adequate mobile film units, and the limitations of the electronic cameras of those days. But they suffered also by being born at a time when national and international figures were still reluctant to suffer the ordeal of television, and indeed felt no obligation whatever to face the cameras in an age when the television audience was limited to a few areas of the British Isles and when sound-radio was still the more popular medium.

The Early Documentaries

The technical break-through came in 1951 and 1952. In the USA, Edward R. Murrow and Fred W. Friendly began a magazine programme called *See it Now* in November 1951, and on December 29th, 1952, they abandoned the magazine format in a historic programme called *Christmas in Korea*, an impressive attempt to express the Korean conflict in human terms. Two months earlier the BBC had shown the first programme in its *Special Enquiry* series, a report from the slums of Glasgow.

See it Now ran as a weekly series until 1958, and *Special Enquiry* ran monthly every autumn and winter until 1957. Both programmes relied upon the personality anchor-man: Ed Murrow for *See it Now*, and Robert Reid for *Special Enquiry*. Significantly both Murrow and Reid were practical reporters with similar backgrounds. Ed Murrow had made his name as a radio war correspondent, reporting to America from a blitzed London. Later, with Fred Friendly, he had been responsible for the radio series *Hear it Now*, whose logical successor was television's *See it Now*. Robert Reid, graduating to radio from the provincial press, was one of the BBC's war reporters, and later

72

was in charge of radio news in the BBC's North Region. When the first *Special Enquiry* went on the air, in October 1952, he was features editor of the *News Chronicle*.

See it Now began nearly a year ahead of *Special Enquiry*, and the British programme owed a great deal to its American predecessor. Its basic approach was similar, and intentionally so. For although the BBC, like CBS, was unable to have an editorial opinion of its own, it could at least have a broad point of view, and it seemed to those of us who were concerned with the birth of *Special Enquiry* that one of the most exciting merits of *See it Now* was the way in which Murrow had seemed to place himself on the side of the audience. His approach was that of the hardened reporter whose concern was to find out the facts on behalf of the viewer, and to let nothing and nobody stand in his way. In choosing Robert Reid we knew we were choosing a man whose approach would be precisely similar, and the fact that he had a slight northern accent added to his earthy, no-nonsense appearance. This was clearly no routine spokesman for the Establishment, but a man to be trusted—one of 'us', rather than one of 'them'. Of *Special Enquiry's* general approach to its subject matter, Robert Reid has this to say:

"The approach was journalistically a simple one. We were aware of a range of social problems which up to then had never been properly uncovered by television. We didn't set out initially to assume the role of crusaders. What we saw as our job was to try to do in television terms what the best newspaper journalism had always done in the way of bringing social problems out into the open, as a matter of public interest. Basically the job was to inform people.

"Up to then television documentaries had been prepared and put on by experts on a particular subject. In our case it was very much the man-in-the-street approach, thinking of all the questions the average viewer would like to ask if he were sitting in my swivel chair before swinging round to the screen to watch the answers coming up in the main body of the report. This approach paid off in two ways. It created the impression that I was lining up with all the viewers, and not posing as an expert on anything; and it engendered a genuine warmth of feeling on my part about many of the social problems we tackled—the slums of the Glasgow Gorbals, for example."

73

Special Enquiry borrowed from *See it Now* the convention of the studio-based reporter who could command, by the turn of a switch, either a filmed report from a colleague in another town or country, or live OB cameras from a remote location. There was a sense in which both Murrow and Reid played the part of TV news editors, calling for reports from their own correspondents.

In the first *Special Enquiry*, a historic programme from the slums of Glasgow (very forcefully directed by Anthony de Lotbinière), Jamieson Clark appeared as the local reporter who had been sent on this particular assignment. When *See it Now* presented two programmes on Africa, Alex Kendrick played a similar role. Both series used film cameras with a flexibility that was new to television in either country, and they forged a basic technique of television reporting which has remained substantially unaltered since then. Together, moreover, they killed the traditional studio-bound programme in which an expert (as opposed to an enquiring reporter) presented, sometimes rather patronisingly, the essential facts of his subject.

Finally, and especially, *See it Now* and *Special Enquiry* were never afraid of an emotional appeal. They respected the head as much as the heart, and they did this from the moment they first went on the air until the day they came off it. The first *See it Now* to abandon the magazine format, *Christmas in Korea*, remains in the memory as one of the sincerest human documents in the history of television, and *Special Enquiry's* exposure of Glasgow's slums still stands up as an attack on man's exploitation of man.

Indeed, each of these series was at its best when attacking. I have already mentioned in these pages Murrow's *See it Now* programme on Senator McCarthy, and it undoubtedly remains a high peak not only in Murrow's own work but in factual television anywhere. *Special Enquiry's* successes were social rather than political, and it was at its best in its reports on Britain's Colour Bar (in which René Cutforth spoke from Birmingham), Smoke Pollution, Dirty Food, and British Teenagers (which brought Denis Mitchell into television for the first time).

Special Enquiry ended in 1957, and *See it Now* in 1958, having blazed a trail that has since been followed by their (often more distinguished) successors. They had learnt how to use the TV reporter with a film crew, working fast in difficult

74

conditions. They had found the merit of the accurate recon-struction—thus the *Special Enquiry* into the decline of the British village re-staged a meeting of villagers that had taken place some months previously in the local school, and did it *verbatim* from the minutes of the actual meeting. They had stumbled across the technique of counterpointing extracts from the contrasting statements of several people with different views, thereby achieving the essence of genuine controversy without the time-consuming formality of a conventional debate; and they had discovered that the policy restrictions of television did not prevent a current affairs programme from taking a firm moral stand.

Unfortunately they suffered from being born at a time when leading figures (especially in Britain) were still frightened of appearing on television in programmes of controversy, and when the conventional pressure groups had a stronger hold on television executives than they have now. A *Special Enquiry* into British railways was actually cancelled because the British Transport Commission, which by definition had the right to prevent film cameras from going anywhere near a railway station or a train, objected to the programme's terms of refer-ence. Such a cancellation would be impossible today. As for *See it Now*, it eventually lost its constant sponsor (ALCOA), and Murrow, asking for leave of absence, complained that most of television "insulates us from the world in which we live".

In Britain, between March 1957 and January 1963, there was only one continuous TV news documentary, ITN's *Roving Report*. This was a much simpler programme than either *Special Enquiry* or *See it Now*, and its basic technique was that of straight reporting. It turned its back on production gimmicks, its film editing was straightforward and direct, and it remained in essence an extended news story.[1] Its length varied from 15 to 30 minutes, and sometimes it adopted a 'magazine' format, including separate stories within the same programme. It never had a constant anchor-man—a Reid or a Murrow—and often used ITN's own news reporters in succession. It maintained a consistent quality for nearly a decade, without ever joining that small group of programmes which demand to be seen.

More exciting than *Roving Report*, though its life was shorter

[1] So indeed did BBC-2's *Enquiry* series (for some reason no longer 'Special') which lasted for some eighteen months.

and its subject-matter confined to the United Kingdom, was Granada's *Searchlight* series, produced from the autumn of 1958 until 1960 by Tim Hewat. It had that simple directness which, allied to a fierce crusading zeal, has since characterised nearly all of Hewat's work. It was essentially—or in retrospect seems to have been—a series which specialised in the investigation of social scandals, and several of its subjects had already been treated by the BBC in *Special Enquiry* : Dirty Food, Teenagers, and Child Cruelty, for example. But its method was more direct, its tone sharper, and its impact more startling. It was more interested in issues than in people (if it had a serious weakness it was perhaps that it seemed to regard human beings as mere statistics) and it generated more indignation than compassion. Its significance was that it was tougher and less comprising than any British television current affairs series had so far dared to be. When it ended it left a gap which was filled two years later by another Granada series, also with Tim Hewat as producer, but this time with greater resources, both financial and technical : *World in Action*.

Despite *Searchlight*, from 1957 to 1963, British television relied for its current affairs coverage mainly on its magazine programmes. These were the years of glory for *Panorama* (edited successively by Michael Peacock, Rex Moorfoot, Michael Peacock again, and Paul Fox), *Tonight* (edited for nearly all that time by Donald Baverstock), and *This Week* (with a succession of editors, and often beating *Panorama* at its own game when it was in the charge of Cyril Bennett, Peter Morley, and Jeremy Isaacs). The magazine programmes took the conception of the mobile reporter from *Special Enquiry* and *See it Now*, and sharpened his approach, both verbally and in terms of film technique. They made less use of the studio, but far greater use of the newly available 16 mm film cameras, and there is certainly much truth in their claim that they could pack as much into ten or fifteen minutes as *Special Enquiry* managed to cover in three-quarters of an hour.

There is much truth, certainly; but no one in his senses can claim that a complex subject of national or international concern can effectively be handled by a reporter, however skilful, within the boundaries of a magazine story. The digest approach was undoubtedly fashionable, but there were many practitioners in British television at that time who felt the need for a regular programme which could handle major subjects in considerable depth. There were, it is true, occasional programmes which did this, and many of them were very fine (for instance Anthony de Lotbinière's documentary on capital punishment, Derek Holroyde's remarkable series on British prisons, Richard Cawston's investigation of the British National Health Service, Peter Morley's *Two Faces of Japan* and Granada's investigations into venereal disease and homosexuality), but apart from *Roving Report* there was no constant series of news documentary in Britain between the death of *Special Enquiry* and the birth of *World in Action*.

US News Documentaries

In the USA the gap which followed the end of *See it Now* lasted only a year. On October 29th 1959 the first of the new *CBS Reports* was transmitted: *Biography of a Missile*, introduced and narrated by Murrow, which followed the story of a missile from the drawing board to the firing range, and included statements from Dr. Werner von Braun and Dr. James van Allen. Since then *CBS Reports* has covered subjects as varied as the population explosion, death on the road, racial tension, the problems of President de Gaulle, Britain since the war, the world's water supply, East Germany, American Conservatism, the European Common Market, the work of Allen Dulles and the Central Intelligence Agency, the Congo, South Africa, American undertakers, and the life and times of Konrad Adenauer.

It has never hesitated to be outspoken, and never seems to be afraid of supporting unpopular causes or irritating people of influence. *Harvest of Shame* (1960) was an investigation into the sad condition of migratory farm workers in the United States, *Biography of a Bookie Joint* (1961) dealt with the operations of an illegal gambling establishment in Boston. *East Germany—The Land Beyond the Wall* included an interview, rare on Western screens, with Walter Ulbricht. *Thunder on the Right* was a forceful exposé of right-wing American political groups. *The Other Face of Dixie* had the courage to visit four cities which had actually met successfully the challenge of racial conflict.

"News media", Fred Friendly said, "are often criticised for reporting violence and controversy but not going back to see

77

how the wounds have healed. This *CBS Reports* was an attempt to do just that."

A list of eminent personages who have appeared in *CBS Reports* reads like a Who's Who of the global Establishment: Ayub Khan, Willy Brandt, Allen Dulles, the late Hugh Gaitskell, J. K. Galbraith, President Eisenhower, Averell Harriman, King Hussein of Jordan, Herman Kahn, the late President Kennedy, Robert Kennedy, Walter Lippmann, Chief Albert Luthuli, Harold Macmillan, Robert McNamara, Krishna Menon, Guy Mollet, Jean Monnet, Robert Moses, the late Jawaharlal Nehru, Richard M. Nixon, the Shah of Iran, Janio Quadros (then President of Brazil), Nelson A. Rockefeller, Dean Rusk, Bertrand Russell, General Salan, Jacques Soustelle, Generalissimo Trujillo (former dictator of the Dominican Republic), Harry S. Truman, Walter Ulbricht, and Konrad Adenauer.

Ed Murrow left *CBS Reports* in 1960 when he joined the USIA in the Kennedy administration,[1] but Fred W. Friendly remained in charge of the series until the summer of 1964. At present its permanent team consists of a director of operations, ten producers, an associate producer, six cameramen, six film editors, six sound technicians, a production manager, and the use of more than a dozen reporters. Of *CBS Reports* Fred Friendly himself once wrote:

"It would be simple to provide a prospectus for CBS Reports, *listing ten or a dozen subjects on which we are currently working. We are always working on ten or a dozen subjects. Some are completed in a matter of months; some take years; some are never finished. We are essentially a news series. We schedule some topics at the last minute—though never without a substantial portion of earlier research and production—and we do change broadcast dates to accommodate the pertinent developments.*

"Every day there is more for the people of the world to know; and every day, what we don't know can kill us. We of CBS Reports *believe that our job is to try to cast a little light, create a little more understanding of what bothers people, what helps people, what can kill and what can save. Something that Dr. Frank Stanton said when we were about to start* CBS Reports *provides the most succinct statement of what we hope has been*

[1] His death in 1965 was mourned by everybody who had ever worked in factual television, whether they had ever been privileged to meet him or not.

78

accomplished and what still remains to be done. 'It is no exaggeration', Dr. Stanton commented, 'to say that the United 'States
is probably better informed today than ever in history. Nor is it
an exaggeration to say that the need has never been greater than
today.' "

A few months after the start of *CBS Reports*, NBC began its
White Paper series, produced by Irving Gitlin with the help of
Albert Wasserman, and for its first transmission it chose *The
U2 Story*, a careful and often exciting dossier of the incident in
which an American U2 aircraft was shot down over Russia.

White Paper was not as frequent a series as either *See it Now*
or *CBS Reports*, and from the beginning it aimed to present a
sixty-minute programme every two months. Its purpose, however, seemed at the time to be more precise, and possibly more
fearless, than its rivals: "To point its cameras squarely at some
of the major issues, trends, and developments which many fear
are sapping America's vitality or may suddenly explode into
major threats to our way of life".

Certainly this was a fair description of the second programme
in the series, shown in May 1960, and called *Sit In*. This was an
analysis of one particular incident in the battle against segregation—the occasion in Nashville, Tennessee, when negro custo-
mers had entered a café and refused to leave. Apart from its
fearless honesty (and American television has been consistently
outspoken in its treatment of racial conflict) this programme,
even more than its predecessor about the U2, made fine use of
television's ability to counterpoint the present and the past.

Using both news material that had been shot at the time of the
incident, and more recent coverage from a Nashville which, at
least in outward appearance, was calm and settled, it was able
to let the present make its own comments on the past, and the
past to attach its own moral to the benevolent and sometimes
empty phrases of the present. Negro students who had taken
part in the 'sit in' not only expressed their considered views on
the problem in the light of what had happened, but also described the incident itself, looking back on it as participants.
The local Mayor, a significant figure in the proceedings, spoke
of the present and the future and also, like the students, described the actual incident in his own words and as it seemed to
him in retrospect.

In this way *Sit In* was able to look at the Nashville incident subjectively, through the eyes of those who were personally involved in it, and this device gave an extra dimension to what might otherwise have been just another objective report. There was also a considerable fascination in being able to compare how people *said* they had thought and behaved in a time of crisis with how they had actually behaved.

Occasionally *White Paper*, without openly editorialising, has contrived that men should condemn themselves out of their own mouths and by their own recorded behaviour, and an excellent example of this was the film about the negro demagogue, Adam Clayton Powell. Mr. Powell at one minute was 'living it up' with the 'Big White Folks', at another was relaxing informally in his Puerto-Rican hide-out (the implication being that he had chosen it as a way of appealing to the Spanish speaking population of his Harlem constituency), and at another was behaving like the popular misconception of an American politician among his poorer coloured supporters. Every shot in the film was true, every word spoken was authentic (and nearly all of them were spontaneous), and there was no routine commentary to give us an objective view of Mr. Powell. The comment, and it was very powerful indeed, came from the editing, from the juxtaposition of images and speech.

White Paper, as a series, has also made considerable use of the cross-cut interview, using selected sentences from the statements of several people, and cross-cutting them into a fast-moving argument. Yet its ambitions and its technique have sometimes been ahead of its subject-matter. *The U2 Story* and *Sit In* were followed by the more routine *Panama—Danger Zone*, and *Angola—Journey to a War*. Although the last-mentioned had considerable scarcity value, and was neatly directed and narrated by Robert Young, these were the conventional themes of roving current affairs series. *Battle of Newburgh* (about local welfare scandals) and *The Business of Gambling* were subjects nearer home, though whether they were explosive enough to be fairly regarded as matters which 'are sapping America's vitality' or as 'threats to our way of life' must remain a very open question.

A third American network, the American Broadcasting Company, began its own major current affairs series, *Close-up*, in the autumn of 1960, and ran it for three years. Like *White*

Paper, but unlike *CBS Reports*, *Close-up* occasionally explored the subjective approach, and did so with a thoroughness which was new in American television (where the objective reporter seems in danger of degenerating into a sacred institution). Thus, *Walk in My Shoes*, made by Nicholas Webster, was an attempt to show what life looks like to a Negro.

More significantly, it was ABC which took the considerable gamble of encouraging the 'cinema verité' team of Robert Drew and Richard Leacock. Drew and Leacock, perhaps inevitably, also tackled the problem of negro rights in *The Children are Watching*, a film about the attempt in 1960 to integrate the public schools of New Orleans. In this film, as in *Walk in My Shoes*, *Close-up* seemed to be breaking new ground, not only in actual technique but in its efforts to get into the skins of those men and women whose lives were most closely affected by whatever problem the programme decided to tackle.

Sometimes these men and women were ordinary and not at all in positions of authority, but at other times they were those who had the responsibility of making delicate executive decisions. *Crisis: Behind a Presidential Commitment*, by Gregory Shuker, was a film which took its cameras into the offices of President Kennedy and his brother Robert during the delicate days when Governor Wallace was threatening to bar negro students from the University of Alabama. Richard Leacock made *Yanki—No!* for the *Close-up* series—a film about the balance between the respective influences of the United States and Communism in Latin America. This also was a film which had the considerable merit of avoiding an interviewer (though it had a narrator) and thereby seeming to get closer to its subject-matter than has sometimes been the case in *CBS Reports*.

C'est la Guerre, about the war in Algeria, was another exercise in immediacy, in which the cameras stayed with a patrol both before, during, and after a dawn attack. Unfortunately— for this viewer anyway—some of the earlier sequences seemed curiously artificial, and the attack itself looked like any generalised war sequence. Yet *Close-up*, even when least successful, had a recognisable style of its own, and usually had a 'different' look about it; and if its principal producer, John Secondari, had done no more than introduce Drew and Leacock to the television screen he would have amply earned our gratitude.

In referring at such length to *See it Now*, *CBS Reports*, *White*

F   81

Paper, and *Close-up* I have selected those current affairs series which seem to me to have been the most seriously significant in American television. It is only fair to say that they are merely the highest peaks in a long range of mountains. *White Paper*, for example, followed *Outlook* (by Chet Huntley and Reuven Frank), and both Chet Huntley and David Brinkley, NBC's distinguished pair of topical reporters, for several years have had their own regular half-hour programmes. CBS ran its *Eyewitness to History* for several years. ABC runs a thirty-minute *News Report* every Thursday, and all the major networks have recently stepped up their output of news specials, a form of 'instant documentary' at which American television is particularly expert, and in which commercial sponsors have lately become admirably interested.

The firm of Xerox, having sponsored an NBC special on *The Kremlin*, agreed to sponsor six more documentaries from the same company. The Humble Oil and Refining Company last year bought 26 NBC news specials and another 25 were bought in advance by The Savings and Loan Foundation. *CBS Reports* is sponsored by Travelers Insurance; ABC's sixty-minute film, *The Soviet Woman*, was bought by Philco. I mention these precise examples as evidence of the growing realisation in a hard commercal world that the documentary need be neither dull nor minority. As Mr. Richard L. Tobin put it in the issue of *Communications* for March 14th, 1964:

"The day of the news commentator is dead. The day of the documentary is at hand. It is at hand because the public tunes in to this sort of news show as it never has before, and with good ratings, sponsorships are easy where once they were pioneering. Ever since that excellent old series The March of Time, *on radio and newsreel, we must admit to long-term partiality for the documentary as absorbing entertainment. We're happy to have company, and delighted that advertisers are flocking to a worthy standard."*

The US Pattern

It is possible to admire Mr. Tobin's sentiments without praising his literary style, and the discovery by wealthy sponsors of the news documentary, however belated, is as good an excuse as any for throwing hats in the air along the length of Madison Avenue. Moreover it is one reason, and arguably the most

82

effective one, why television in the United States has now evolved a logical pattern for its treatment of news and current affairs. The main news programmes in the principal networks are now thirty minutes in length, a time which allows for comment on the news as well as the straightforward presentation of the facts.

In addition, the production of news specials has increased dramatically in the past two years; at the time of writing, some 400 news specials, all produced by Chet Hagan, have come from NBC alone. This combination of news-with-comment and special programmes mounted at short notice provides a continuous flexibility which at present is one of the main reasons why current affairs coverage in the USA is able to be both immediate and deep.

Reinforcing this topical activity are the more considered documentaries, and it is in the nature of American television that these should be scheduled as a series, appearing for convenience at the same hour of day and at regular intervals of time (usually weekly). This form of planning combines the maximum of topicality with the maximum of considered comment, the merits of the well-informed daily newspaper with those of the knowledgable political weekly. For the ideal at which all those concerned with news and current affairs should aim must surely be this: news of the moment, presented at the same times daily, and with one news programme at a peak evening hour which can be regarded as the 'main' bulletin of the day; immediate comment on the news, which will fill in whatever background may be necessary, and which will allow time for longer interviews than a normal news programme can allow with those who are today making the news; nearly-immediate news-documentaries, for which the most suitable length would seem to be thirty minutes, and which are television's substitute for the topical feature piece in the daily newspaper, and which have time enough to treat each subject in reasonable depth; lastly, the documentary which is not tied to a particular news story on a particular day, but which has been prepared with great care over a longer period of time, yet is nevertheless related to the news by confining its subject-matter to those themes which are directly concerned with the continuing issues of the age in which we live.

This ideal pattern may not as yet be perfectly realised in any of the world's television producing countries, but I believe that the United States is closer to it than anywhere else.

The Documentary in Britain

The five-year gap which stretched in Britain from the end of *Special Enquiry* to the beginning of *World in Action* had in truth more to offer than *Roving Report*, and the two-year *Searchlight* series. One is forced, in surveys of this sort, into generalisations which at once have to be modified. This was also a period which contained some of the most distinguished single programmes ever made within this field. One recalls with admiration Richard Cawston's fascinatingly detailed survey of the National Health Service, Anthony de Lotbinière's film on capital punishment, Rediffusion's *Two Faces of Japan*, by Peter Morley and Cyril Bennett, Granada's reports on homosexuality, venereal disease, and the contraceptive pill, and the same company's *Sunday in September*, a stop-press film by Tim Hewat and James Hill about the CND's 'sit-down' in Trafalgar Square. Yet this remained a period of sudden excitements rather than of expected pleasures. These were the years of the personal documentary, when the men who flourished were the essayists of British television: Denis Mitchell, Philip Donnellan, John Schlesinger, and Ken Russell. Current affairs, from 1957 to the end of 1962 was largely confined to *Panorama*, *This Week*, *Tonight* and (at the end of that period) *Gallery*.

World in Action, with Tim Hewat as its executive producer from its first programme until the summer of 1964, very soon became such a landmark in the normal week's television that it was hard to imagine the years when it had not existed. Rarely announcing its subject-matter in advance, it has always been willing to scrap a planned programme if the news demands it; thus a prepared report on British athletics was postponed in two successive weeks, the first time because of a decision to cover the Aberdeen typhoid epidemic, and a week later because of the death of Lord Beaverbrook. Although normally running for thirty minutes (or just over twenty-five on the screen, allowing for commercials) it has sometimes sought and deserved rather longer. In the early autumn of 1963 it presented a 40-minute special on South Africa, and when the cruise liner *Lakonia* sank at sea it once again extended its normal running time to contain a detailed reconstruction of what had apparently happened, told

84

by passengers and crew, with additional evidence from the captain of a British ship engaged in the rescue work and from a spokesman of the Greek company which owned the *Lakonia*.

A list of *World in Action* contents would include subjects as far apart (in every sense of the phrase) as Franco's Spain, Moral Rearmament, the family of Sir Alec Douglas-Home, the views of boys aged seven whose generation will provide our national leaders in the year 2,000, Cyprus, dirty food, heart disease, the mood of Dallas after the assassination of President Kennedy, the Great Train Robbery of 1963, the Beatles in New York, Zanzibar, the Welsh steel strike of 1964, the life of a fashion model, and the position of the Church of England.

That list, of course, is not especially impressive by itself. What is important about *World in Action* is its radical departure in technique and attitude from what had become the accepted practice in British television. This departure assumed two forms; the series had neither personal reporters nor visible interviewers, and it frequently took, or seemed to be taking, an editorial 'line'.

To present a current affairs series in one of the mass media without using a team of reporters is not to do anything new. In the cinema *The March of Time* (in the USA), *This Modern Age* (in Britain), and the programme's namesake *World in Action* (in Canada) had functioned successfully for many years with a straightforward narrative spoken by an unseen voice. In American television both *White Paper* and *Close-up* have dispensed with a visible reporter, and in Britain *The World is Ours*, which owed too much to the cinema to be wholly successful in its own medium, had also relied upon a straight narration. But by 1962 the association of 'current affairs' with teams of friendly and familiar reporters had become axiomatic in Britain.

The Approach of World in Action

We were no doubt due for a change anyway, and *World in Action*'s decision to adopt what was in fact a pre-war cinema technique seemed at the time to be a startlingly courageous novelty. The use of two contrasting voices for the narration, the complete absence of interviewers, the way in which those who made synchronised statements did so straight to the camera instead of to an intermediary, the fast cutting—all these devices combined to give the programme a new look and a new force.

85

Instead of being, or seeming to be, the personal and professional views of a named and experienced team of publicly admired journalists, *World in Action* had the appearance and drive of a self-confident editorial. The voices we heard had names, certainly, but we know they were merely readers. The credits at the end of each issue included a production team and the name of the producer responsible for each issue was publicly displayed. But the significant credit was the last one, to Tim Hewat as executive producer, and it was perhaps inevitable that the views expressed by *World in Action* came to be regarded as the views of Mr. Hewat. Or, if not the views of Mr. Hewat, then the views of his employers, the Granada company.

The essential difference between *World in Action* and the rest of British current affairs output was described to the present writer by someone who is himself much concerned with the same area of subject-matter in these words:

"It has always been a tradition in our current affairs programmes that we should present the facts as objectively as we can, and should collect and make available all the relevant opinions on those facts. Thereafter we should allow the audience to make up its own mind as to who is right and who is wrong. This is one reason why we have employed distinguished and trusted journalists, whose appearance on the screen is, or should be, a guarantee of integrity. But World in Action *was different. It not only seemed to express an editorial view, but it did so from a position of glorious anonymity. It suggested, sometimes openly, sometimes obliquely, what the viewer should think about the subject under review. It did not leave him to make up his own mind. It made it up for him."*

It would be unfair, however, to exaggerate the uniqueness of *World in Action*'s editorial attitudes. For there are many areas of subject-matter in which impartiality is not only undesirable but positively anti-social. Neither *This Week* nor *Panorama* has pretended to be unbiased about colour prejudice, crimes of violence, the slums, Fascism, Communism, and the Governments of Portugal and South Africa. Impartiality, it would seem, depends as much on the subject chosen as on the subsequent treatment of that subject. This, essentially, is the view of Tim Hewat, who expresses his attitude to 'editorialising' in these words:
86

"The real key lies in what you decide to do programmes about rather than how you do them. The original choice is the fundamental thing. For example; one decides to do a programme on 'The Drunken Driver'—which indeed I once did. The acceptance of this as the starting point for a programme sets down, almost completely a strong editorial line for the programme. The word 'drunken' is loaded, and all the thoughts surrounding the 'drunken driver' are loaded. Because the drunken driver is so clearly a menace, there can be no balancing view of any strength. The programme I did, which was entitled Slaughter on the Avenue, was a slap-bang editorial from first to last minute."

Difficulties of the Impartial Approach

That is true of a great number of possible subjects, though I myself suspect that most of them are social rather than political. Tim Hewat, however, goes much farther than this, arguing that absolute impartiality is a condition of mind which most human beings find hard to achieve. He writes:

"One goes into some subjects with a prejudice or a belief that one wants to see borne out on the screen; conversely, one goes into other programmes without preconceived beliefs but in a spirit of enquiry and investigation. Having made the investigation, and being satisfied that it has been done thoroughly and fairly, then I think it is the responsibility of the producer to draw conclusions from the information. I do not think it is right to be a professional fence-sitter; no one in life is like this. (Having looked at any girl, and digested the information of curves, face, smile, etc., one is entitled to draw the conclusion 'I would like to know you' or 'I would not like to know you'.) Having drawn some conclusion, I think one's view and conclusion should be evident from the programme and should not be disguised. At the same time one must not suppress the evidence which disagrees with this conclusion. As far as time and facilities permit, one should present the whole story, but in doing so, one should make clear one's stand on the issue."

This is an attitude which places the producer in a position of considerable eminence. It seems to presuppose a state of affairs in which the television organisation appoints a producer of

87

current affairs programmes and thereafter allows him unlimited freedom to make public the conclusions which he personally has deduced from whatever evidence he has had the time to study. Having selected its producer—no doubt with great care— it leaves him alone. The initial selection of current affairs producers is therefore all-important :

"The search for balance across a whole broadcasting network is, I accept, desirable. Because all beliefs are fundamentally prejudices this can only be achieved by a wide selection of producers of differing attitudes. I am surprised that the broadcasting authorities never seem to concern themselves with the problems they might have with, say, nine Socialist producers in action, five Conservatives, one Fascist, two Communists, and a flat-earther. This is clearly an unbalanced panel of producers. I think they should ponder on the balance of producers rather than concern themselves so much with one sentence of one interview or one segment of a programme in isolation."

That is a forceful argument, but I imagine the broadcasting organisations themselves would reply that they have in fact managed to achieve an all-over balance within single programmes as well as within a long series, and have done this without enquiring too deeply into the political persuasions of individual producers. They accept that no man can be a fence-sitter by nature (or if he is, then he is likely to be a very unstimulating human being), but they have found that intelligent and sensitive producers are in fact capable of expressing all sides of a question without obtrusively imposing their own personal views. Tim Hewat's approach is certainly a very honest one, and makes for very exciting, because very committed television. That its full implications could be completely accepted by our television organisations, operating as they do within limits which exclude bias or prejudice, is—as Tim Hewat might possibly admit—very doubtful indeed.

What we can say for certain is that his approach makes for lively television; we can know that on two occasions *World in Action* was stopped by the ITA in advance of its transmission. The first occasion, in 1962, was its report on Britain's defence expenditure, and the second, in 1964, was its enquiry into the financial support given by the state to British athletics. Both programmes were strictly, even terrifyingly, factual. The precise sums of money spent on the three arms of the Services were listed in the programme on defence expenditure, the items (weapons, ships, aircraft, etc.) that were developed or purchased with that money were shown, and the occasions were carefully listed when a project was scrapped or became obsolete or was left incomplete. The conclusion which any unbiased viewer would have reached by the end of this dismal catalogue was that as a taxpayer he had been milked by successive governments of both parties who had taken his money and wasted it by a series of errors and miscalculations on pieces of defence equipment which far too frequently were useless or obsolete before they were in service, or were rendered obsolete shortly afterwards.

What the programme did *not* do was to call in either a politician who could answer for those who had authorised the spending of the money, or a defence expert who could help to explain why such policy errors—if indeed in the light of the facts known at the time, they were errors at all—came to be made. It was presumably this absence of a chance to reply which caused the ITA to take the action it did. The producers of the programme felt this to be an occasion when the facts spoke for themselves, and needed no further comment or discussion, and Tim Hewat has pointed out that the programme was about Britain's defence *expenditure*, not about Britain's defence policy.

Moreover it is interesting that the (then) defence correspondent of *The Guardian*, Mr. Leonard Beaton, who appeared in a BBC *Panorama* programme which ironically included a section of the banned *World in Action*, expressed the view that although the programme was open to the accusation of bias it should in the public interest have been screened.

The *World in Action* on British athletics (with Derek Grainger as executive producer) was a similarly factual presentation of a state of affairs which, assuming its accuracy, clearly implied that British athletes would do a great deal better for their country at the Olympic Games if they received as much official support, in terms of finance and amenities, as did the majority of the other competing countries. Comparative statistics were shown, and witnesses were produced in the form of athletes and those professionally concerned with athletics.

Again, as in the programme on defence expenditure, the

89

thoughtful viewer would come to a very definite conclusion: that Britain should devote more money and resources to athletics. This conclusion, however, could be interpreted as a party political one, for the House of Commons had debated this very subject on the eve of the programme's scheduled transmission, and the Government had been very much on the defensive. The whole question of Britain's attitude to amateur sport, instead of being a non-party discussion, had become yet another battle between Government and Opposition, and *World in Action* had invited no one from the Government to make the case for the present state of affairs. The programme was therefore technically biased.

The sad aspect of all this is that a policy of impartiality, as at present exercised by the BBC, the ITA, the American networks, and most of continental Europe, is sometimes liable to suppress the truth. For it does not follow that by balancing one opinion against another, by carefully giving each side a fair share of programme time, a truthful picture is achieved. To present to the audience the opinions of all those taking part in a particular controversy, whether it be defence expenditure or the way in which the British government treats amateur sport, is too readily regarded as an admirable way of covering current affairs. Present all the facts and all the opinions, so the theory goes, and the viewer will himself decide on the truth. The snag is, alas, that he is unlikely to do anything of the sort, for the truth does not necessarily lie somewhere in the middle. It may, in political terms, lie sometimes on the Right and sometimes on the Left.

Assuming, for argument's sake, that the way in which successive British governments had spent the people's money on defence was truly scandalous, then is it not in the public interest that the scandal should be exposed? If it is possible to be 'partial' about drunken drivers, or the Government of South Africa, or Negro Rights, or the slums, why not be 'partial' about everything? The answer, of course, is too obvious for me to have to state it. I merely make the general point here that impartiality, although no doubt the only acceptable policy for responsible television organisations in a democratic society, is not entirely satisfactory and does not inevitably, or even frequently, lead the prejudiced viewer to a position of truth and light.

Four Examples

This policy dilemma arises, of course, in every current affairs programme, but it is at its most acute in the documentary, where the programme is long enough to have an impact in depth, and where, again because of its length, the producer has less excuse than usual for making erroneous generalisations or pleading that he lacked time for the inclusion of this view or that. I would like here to give four examples of particular programmes, and to consider them not only in the broad context of current affairs policy, but also with regard to their detailed technique and to my own political and social prejudices.

I have chosen them all, fortuitously, from the output of the BBC: *On Call to a Nation*, made in 1958 about the British National Health Service, and both written and directed by Richard Cawston; *Capital Punishment*, directed in 1960 by Anthony de Lotbinière, with a commentary by Patrick O'Donovan; *Death in the Morning*, a film about a fox-hunt, written and spoken by Alan Whicker and directed by Jack Gold in 1964; and *Supersonic*, a report on the Anglo-French aircraft, the *Concorde*, written and directed in 1964 by Richard Cawston.

I have chosen these as films of considerable intrinsic merit, on matters of vigorous controversy, and dealing with subjects about which I myself have clear personal views (or prejudices).

On Call to a Nation was made ten years after the beginning of Britain's National Health Service, as an objective analysis of that service. It dealt with each aspect of the service in turn (general practitioners, hospitals, dispensing, and so on), it relied for its controversy upon the opinions of those actively concerned (GPs, consultants, chemists, opticians) who spoke directly to the film camera without being prompted by an interviewer, and the main narrative was carried by a factual commentary written by the producer/director and read by Colin Wills. The film lasted over an hour and was carefully prepared for several months.

It was, I think, a completely effective film, presenting the facts of the Health Service clearly and concisely, discovering all of its merits and problems, choosing speakers who made their points from their own experience, and remaining—like the rest of Richard Cawston's work—itself beyond (or perhaps above) the battle on which it was reporting. Anything which was either partial or debatable came from the mouths of the men who worked within the Health Service; the commentary limited itself to a statement of the proved facts. The viewer was left to form his own conclusions, and this, of course, is where his personal prejudices began to operate.

The conclusions which I myself reached at the end of Cawston's film were, perhaps inevitably, the conclusions that I wanted to reach; that the Health Service was a major contribution to social progress, that its achievements were already a justification of its existence, but that a revolution as dramatic as this had caused its own problems, mainly of an organisational kind. In brief, I concluded that although the Service was not everywhere functioning as smoothly as we might wish, it was nevertheless a glorious thing to have introduced, and was without doubt an institution of which the British ought to be justly proud. I admired the absence of emotion in a subject which lends itself too readily to cheap appeals to pity or sympathy or anger, and I felt at the end of the film that I knew all that a layman needed to know, and that I had witnessed a completely impartial and thoroughly documented investigation.

Because the conclusions I drew were the conclusions I wanted to draw, I regarded On Call to a Nation, apart from its technical merits, as an admirable piece of work. So, in fact, did most of the public and critics. Its impartiality was never challenged, and even the organised medical profession was silenced.

Capital Punishment used the same technique as On Call to a Nation. It told its story by a direct narrative, this time both written and spoken by Patrick O'Donovan, and it relied for its controversy upon the spoken comments of people particularly involved and whose views commanded respect even from those who most bitterly opposed them. As subject-matter for a documentary film, capital punishment differs from the Health Service in three essential ways: first, it is not so obviously a party political issue[1]—on the face of it there is no reason why a Tory should support capital punishment and a Socialist oppose it, or vice versa; secondly, it is something which produces an immediate and enormous emotional response, so that an objective assessment becomes, both for the producer and for the audience,

[1] When it was at last the subject of new legislation in the House of Commons its fate was decided by a free non-party vote.

almost impossible; and thirdly, it is not an essentially visual subject, but one which might seem as effective a programme for sound radio as for television.

Anthony de Lotbinière's film either conquered or subtly avoided these pitfalls. Like *On Call to a Nation* it finally impressed by the weight of the evidence it collected: from lawyers and administrators of justice to men convicted of murder, from the experience of the past to the current experience of those countries which still practised capital punishment and those who did not, from impartial investigators to a former British hangman. Again the commentary was scrupulously factual and altogether without emotion, and again the witnesses spoke to us from the screen without a visible intermediary.

Capital Punishment was a model of impartiality in an area where partiality, in every other medium, has long been the custom, and it gained in impact by being so carefully unemotional, by confining its argument to the known facts in several countries, and by accepting the emotional undertones of the subject as just one of those known facts.

The emotion, however, could not be entirely removed. It was there, in the quoted statements by lawyers, condemned men, police. Even the calm and possibly dull statement of his duties by the public hangman packed a tremendous emotional punch merely by allowing us to see for a minute or so the face of a man who had accepted the orders of society to kill other men.

My own conclusion, as at the end of *On Call to a Nation*, was to reinforce my personal prejudice—that capital punishment is certainly immoral and probably ineffective, and should therefore be abolished. I believe that Albert Camus's famous essay on the subject has long since said all that needs be said. Anthony de Lotbinière's film did not persuade me otherwise, and I doubt whether, despite its many excellences, it could hope to persuade anyone out of his passionate convictions one way or the other. Nevertheless it remains, I believe, the most complete document prepared for popular consumption on this subject of enormous importance.

Death in the Morning, as its provocative title implies, was also about the taking of life. Moreover it was concerned with the taking of animals' lives, and this, in Britain, is a highly emotional matter indeed, especially when the animal is as pretty and furry as a fox. Fox-hunting, or blood sport, is a subject at

93

least as dangerous to handle as the execution of murderers, and once again the BBC presented us with a film of total impartiality. Yet in one essential aspect *Death in the Morning* differed violently from both *On Call to a Nation* and *Capital Punishment*. It was a highly emotional work. This was partly due to its remarkable photography (by Peter Hall), which created moments of great beauty as well as moments of provocative visual comment, and partly the result of Alan Whicker's commentary, which achieved its impartiality by stating the cases for and against fox-hunting with equal vigour and with a prose style which was anything but 'deadpan'.

The technique of the film was quite unlike that of *Capital Punishment* and *On Call to a Nation*. Not only was this a film about a particular Hunt (the Quorn, the most distinguished of them all) but it deliberately confined itself to that Hunt. It did not go off in search of a global view, or make references to bull-fighting, or enter the office of this pundit or that. It remained firmly rooted in the English countryside in rather bleak weather, and its central figures were the huntsmen (and women), their dogs, their horses, and the fox. Nor did anyone speak directly to camera—though there was at least one moment when the fox seemed about to do so—but were openly interviewed by Alan Whicker in the sharp, provocative manner normally associated with his performances in the magazine programme, *Tonight*. Moreover Whicker appeared himself now and then, facing the camera, and addressing us on the subject of blood sports—and this was perhaps the film's main weakness.

Although it was in many ways a quite brilliant programme, I personally found it ultimately unsatisfactory, not because of what it was but because of what it might have been. It could have been, and in my view should have been, a subjective portrait of the Quorn, an essay in which the only people who spoke were the members of the Hunt, and which had neither a written commentary nor an interviewer. This, indeed, is what Jack Gold and his cameraman seemed now and then to be trying to do, with their splendid sequences of the chase, and the lovely shots of the landscape at what is normally an uninspiring season of the year. A film of this sort would, I think, have given us a profounder insight into the minds and impulses of those who hunt foxes than *Death in the Morning* succeeded in doing. Moreover it would have avoided the artistic conflict which arose now and

94

then between the exciting visuals (which cried out to be played with only the natural sounds of the moment) and Whicker's equally exciting commentary (which did not always relate directly to what we were seeing). The film's problem, presumably, was how to argue the case for and against fox-hunting in the context of a film which was essentially one of action rather than of talk or ideas, and which allowed little opportunity for the anti-blood-sporters to state their case. The case was stated, fairly and admirably, by Alan Whicker, but he seemed sometimes to belong to another film altogether.

How did *Death in the Morning* affect my own prejudices? Despite my reservations about its technique, I confess that I was more persuaded by this film than by any of the others in my haphazard list. My general attitude has always been to oppose fox-hunting, without seriously considering why I did so. It was one of the merits of *Death in the Morning* that it went some way to explaining not only why so many of us oppose blood sports but it also indicated very firmly how illogical we were.

I am now sure that my opposition was never against blood sports as such—it could never have been, for I have always admired the bull-ring—but was merely a reflection of my hostility to those who indulge in it. I suppose that I must have instinctively regarded it as a visual symbol of an outmoded landed gentry and an old-fashioned way of life, something which a progressive nation should have thrown overboard long before the mid-twentieth century.

My opposition was thus no more than a reflection of my own social and political prejudices. I am now grateful to Alan Whicker for explaining this to me. I am also grateful to him for asking why I, and those like me, manage to oppose fox-hunting without condemning fly-fishing. On its chosen current affairs level, therefore, *Death in the Morning* was for me a highly effective film which caused me to reconsider my prejudices; and this, no doubt, is of more significance than my professional reservations about its technique. But the essential thing about *Death in the Morning* is that it did not take sides in what is a highly-charged controversy. It behaved impeccably in accordance with the rule of impartiality.

With *Supersonic*, Richard Cawston's film about the Anglo-French supersonic aircraft, the *Concorde*, we are back to the technique of *On Call to a Nation* and *Capital Punishment*. The narrative is carried by an off-screen voice (in this case Cawston's words were read by Michael Flanders), and the argument is advanced by a series of expert protagonists. Those who appeared in the film were the men most personally and professionally concerned, not only with the development of the Concorde but with the American project for an even larger supersonic passenger aircraft, and also those best placed to criticise the broad policy of encouraging supersonic flight.

These were not the opinions of television reporters (however perceptive) or professional air correspondents (however well-informed and persuasive), but the views of men who had become personally involved in the debate about supersonic aircraft in general, and the *Concorde* in particular. Like *On Call to a Nation* and *Capital Punishment*, *Supersonic* had above all other merits the appearance of authority, for it is not enough that impartiality should be preserved: it must also *seem* to be preserved. A film with such a cast list could scarcely fail to impress. The viewer was offered the expert opinions and then left to form his own conclusions.

Perhaps *Supersonic* failed somewhat on the aesthetic level, as a film was bound to fail which concerned itself with an aircraft that had not even been built. There was an inevitable shortage of visuals, and a repetition of conventional shots of hangars, models, workshops, offices, drawing-boards, and parts of aircraft under construction. Yet this did not greatly matter, for *Supersonic* was an argument rather than a work of art, and on this level it easily held one's attention for the whole of its seventy-five minutes.

World in Action, it so happened, had earlier tackled the same subject in a programme produced by Mike Wooller, but with some important and expected differences; it was much shorter (only twenty-five minutes) and constantly sharper. Its narrative, instead of presenting the background facts and introducing the witnesses, was itself charged with a mood of emotional enquiry —are we spending too much money on the *Concorde*, will the American plane supersede it, will it be safe, what about the damage caused on the ground by supersonic bangs (and so on)? The witnesses were generally less impressive, and had less time in which to state their cases. Although this was not a *World in Action* which came to any open conclusion, it asked so many sharp questions and received so many half-convincing answers

96

that one was left with an impression of hostility—and I hope I am being fair here; certainly this was the impression which the programme left with me. It was shorter, faster, more pointed, and more exciting than *Supersonic*. *Supersonic* was longer, more thorough, much deeper, better photographed and more imaginatively edited (presumably because so much more time was spent in its preparation), yet less compulsive. But—and this is surely the important point—I found myself trusting *Supersonic* more readily than the *World in Action*, just as I am more likely to trust a long official report than a short editorial in a tabloid newspaper. *World in Action* generated more heat, but *Supersonic* produced more light.

Documentary Technique

It is clear, I think, that programmes which treat public affairs in depth—I have called them current affairs documentaries in this chapter—have become an established, even a necessary, part of television's normal programme schedules. The techniques they employ vary from place to place and producer to producer, but it is possible, I think to risk a few generalisations.

Most current affairs documentaries have so far been made as films. There have been exceptions to this, of course, and the original pattern of 'studio-interview plus film-inserts' crops up from time to time. But film remains the more normal method, and for the programme which is prepared quickly it must be film that is shot with equipment as mobile and as sturdy as that used for news. A series like *World in Action* needs to get its cameras into situations where lightness and portability are essential to success and many of the most exciting sequences in *White Paper* have been shot by cameras whose main merit was their unobtrusiveness. Tim Hewat has underlined this very forcibly:

"Fundamental to most current affairs features is speed and mobility. The ideal unit is the motor car: one car, with room for four or five people plus limited equipment and baggage. The four people should be: producer/writer, cameraman/director, sound man/driver, and researcher/driver. A fifth would be the reporter, if you need one. An electrician is rarely required, but when one is he can be hired locally. A separate director is a dying

thing on these programmes as he is a time-consuming go-between; I think there should be a two-way development—of directors who learn to handle the camera and cameramen who learn to direct shots."

That refers, of course, particularly to films which are fast and topical. Most of Richard Cawston's films, on the other hand, have been made on 35 mm stock, with a technical crew of normal size, and for the most part in situations which are carefully prepared. *CBS Reports* also prefers to work on 35 mm film, and manages to achieve a remarkable spontaneity despite the physical size of the equipment. We can also assume that video-tape will begin to take over from film, in this field as in many others, as its mobility increases and as the ability to edit it becomes faster and more precise.

There are three normal ways of carrying the narrative in a current affairs documentary : by the use of a visible-reporter-narrator, as in *CBS Reports*; by the use of an off-screen voice (or voices) as in *World in Action* or *Close-up* or the films of Richard Cawston; or by the use of a subjective first-person narrative, as in *Walk in My Shoes*. If I were to hazard a guess at the future, I would suggest that we are likely to see more documentaries that are conceived, shot, and narrated from a personal viewpoint—an industrial dispute seen through the eyes of a trade unionist, a political battle seen by one of the contestants. *CBS*'s film about Lester Pearson, in which the camera followed him about his normal business in the manner of 'cinema-verité'—are examples of what might be done, granted the willing co-operation of those concerned.

The subjective view—looking at a subject or part of a subject through the eyes of one of the participants has been a popular device for many years, and to lay a voice-track behind silent pictures is nowadays almost a cliché. At its best it can add an emotional force which objective narration, however skilfully written, can rarely match. I recall a sequence in *The Trials of Charles de Gaulle* where a citizen of Algeria, a liberal and humane man, described the conditions in which the Arab population lived when he was a boy, and the film camera showed us those conditions in shots which were carefully composed to suit the mood and the content of the man's spoken words.

Only an eye-witness of a riot can hope to convey to us something of what it was like to be there at the time. Pictures alone cannot do it effectively, nor can a well-prepared or even brilliantly written professional commentary. It is this feeling of 'being there', of oneself being placed on the spot as a participant, which is one of the principal strengths of the current affairs documentary.

In Other Countries

In this chapter I have deliberately confined my remarks to current affairs documentaries in my own country and in the USA. I have done so partly because I prefer to write of programmes which I have myself seen than of those which I have not, partly because these are the two countries which historically have pioneered this particular form of television, and partly because what I have written in general terms of Britain and the USA is valid, *mutatis mutandis*, of many other countries as well. There are, of course, policy variations from place to place. There is a restriction on editorial freedom in the Communist countries, in Spain, in the United Arab Republic, in Ghana, and (alas) in France. In Italy the shadow of the Vatican often seems to influence programmes deviously rather than directly— though this is usually denied and always hard to prove. Even so, what our documentaries have in common is far greater and more significant than their differences.

It seems generally true that most of the television-producing countries have shared Britain's preference for the magazine programme rather than for regular series of longer documentaries. In France the most conspicuous programme of current affairs has long been *Cinq Colonnes à la Une*. In Italy it has been the weekly magazine *TV-7*, in Germany the two magazines *Panorama* and *Report*, and in Australia *Four Corners*. Nevertheless there are current affairs documentaries which have stayed in the memory of this particular and occasional viewer of European television. The French series *Faire Face*, for example, by those distinguished television journalists, Etienne Lalou and Igor Barrère, which investigated domestic social problems, and whose subject-matter often overlapped that of *Special Enquiry* and *Searchlight*—birth control, racialism, housing, prostitution. There was the impressive Italian programme on life imprisonment by Ugo Zatterin and Brando Giordani, whose frank interviews with prisoners would have impressed me rather more had

99

I not already seen Derek Holroyde's remarkable series on British prisons for the BBC.

More startling, at least to the foreign viewer, was RAI's report from Milan on those ignoble citizens who have set up as slave dealers, trafficking in the poorer workers in the South. There was the fine Japanese documentary on the snowstorm which swept the north of the country early in 1963 and which had the startlingly charming title *Niigata Combating the White Devil*. Among the many admirable documentaries from Poland one recalls particularly *Investigation*, a film which dealt in *verité* terms with an actual crime—the arrest, the interrogation, the trial, and the sentence.

West Germany was responsible for the ambitious but for me not entirely successful *Searching for Europe*, in which several eminent Europeans—they included Sophia Loren, Henry Moore, Rebecca West, Carlo Menotti, and Sena Jurinac—tried to discover what Europeans have in common. Less pretentious, and much more of a straight report, was *The Dying Legion*, a frank exposé of the Foreign Legion which made one wonder just why this particular subject had never apparently been tackled before —or at least never so frankly. Another theme which has mysteriously been ignored elsewhere emerged from the Belgian film *Coeur à Vendre*, an analysis of the methods and impact of women's magazines.

The techniques which I have described in detail in terms of television in Britain and the United States recur throughout the world. Differences are of national temper and emphasis rather than of method. I find myself, as a final thought, repeating what I have already written about the magazine programme, that this is a rich field for international co-operation, and yet such co-operation has been virtually non-existent.

The most conspicuous attempt at international co-operation in the documentary field has been the work of Intertel, a filmed series produced by Rediffusion, WBC/NET (USA), the Australian Broadcasting Commission, and the Canadian Broadcasting Corporation. This group has so far made highly competent films in Viet-Nam, Iran, Britain, Italy, Ghana, Pakistan, Cambodia and Kenya. Each film is the responsibility of a particular network, and is thereafter shown by all the organisations which contribute to Intertel; the total audience is estimated at between forty and fifty million.

I have myself attended more than one international television conference as a delegate, and although we have all exchanged pious intentions, little has ever come of it. Eurovision, which began with such high hopes, has failed miserably in the field of current affairs; *European Journal* is as far as we have reached, and that is a magazine programme. Yet in a field where countries share so much in common, it seems a pity that there is so little professional contact between the documentary producers of different countries. There is happily rather more contact on the personal level, but that is a different matter. It is surely sad that a form of television which, as we all know, can play such a constructive and responsible part in the formation of public opinion and of social attitudes should be restricted, in practice if not in theory, to a policy so parochial.

If individual national networks can independently make programmes about such subjects as housing, racial prejudices, crime, medical care, and education, how absurd it is that they have so far proved themselves incapable of combining together to produce a series about problems of this kind which affect the lives of all their audiences, regardless of nationality. The social and civic merits of responsible current affairs television are too important to be so restricted at a time when national barriers are disintegrating and the world is becoming every day a little smaller. A form of mass communication which can penetrate frontiers without a permit is being kept at home for reasons which by any standards are absurdly inadequate.

REPORTING AND REPORTERS

THE majority of television programmes in the field of current affairs involve the use of reporters and reporting. Television reporters are ready to cross the world at a moment's notice if their Editors ask them to. They are prepared to interview a President or a Prime Minister. The words they use are almost always their own, and so are the questions they ask. Their responsibility is enormous, and their activities, inevitably, are controversial.

"Millions of us", wrote the Daily Mail, *"have seen interviewers adopt an aggressive and hectoring tone, as though the man or woman in the chair had committed some offence they wished to hide."*[1]

Sir Linton Andrews, formerly Editor of the *Yorkshire Post*, is less worried:

"It seems to me that television is developing, expanding, and enriching the role of the journalist in a way of vital importance to civilisation. These television journalists who cover the world and report so many turbulent scenes are in the tradition of the great war correspondents and special correspondents. They are giving it a new lustre. They are making much in the news clear to us all. The British public are better informed than ever before."[2]

Robin Day, one of the ablest and most experienced of television reporters, has correctly written,

"Nothing on the British television screen has provoked more argument than the television interview. During the past few

[1] Quoted by Robin Day in *Television, a Personal Report*, Hutchinson 1961, page 98.
[2] In *TV Times*, February 28th, 1964, page 8.

years, television interviewing has become a force in public affairs, a new branch of journalism, a source of front-page news, and a talking point for viewers everywhere.'[1]

Accusations of Bias

It has been suggested that television interviewers are some-times both biased and rude, that from their journeys to the other end of the earth they occasionally return with reports which are unfair and inaccurate, and that in any case they have assumed an importance in world affairs which is equal to and sometimes even greater than that of the nations' statesmen, who indeed are far too ready to perform for them like happy puppets at the mere notion of television's vast audience. Thus James Mossman's report from the Yemen for *Panorama* was regarded as biased in certain places and by certain people, in Westminster as well as in Cairo; and when Felix Greene returned from China with a series of personal films the producing company in Britain felt obliged to follow each one with a statement in the studio by a correspondent of *The Times* who seemed to suggest, in the nicest possible way, that Mr. Greene's survey of China was in some respects incomplete.

On the occasion of the British Conservative Government's 'pay pause' in the autumn of 1962 James Mossman, in *Panorama*, conducted an admirably frank interview with the Chancellor of the Exchequer (at that time Mr. Selwyn Lloyd), but it proved to be too admirable and too frank for many of the Government's supporters, and even as objective a person as the television critic of the *Sunday Times* was inspired to use it as the starting point of a leader-page article on the fairness or otherwise of contemporary television interviewing.

John Freeman's splendid interview with the (then) Communist president of the Electrical Trades Union was condemned as 'trial by television' by several Labour MPs who were sufficiently provoked to write to *The Times* about it—a course of action which in itself proves how desperately in earnest they were.

Robin Day has put the matter with an excellent lucidity:

"No sooner did television begin to show signs of virility than the cry went up for its castration."

[1] *Television, a Personal Report*, page 91.

The issue, of course, is a serious one. It arises out of the fact of television's tremendous power and influence, and therefore out of the power and influence which its reporters and inter- viewers themselves must assume. It is of course perfectly easy for a television reporter to come back from, say, an 'emerging' nation with a filmed report that is biased or incomplete, though most of the complaints of bias in this field have come from pressure groups and organisations which can hardly claim to be without prejudice themselves.

Similarly, it is technically an easy matter to distort a filmed interview with a national leader, and it is even possible, through the black art of the film editor, to represent him as apparently saying the exact opposite of what he actually said. I have heard of one or two occasions when this was assumed to have been done, though I have neither known personally of such sinister distortions nor have met anyone sufficiently corrupt to want to perpetrate them.

It is also true that a television interviewer can be very tough with a politician in a live studio, and that this toughness might, in the eyes of the politician's self-appointed protectors, appear to be evidence of bias on the part of the interviewer. Yet it is not without significance that professional politicians themselves hardly ever complain of their treatment, and there has so far been no evidence that our political leaders are so scared of the handling they receive that they intend to give up their television appearances altogether. I have rarely yet seen a politician pro- test to his interviewer after a broadcast, though I have often seen them share an amiable drink together when the programme was over.

Television Can Alter Facts

Yet . . . how can the television reporter guard against his own prejudices (for we must assume that as he is a human being he cannot be altogether free of them) and how can his producer help him to be fair and objective? When, in an interview, does integrity slide into bias and objectivity into impertinence? By what means can television ensure that its honest endeavours at factual reporting do not become a means whereby the tail of the tiny screen wags the dog of the political arena? Is there not a real danger—and here I am thinking in terms of the working of political democracy itself—that the television studio might become (indeed to some it has already become) more important than the House of Commons or the White House?

Robert Kee, himself a distinguished television reporter, referred to a television appearance of Sir Alec Douglas-Home in these words:

"All Britain was glued to what the Prime Minister was saying in answer to questions about the state of the nation, while relatively little mass attention had been paid to what he may or may not have said about it in the House of Commons. Moreover, he was putting himself out to answer these questions with a more obliging wish to please and without restriction as to range in a way he would never have done in the House of Commons. His questioners were all highly competent men, but they had been elected by no one to search out national policy in this way, and yet he was behaving towards them as if he had some responsibility towards them."[1]

This, it may be argued, is an unsatisfactory state of affairs in a political democracy. Even less satisfactory, and much more subtle, is the problem raised by Alex Kendrick, of CBS News:

"What often worries me about reporting by television is not so much that it distorts whatever it chooses to cover, but that it has a way of changing its essential nature. Television reporting is still such a conspicuous business; a newspaper correspondent can go around with a notebook and a pencil, and he can go away quietly into a 'phone booth and send his stuff home—or else he can send a cable. But if he happens to be a television reporter he brings with him, at the very least, a cameraman and a recordist. He himself, simply because this is television and he is therefore expected to be visually as well as aurally conspicuous, is obliged to be seen by his camera and heard by his microphone. Eventually the result of what he does, and what his technical assistants do, is seen by millions of people and quite often all over the world.

"This means, simply, that television reporting, unlike reporting in any other medium, is something of an occasion. The makers of news, the politicians or the rioters or the men of action, are very well aware that television men are among them, and of course they behave accordingly. The danger is that the rioters will riot more dramatically, the politicians will speak

[1] In *The Spectator*, March 6th, 1964, page 309.

more carefully, and even the military will time their activities to suit the demands and the convenience of television. Instead of spontaneous truth we get a public performance. A leader of state will behave in one way to an informal, partly off-the-record group of newspapermen, and in quite a different way if he knows that his press conference is being recorded for television. The organisers of a political demonstration will, if they know that TV men are amongst them (and how could they fail to know it?), be tempted to 'produce' their demonstration with the little screen in mind; they are less concerned with impressing the mere hundreds of people who happen to see the demonstration with their own eyes and far more concerned with the impact of what they are doing upon the millions of people who will watch it by television.

"Quite often a reporter of undoubted integrity will ask that a particular piece of action, planned for today or tomorrow, might for his sake take place the day after. Men of the United Nations, for example, might in Africa or Asia be doing a job which is essentially newsworthy, but they might not be doing anything very interesting on the day or two when the television reporter, who has flown in with his technical crew, happens to be there. So he asks whether they would be willing to change their plans. Naturally they are excited at the possibility of their activities being seen by a vast audience. The temptation to change their timetable is great, and as often as not they will agree to change it.

"The reporter's story is essentially true, but in order to get that truth he has been obliged to distort the reality which he went out to record. It is not so much that his story is false, but that the truth itself has changed, just as a Presidential press conference takes on a new form by the very fact of being televised. The words of the President are true words, but if television had not been there he might never have said them—or he might have said them differently. The television reporter himself might perhaps feel obliged to ask a question, not so much for the sake of extracting information but in order to assure his own public that he is there, battling away for their sakes. Not only that, but he must sometimes feel tempted to ask a particularly tough question, so that his admirers by their TV sets can applaud his vigour and his no-nonsense attitude.

"We have reached a period in human history when political

decisions might well be taken for the sake of the television audience, when the tactics of wars might be modified to suit the convenience of television technicians, and when riots and demonstrations might be so timed that they can be sure of full TV coverage—you will rarely, for instance, get two riots in the same area at the same moment, for the organisers of riots know perfectly well that the maximum television coverage can only be achieved by one riot at a time.

"What I'm suggesting is that television, partly because it is so conspicuous a thing, and partly because its audience is so enormous, has got itself in the position of being able to change the very nature of the events which, in theory, it is there merely to record."

I agree with Alex Kendrick about the importance of these dangers. Indeed they lie at the very heart of any attempt to assess television as a social and political phenomenon. At the same time one is forced to admit not only that there is precious little to be done about it, but that television's activities in this respect are in essence no different from those of the Press or the radio. Robin Day, for instance, maintains quite correctly that "the newspaper correspondent has always asked questions at press conferences, has always tried to persuade people to make their plans suit his own convenience, and has always done his very best to 'get a good story'. The difference is of degree rather than of kind. Television is both more conspicuous and more powerful. But the problem is not really a new one."

Moreover we must admit, I take it, that to exclude television from those occasions and places where contemporary history is being made is to give an unjustifiable slap in the face to the most powerful means of communication yet invented. If we believe that in a democratic society the public should be well and accurately informed, then we must also support television's claim to be allowed to report events and decisions without restriction. That it might sometimes change those events, or even alter those decisions, is a price that we have to pay. All we can hope for is to minimise the danger, by appointing television reporters of integrity and then encouraging them to seek the truth before their own popularity. That Alex Kendrick should feel the danger of his position as strongly as he does is the best evidence that he is the right man in the right job.

107

Indeed, the answer to most of the questions which disturb those who are critical of television's role in public affairs is that television organisations should be careful to appoint the proper people as reporters and producers and then, having appointed them, allow them to get on with it. They have, after all, the advantage over their fellows in written journalism that they are actually commanded to be fair and objective; not for them the gay contortions of men whose main concern is to fit the facts to whatever may be the favourite thesis of this press baron or that.

Reporting Technique

Nobody will praise a television reporter who shows evidence of bias, and if he does it often enough he will be caught out so openly that he can scarcely remain in the job. He must, in view of his unique importance, be constantly on his guard, and it might be worth suggesting here a few general principles which, in the light of what I have just written, have become, for the television reporter, a form of technique. For technique in television is not always a matter of equipment and visual skill; it is sometimes more concerned with men and with ideas:

1. The television reporter will have at the front of his mind the necessity to reflect all sides of a controversy. This means showing whatever pictorial evidence seems to support each successive point of view, and it also means seeking out and probably interviewing the spokesmen of all sides.
2. If he finds himself responsible for reconstructing an event which in reality took place in his absence he should in fairness admit that it is a reconstruction.
3. Much of his work will consist of recording interviews overseas and on film. On each occasion he will almost certainly shoot each interview at three or four times its ultimate length. Therefore he must be especially careful that when he comes to edit the final version he does not distort the point of view of the person being interviewed. Often this process of editing will take place at home, and while he himself is still abroad; so his instructions should indicate clearly those parts of the interview which are, for whatever good reasons, essential. It follows that his wishes in this respect must be obeyed by his producers.

4. As he will frequently send his reports home with a commentary recorded 'blind' some thousands of miles away, he should be careful that his editing instructions are clear and simple. It is possible for the truth to be accidentally distorted through lazy or sloppy paper-work.

5. Whenever he adds his own personal views to his pictorial statement of the facts he should be careful that they are recognisable as such. Thereafter it is the responsibility of his producers to decide whether or not those private views should be transmitted. In fact, most of the criticisms of bias which I myself have come across have been directed less at the pictures or at the general approach to the subject-matter as at the words, and sometimes the opinions, of the reporter himself. In stories overseas he has, of course, the considerable advantage of having been there. Thus James Mossman's report from the Yemen was by an experienced journalist who had visited both sides of a civil war, whereas many of his critics had visited only one side (or else had not been there at all). Felix Greene had recently been to China, but the gentleman from *The Times* who supplied the 'necessary' corrective had not.

6. Most television reporting assignments are tackled very quickly, and we all know that speed has its dangers. So does condensation, and there have been many occasions when a television reporter has had to handle the state of a nation (albeit a small nation) during a visit which has been limited to three days and in a screen story which has run for less than ten minutes. These are the hazards of the profession. What they mean is that the reporter must be particularly careful in his briefing (often a self-briefing) and in his selection of whatever information and people seem to him to be important. Yet the mere fact that he has to take pictures and must be seen talking to this politician or that is a guarantee that he will never slip into the lazy newspaperman's habit of writing his story without moving from his bedroom telephone or the hotel bar. This is indeed a serious point. The simplest demands of television impose their own discipline on the reporter.

7. Although this is a medium of pictures, words are still arguably the most important tools of the television reporter. Therefore he must be able to write well. Indeed

many stories depend entirely upon words; what pictures, for example, can an American reporter add to a piece about an important debate in the House of Commons? Should he be seen standing in front of the Palace of Westminster? Should he insert stills or moving film of the politicians who have made the most significant speeches? If, let us say, the subject of the debate was Britain's Defence policy, should he cut in shots of missiles or aircraft? Or should he simply face the camera in a studio? Whatever he does, the final effect of his piece will depend on the words which he writes and speaks. Similarly a reporter's commentary to a filmed story is what adds point and significance to the pictures. The art of television journalism still relies on good writing, and the reporter who writes flabbily will never be a neat one.

The principles which determine the approach to television interviewing deserve separate mention, and one of them, certainly, is fundamental. It is that the person being interviewed must never be allowed 'to get away with it'. Programmes of current affairs deal largely with politicians, and politicians are chronically wedded to the rightness of their own causes. An objective politician, at least on television, is a contradiction in terms. Television provides him with the largest platform ever constructed by man, and he would like nothing better than to be permitted the liberty of airing his views on it without dispute or challenge. He would like his questioner to ask him 'stooge' questions, which of course he would prefer to know in advance, rather as de Gaulle conducts his press conferences. But this, very clearly, is something which in democratic countries cannot be permitted. In Britain we have time set aside for such junketings and we call them Party Political Broadcasts.

A Code for Interviewers

The function of the television interviewer when he tackles a political leader is essentially simple, and Alex Kendrick describes it as "the job of extracting information, on policies and controversies; it should never be the privilege of the interviewer to be cleverly provocative, but his duty is to find out what the man's views are on the major issues of the day. He is entitled, obviously, to press for answers, and to resist attempts at evasion.

But beyond that he should not go." Robin Day has written a 'code for television interviewers', which is worth quoting in full:

"1. The television interviewer must do his duty as a journalist, probing for facts and opinions.

2. He should set his own prejudices aside and put questions which reflect various opinions, disregarding probable accusations of bias.

3. He should not allow himself to be overawed in the presence of a powerful person.

4. He should not compromise the honesty of the interview, by omitting awkward topics or by rigging questions in advance.

5. He should resist any inclination in those employing him to soften or rig an interview so as to secure a prestige appearance, or to please authority; if after making his protest the interviewer feels he cannot honestly accept the arrangements, he should withdraw.

6. He should not submit his questions in advance, but it is reasonable to state the main areas of questioning. (An exception is the non-controversial interview, i.e. factual questions to an expert when the programme demands answers for information only.) If he submits specific questions beforehand he is powerless to put any supplementary questions which may be vitally needed to clarify or challenge an answer.

7. He should give fair opportunity to answer questions, subject to the time-limits imposed by television.

8. He should never take advantage of his professional experience to trap or embarrass someone unused to television appearances.

9. He should press his questions firmly and persistently, but not tediously, offensively, or merely in order to sound tough.

10. He should remember that a television interviewer is not employed as a debater, prosecutor, inquisitor, psychiatrist, or third-degree expert, but as a journalist seeking information on behalf of the viewer."[1]

[1] In Television, a Personal Report, pages 108–9. This valuable book contains what I think is still the best description of the work of the television reporter.

The matter could well be left to rest there, but I will risk three further observations of my own. The first is that because an interview, however careful the interviewer and however civilised the person interviewed, is to a great extent something which is spontaneous and unprepared, there is always the possibility that it might develop into an apparent clash of personalities. The interviewer might feel obliged to ask a searching supplementary question, the person interviewed might resent it (or pretend to resent it, for most politicians are actors at heart), and the viewers of the programme might find themselves enjoying a 'scene'. The interviewer will always try to prevent this from happening, but he may not always succeed, and anyway his duty remains that of asking the most relevant questions, and pressing for an answer. The point I am making is that some of those occasions when an interviewer has been accused of rudeness have resulted from a refusal by the person interviewed to answer directly, and the following refusal by the interviewer to let him get away with it.

My second observation is that the interviewer's proper insistence on asking the most relevant questions can sometimes be taken for bias; for the most searching themes are frequently those which are the subject of intense inter-party dispute. The interviewer who questions a Labour Minister therefore runs the constant risk of seeming to be asking questions from a Conservative point of view. The sharper the questions are, the more biased the questioner appears to be, and therefore the more conscientious he is the more he seems to be in open opposition to the man he is interviewing. In the long run, of course, he can acquit himself of the charge of bias by showing that if he appeared to be a Tory last week he also, by the same token, looked very much like a Socialist this week. But those who are quick to discover evidence of prejudice in men who do not openly support their cherished ideals are unlikely to be capable of such a long-term attitude.

My third observation is that television reporting is perhaps in danger of becoming over-centralised. The contents of programmes are become increasingly controlled from 'headquarters' by television executives who are inclined to push the individual reporter into being a man who merely provides items to order. The men in charge of television programmes may be professional television men but they are not always professional reporters, nor do they know exactly what is happening a few thousand miles away. They are the creators of concepts, the devisers of neatly-constructed programmes, juggling with men and ideas and facts, whose aim is to make a programme which is exciting as well as true. I believe it would be a pity if the independence of the foreign correspondents of television were to be whittled away simply because distances have become meaningless and television executives increasingly powerful. The reporter is too valuable a part of television's public integrity for him to be demoted into a mere stooge.

TELEVISION AND PARTY
POLITICS

TELEVISION'S power, real or assumed, to influence people and even to change their minds is why in democratic societies its handling of political controversy is regulated by written rules which demand absolute impartiality. It was on the charge of political bias that *World in Action*'s report on defence expenditure was cancelled, and if such incidents are rare it is not because formal vigilance is slack but because television producers know the rules so well. Moreover because this is the area of subject-matter which is most constantly and carefully scrutinised, as much by the broadcasting organisations themselves as by the Party machines, it is arguably the area in which production techniques are more often determined by the demands of public policy than the excitements of art. I have already discussed television's treatment of current affairs. What I propose to consider in this present chapter is its handling of party politics—political broadcasting and the techniques employed during national elections.

The Effect on Voting

That the political parties should themselves be nervous of television's potential influence on their fortunes is understandable; what is much less certain is whether such instinctive nervousness is really justified.

A British company, Research Services, carried out some post-broadcast inquiries into the effect on the viewing public of the Labour and Conservative broadcasts which preceded the General Election of October, 1964, and the results scarcely indicated a passionate excitement at what the telepoliticians had to offer.

A summary of the conclusions of this research was published in the *Observer* (London) on October 11th, 1964:

"The sound had been turned down in one out of every eight homes until the politicians left the screen. And of those viewers who did listen a remarkably high proportion were unable the next day to recall accurately any points made by the parties. Surveys on each post-broadcast day . . . have also shown a trend for viewers to get more bored with the politicians as the series of broadcasts has gone on. . . . Research Services has also asked viewers whether they understood the points made by the particular speakers. On this rating Heath is very near the bottom, with two-thirds of his listeners not knowing what he was talking about. Brown comes just about top. Only 17 per cent failed to understand him. . . . Non-comprehension of Cross-man was 27 per cent. . . . Most people, irrespective of their politics or the performers, said the broadcasts had no effect on their voting intentions—they had merely been reinforced."

This of course is to generalise about a particular election, and one moreover which seemed to lack those issues which raise public interest to a frenzy of excitement and then violently divide it. It is in any case quite clear that television has now and then very considerably affected the course of national politics, and usually by its talent for highlighting a particular issue or a particular confrontation of personalities. A very famous example of such an occasion was in the summer of 1952, when the integrity of the Republican nominee for Vice-President of the United States was attacked by the charge that he was supported by a private and secret 'slush fund'. A very pertinent comment on what followed was made, as much in alarm as approval, by Governor Robert F. Bradford :

"Then came television. One speech, perhaps the largest television audience in history up to that time, and the slush fund charge as a factor in the campaign completely disappeared. Granted that it was an extraordinary speech; granted the situation was made to order for television—high drama, a young man defending his honour in the presence of his attractive wife, before a jury consisting of every voter who could get within earshot of a video screen—the fact remains that such a thing had never happened before, and that it could have happened in no other medium."

Such occasions as that, 'made to order' as Governor Bradford wrote, are rare, even at election time. A less dramatic example, though arguably it affected the outcome of the campaign, was the confrontation between John Kennedy and Richard Nixon in 1960.

Whether television, at any particular moment in a political battle, can have an effect on the voting audience, must depend on the issues involved and the personalities concerned. The party television broadcasts in Britain in 1964 came at a time when the public was bored with politics (the actual vote on Polling Day was lower than usual), the issues were stale, and the politicians generally unstimulating. The opposite was probably the case in the Presidential Election in the United States a month later, where the personalities (especially Goldwater) were more provocative, the issues more dramatic (especially those relating to the Negro problem), and where a deep emotional undertone was provided by the ghost of John Kennedy.

Generalisations are difficult, but it is certainly important to accept that although professional politicians either fear television or admire it, depending on whether they are themselves good performers or not, there is no conclusive evidence to suggest that political broadcasting by television must always affect the direction in which votes are ultimately cast.[1]

There are no doubt several reasons for this, and one of them, almost surely, is the public's suspicion of propaganda. In Britain, as in the United States, the 'party broadcasts' are the only occasion when television is permissibly propagandist. The programmes are made by the political parties with the single purpose of vote-catching. They are examples of unconcealed special pleading, in which truth is selective and the opposite view is quoted merely in order to be demolished. That the audience, on all the available evidence, takes unkindly to such activities is partly due to its own good sense, but is also a credit to the admirable objectivity with which television organisations normally handle matters of controversy. After five years of *Panorama*, *Gallery*, and *This Week*, the British public could be excused in 1964 for finding the parties' own performances naïve, unpersuasive, and even slightly vulgar. After a decade and a half of party television broadcasts we seem to have reached a state

---

[1] One reason for the public's hostility to party broadcasting in Britain may well be the fact that the programmes are carried at the same time on all three channels. That there is no alternative programme available whenever a party broadcast is on the air is almost certainly a cause of widespread resentment.

of affairs where, as Research Services discovered, "most Conservatives described the Conservative programmes as 'very good' and most Labour supporters said the same for Labour."

The Case for Party Political Broadcasts

Is there even a case for specifically 'party' broadcasts in democratic societies whose television services provide non-party coverage of news and current affairs which is admirably comprehensive? Despite the proved ineffectiveness of party broadcasts the answer would seem to be that our politicians, always reluctant to sacrifice any opportunity of speaking directly to the voting public, are never likely willingly to give up the chance of addressing an audience which is several thousand times larger than can be obtained anywhere else. Moreover it is hard to deny that in political democracies Prime Ministers and Presidents (and their potential successors) should be granted the opportunity of making their cases in public; and the most public way of doing so in the second half of the twentieth century is through the medium of television. The course of party political television will be determined in the future, as in the past, by factors which have everything to do with the principles and the realities of politics, and little or nothing to do with the arts and techniques of television—or, for that matter, with the real wishes of the audience.

Choice of Technique

Nevertheless it continues. The techniques it employs are usually, though not always, simple. Simplicity is to some extent forced on the parties by their own lack of television expertise, behind the cameras as well as in front of them. For although in Britain the party broadcasts are presented from BBC or ITV studios the role of the staff producers and directors is limited to technical advice and technical action. Faced with a medium whose importance they realise but whose complexity they find frightening and whose areas of effectiveness they know only at second-hand, the organisers of the party broadcasts are inevitably tempted to present their offerings with the utmost simplicity. Moreover it is doubtful whether a busy senior Minister, at the height of an Election campaign, can have the time or the energy to do more than sit down before a camera and speak. His instincts are to do what he believes to be safe, and what he presumes he can do best. Discussions and debates frighten him, especially if they are genuinely spontaneous, for they contain the possibility of disaster. Seated before a camera, speaking a carefully prepared text in a manner which he, if no one else, regards as human and sincere—this is something he understands and is prepared to tackle.

It so happens that this is in fact almost always the correct decision. The more ambitious the party broadcasts have been in terms of television technique, the less effective they have tended to be. Discussion programmes of various sorts have been attempted in the past, but they have lacked conviction by seeming, rightly or wrongly, to be 'rigged'. In the General Election of 1964 the most persuasive broadcasts were probably those by the three party leaders themselves. Yet I believe that greater risks could be taken by those who control party broadcasting, though admittedly they are restricted by the limited transmission time available. Richard Nixon's 1960 experiment, when he sat in a TV studio for several hours, answering questions put to him spontaneously by telephone, would have been ineffective in Britain because the length of time available was an essential ingredient of its success. Time, as well as technical inexperience, is why political broadcasts in Britain take the form they do.

The most interesting of the British party television broadcasts in 1964, though not necessarily the most effective, were a set of films produced for the Conservative Party by Jeremy Murray-Brown, an experienced television film-maker who for several years had been a producer for *Panorama*. Murray-Brown used the proved techniques of the television magazine programme— the objective report behind crisply edited shots of schools, housing estates, etc., the *vox pop* of citizens in the street expressing their spontaneous opinions, the brief but relevant statement by the appropriate Minister. To these he sometimes added the technical devices of the television commercial; the dramatised sequence with the typical young married couple, the crisply written dialogue, the smart and slightly *avant-garde* editing.

The merits of these films were hotly debated at the time. The case against them was that they tended to cheapen British politics by reducing an occasion of serious national concern to the status of a slick advertisement, as though the choice of Conservative or Labour or Liberal were a matter of no more signifi-

118

cance than choosing one detergent rather than another. Jeremy Murray-Brown himself defends his method by arguing that *"a Party which is eager to show itself as a genuinely modern Party, with contemporary ideas and with its eyes on the future rather than on the past, should in its political broadcasts choose the most modern methods of television presentation. It would have been wrong for the Conservative Party in the mid-1960s to rely upon the television techniques of the 1950s. A Party which is up to date must look up to date, and this is as true of its television programmes as of everything else."*

Murray-Brown also believes that the most successful of the Party broadcasts were those shown before the campaign proper began; far from conceding that they failed, he maintains that they played a considerable part in ensuring that the Labour majority was so narrow. I think myself, though in these matters it is hard to prove anything conclusively, that Murray-Brown's programmes fell between two utterly opposing forms of television. They were not sufficiently objective (how could they be?) to pass as fair and impartial reporting in the *Panorama* manner, and yet they were too responsible and essentially too serious to pose as television commercials.

Professional Political Broadcasts

There can be little doubt that the most effective programmes transmitted at times of national political drama are those which are produced in the ordinary way by professional television organisations. During the British General Election campaign of 1964 the best programmes, both as television and as politics, were probably those of the BBC in which the Party leaders answered, unrehearsed, questions sent in by viewers and put on their behalf by Robin Day. A series of confrontations between Ministers and their shadows would no doubt have been even more effective, but the Conservative Party and the (then) Prime Minister, Sir Alec Douglas-Home, held the legitimate view that programmes of that sort would tend to convert the campaign from one of serious national issues to one of personalities.

A single confrontation did, in fact, slip through the net: Sir Keith Joseph (Minister of Housing) faced his 'shadow' opponent in *This Week*. Otherwise television programmes have tended, both in 1964 and previously, to limit their activities to factual reports from the constituencies (Granada in particular had its traditionally admirable coverage in the North of England), to the daily doings and sayings of the Party leaders, and now and then to impartial investigations of some of the principal issues of the campaign—and here *This Week* did a particularly impressive job in 1964, tackling at least one subject, colour prejudice, which the BBC had deleted from its own *Panorama*.

But the law of the land, allied to television's own fears of lapsing inadvertently from the path of strict impartiality, has always had an inhibiting effect on television coverage of current affairs during the weeks preceding a General Election, and indeed there was a time when serious political reporting virtually vanished from our screens altogether at the very time when, one might assume, it was most needed. Things are somewhat better now than they used to be, though some of the restrictions—especially the one which demands that if any candidate should refuse to be seen on television, even in normal News coverage, then none of his rivals can be seen either—are particularly absurd. As Robin Day has rightly written,

"It is fantastic that we still have an election law which does not mention television, and a Television Act that does not mention elections."

Fortunately all the inhibitions and restrictions of the election period are cast aside at 9 pm on Polling Day. Coverage of the election results, both in Britain and the United States, has long been one of the true glories of television. The splendid opportunity which it presents has been described with typical enthusiasm by the person who, above all others, has in Britain helped to forge what are now the established techniques for handling the Election results, Grace Wyndham Goldie:

"The reporting of the result of a national Election gives a superb opportunity to television. Television is most itself when it is showing the viewer something which is happening at the moment, the outcome of which is of importance, and which is not yet known. Such an occasion emphasises the democratic nature of the medium. News is no longer something known to an inner ring and passed on, in a suitable form, to the rest: it is there, happening in front of your own eyes. Every single person, sitting at home and watching on his own set, is as privileged on this occasion as the highest in the land. The sense that this is so

120

*is part of the excitement. Not even the Leaders of the Parties,
watching the results flow in while their fates hung in the
balance, knew earlier what was happening than the shepherd
on the Scottish hills or the factory worker in Newcastle or the
old lady in Bournemouth. Any horse race shown on television,
of course, possesses something of this particular excitement.
But not everyone is interested in horse racing. Certainly not
everyone is interested in politics, either. But no one in Britain
can ignore the fact that a change of Party in the governmental
driving seat must have national repercussions which will affect
every one of us. So, on such an occasion, the suspense of television, the drama of the not yet known, is at its highest, because
what is being unrolled in front of our eyes matters to us and will
affect us.*

*"The potential for television, then, is inherent in the situation.
The problem for the producers is how to capture the suspense,
drama, and natural colour of the occasion, while reporting with
speed, accuracy and responsibility the facts: and to add inter-
pretive comment on a national and local level from Party
Leaders, political authorities, informed journalists and men and
women in the street from all over the country."*[1]

Election Report Technique

The first occasion in Britain when television presented the
results of a General Election was in 1950. The basic principles
involved, and the techniques employed, have not changed at all
since then, nor for that matter is there any essential difference
in approach or attitude between the BBC and ITN. The scope of
the operation has of course increased, and the normal course of
technical advance has brought its own modifications and improvements. But the techniques which Grace Wyndham Goldie
adopted in 1950 have so far lasted for fifteen years and five
general elections without any essential modification.

What are these techniques, and what is the philosophical
approach which underlies them? I would place them in this
order of importance:

1. This is a 'live' programme. Recordings or filmed inserts
   should be used as rarely as possible.

[1] *Journal of the Society of Film and Television Arts*, Spring 1960, pages
10–11.

2. The programme must remain on the air as long as the results are coming in. In practice this means between approximately 9.30 pm and 4 am, and from 8.30 am until the early evening on the second day.
3. The programme is based in a studio, with outside broadcast points throughout the country.
4. Priority must always be given to the announcement of results. To present a result, anything else—interview, OB discussion, studio comment—must give way. The results must be printed clearly and read clearly, and must contain information about Party gains and losses.
5. Granted the priority set down in (4), television can in several ways add to, and help to elucidate the events of the moment:

(a) It can go to selected constituencies at the very time when a result is to be announced.

(b) It can interview national leaders, victorious or defeated candidates, and indeed anyone who is either a part of the drama or is in a position to illuminate it.

(c) It can include frequent assessments of the significance of the results as they come in. These assessments should be helped by visual aids of all kinds.

(d) In addition to obtaining the views of politicians and political experts the programme can canvass those of the ordinary voters themselves; for example the BBC in 1964 had an interviewer in Trafalgar Square on polling night, and another in a café in the City of London on the next morning.

(e) The programme can include character sketches or brief biographies of those candidates whose fate is particularly important. These might be in the form of stills with a live commentary, or else made in advance on film.

6. The programme needs an anchor man with stamina, efficiency, general political knowledge, absolute integrity and impartiality, and a sense of humour.
7. This anchor man will be assisted by political commentators, statisticians, experts in assessing the significance of this trend and that, and interviewers.
8. Anything which adds to the excitement of the occasion

is worth using; computers, for example, played a part in both the British and American elections in 1964, for a computer can be a useful and stimulating prophet, estimating probable developments on the basis of early information.

9. Above all the programme must be clear and un-fussy. Although itself a highly complicated operation it must seem to be simple.

10. To achieve (9) it must be planned in advance. Although a script in the conventional sense is clearly impossible, the fact that particular results are expected at particular times helps the producers to plan a general 'order of battle'. The careful selection of outside broadcast points (e.g. in constituencies which normally declare their results early, or those which are marginal and therefore highly significant) is an essential part of this general plan.

11. The quality of the programme will to a great extent depend upon the quality of the location commentators and interviewers.

This is indeed the very stuff of television, living drama on a subject of immediate concern to a national audience. If the whole of political television were as exciting as its coverage of election results, there would be little cause for complaint.

Televising Parliament

Programmes which are devised and presented by the political parties themselves have become an accepted, if dubious, part of British television, and programmes of a more objective sort, dealing first with the issues and progress of an election campaign and then with the drama of the poll itself, are part of the public duty of any responsible national television service. There is, however, a third way in which the political battle might be reflected by television, and this has not yet been attempted; I mean the televising of Parliament itself.

Such a proposal is, of course, highly controversial—far more so, one might suggest, than it need be. There are some politicians who feel that to have the paraphernalia of television inside the national debating chamber would be an inconvenient intrusion. There are even a few who seem to oppose the idea in principle, just as their predecessors of two centuries ago resisted the sinister notion that the words of parliamentary debates should be taken down and published. To such persons there is something degrading and cheap about the very idea that Members of Parliament, conducting their business in a Palace of privilege, should be seen doing so in the very homes of those who put them there.

The deep fear of the possible consequences of television's invasion of such a precious place is not confined to Britain or to the Members of Parliament at Westminster, and Governor Bradford has expressed doubts of a more reasonable sort which are still widely held on both sides of the Atlantic:

"It has been frequently suggested that it would be a help to the voters if the deliberations of the Congress as a whole or legislative proceedings were televised as a public service. It would be my observation that it would be just the opposite. The business of legislative assemblies for a great majority of the sessions is necessarily dull, drawn out, and unexciting. No attempt by an honest television camera recording the scene could make it otherwise, and the casual viewer would come to the conclusion that Congress or the Legislature was a do-nothing body. In this kind of television, sight could be lost of the fact that to be successful it needs either action, drama, historical significance, or the intimacy of personalities in the scene."

This is indeed a serious point. Clearly it would be impossible to televise constantly the whole of Parliament (in the USA the larger number of available channels makes it possible to transmit for longer periods at a time, as was dramatically proved at the time of the McCarthy hearings), and therefore some process of selection is necessary. This editing procedure would be unfair to Parliament as an institution if it confined itself to the moments of drama, and might be very dull television if it did not. There are of course many occasions which are themselves admittedly dramatic—a Budget debate, the debate on the Queen's speech, an inter-party clash on Foreign Policy, a vote of no-confidence in the Government of the day—and these are times when the problems of the television editor would be those of maintaining fairness and impartiality.

But Parliament's moments of drama are infrequent. Much of what it does and says is tedious to the layman, and yet highly significant to anyone who cares about its broader duties. What is dramatic will usually be important, but what is important

124

is not always dramatic. Moreover there are some activities of Parliament which are fundamental to its democratic purpose, which are rarely quoted by the mass-circulation newspapers, and which would certainly command a place now and then in any responsible coverage by television; near-parochial points made by Members on behalf of their own constituents, protests of all kinds, and the airing, in non-party debate, of examples of grievance and injustice.

Granted that the whole of each parliamentary day cannot be televised, the assumption must be that regular—and perhaps daily—'digests' might be transmitted late in the evening, edited from videotape recorded continuously throughout the same day. Whether each digest would be chronological or thematic would depend upon the activities of the day in question. Presumably each programme would be linked by a commentator whose function, like that of a Newscaster, must be to present the essential facts without ever imposing comments or interpretations of his own.

It is not part of my own concern in this chapter to speculate as to whether such a programme in Britain should be shown by the BBC, the ITA (ITN?), or eventually a fourth (possibly educational) channel, though one must hope that, unlike party political broadcasts, it will never be transmitted by every available service simultaneously. Robin Day, who has long been a leader among those who press for the televising of Parliament, has suggested one possible way in which the programme might be controlled and administered:

"My own preference is that a Television Hansard should be run by an independent unit under Parliamentary auspices, as is the printed Hansard. The Speaker could appoint an editor who would be entrusted with responsibility. If it was Parliament's wish, he could be dismissed. I have suggested an independent unit, because TV coverage from Parliament would in any case have to be 'pool' coverage. There could not be two or three sets of cameras. Staff from the unit could be drawn from both BBC and ITV. The editor would choose experienced political broadcasters to present the programmes. Their job would be linking in the normal way with names and summaries to lead into recorded extracts from speeches."[1]

[1] In Television, a Personal Report, page 210.

The essential problem must be to decide how a Television Hansard shall be controlled and organised. I can see the merits in Robin Day's suggestion that a Hansard Unit should in effect be controlled by Parliament, and have an editor appointed by the Speaker. Such a solution would no doubt allay the fears of many Members who are at present opposed to the very idea of such a programme (though it would give to any would-be editor of the TV Hansard many horrible fears of a quite different sort). Whether our television organisations would share Robin Day's opinion is, I suspect, more doubtful. They have always believed that, being politically responsible and yet outside of Parliament, and possessing the necessary television expertise, they themselves should wherever possible retain the editorial control in matters of political or controversial broadcasting. Indeed the occasions when they have abandoned this control (as in party political broadcasts) have generally proved to be both bad politics and worse television. I can see no reason myself why one of the established organisations (probably the BBC) should not itself control the Television Hansard, and itself appoint an editor. The delicate task of deciding which speaker to retain and which to omit, which sections of a Minister's statement shall be broadcast and which shall not, ought surely to be kept outside the area of processional party politics.

But this is to look to the future. That television cameras will one day be installed in Parliament and Congress seems inevitable. On two occasions in Britain, in 1958 and in 1964, the State Opening of Parliament and the Queen's speech have been televised live, and this in itself has demolished the argument that the Palace of Westminster is not only a privileged place but also a sacred one. In certain other countries parliamentary debates have from time to time been televised—though I must confess that by far the dullest television programme that I have myself ever seen was an unedited relay from the Danish Parliament in Copenhagen. The truth is, surely, that Parliament, which represents the people, cannot for ever cut itself off from the people. If Parliament's activities are reported daily in the newspapers, how can they in logic be excluded from the nation's sitting-rooms?

TELEVISION AND GENERAL
KNOWLEDGE

" *THE glittering cascade of glass marbles tumbled and rattled, and as Sir Lawrence Bragg took away his steadying hand over four million viewers could see the perfect pyramid into which they had fallen, a model of a crystal. And they saw this demonstration in the comfort of their sitting-rooms far more clearly than any member of the audience present that night in the famous lecture theatre of the Royal Institution. Moreover it has been estimated that Sir Lawrence would have needed to be able to repeat his lecture to a full house every night until the end of the century to reach the same sized audience that he had for that single television programme.*"[1]

Those are the words of James McCloy, one of the most experienced and skilled of programme producers in the fields of science and adult education, and they indicate very clearly two of television's enormous advantages as a communicator of general knowledge—it can command the services of those men and women who are recognised leaders in their own spheres, and it can offer them an audience which is literally thousands of times larger than that obtainable in any other medium.

Stimulating Interest

Television may be primarily a source of entertainment, but it can also claim with some justice to have increased the amount of information of all kinds that is easily available to an inquisitive public, and thereby to have stimulated interest in areas of subject-matter of which people were previously ignorant and to which a few were actually hostile. Sir Kenneth Clark has addressed a large and loyal audience on aspects of art which were

[1] *The Journal of the Society of Film and Television Arts*, Winter, 1963–4.

once alien to its experience, and which it would certainly have ignored if presented in a published magazine or within the pages of a book. A. J. P. Taylor has stood alone before a single television camera and gripped millions of laymen by lecturing to them about aspects of history, much as he has professionally held the attention of a hundred students in a university lecture-room. Sir Compton Mackenzie, with the aid of a television film unit, has successfully conveyed something of *The Glory That Was Greece*, and the distinguished archaeologist Sir Mortimer Wheeler has done the same for *The Grandeur that Was Rome*.[1]

In *Victory at Sea, War in the Air*, and *The Valiant Years*, three television organisations (NBC, BBC, and ABC) have made use of newsreel and official film material to compile popular histories of the second world war, and both the BBC and CBS have done the same for the Great War of 1914–18. Television has also assumed the role of the personal explorer: David Attenborough has made 'zoo quests' to four continents; Hugh Gibb has explored Asia with such skill and sensitivity that one of his films, on the uninviting subject of bird's nest soup, was judged to be the best television film of its year at the Cannes Festival; and Adrian Cowell's trilogy about the peasants of the Brazilian outback was by anybody's standards a quite magnificent piece of television. There have been programmes on the virus, on oceanography, on aerodynamics, on relativity, and on almost all of the major diseases which plague mankind. Ronald Kelly has made a remarkable and sensitive film about Picasso, and John Read, in a series called *The Artist Speaks*, has allowed half a dozen contemporary British painters and sculptors to explain their own art in their own words.

On a less erudite level the BBC has presented a *do-it-yourself* series, whose successor was a set of programmes on how to renovate and decorate a not-so-new house, and for which the producer (Stanley Hyland) was allowed to buy a real house and permit his do-it-yourself expert (Barry Bucknell) to work on it in the presence of a few million unseen observers. There have been programmes about holidays, animals, astronomy, marriage guidance, the cinema, gardening, psychiatry, aeronautics, the drama, and about almost every country in the world. Nor have all these programmes been shown during those hours which are

---

[1] Sir Mortimer, in fact, appeared regularly for fifteen years, to achieve the notoriety of a 'TV Personality'.

formally dedicated to education. Many of them appeared at times when men and women switch on their television sets and demand to be entertained.

There is of course, a sense in which almost every television programme which is not purely escapist entertainment in some way adds to the general knowledge of those who watch it. This is clearly true of current affairs, and is arguably true of a great deal of drama. In the weeks which have preceded the writing of this chapter, it has been possible to see on British screens some of the work of Ibsen, de Montherlant, Shakespeare, Tennessee Williams, T. S. Eliot, Sophocles, and Jean-Paul Sartre. For those who are denied access to the live theatre, television, like sound-radio before it, is a very acceptable substitute.

If one includes within the term 'general knowledge' all of serious drama and all of current affairs, then the happy con clusion must be that over 40 per cent of the output of British television comes within this category; an effective answer to those who still maintain that television is generally trivial and time-wasting.

Dangers of the Popular Approach

This apparently happy state of affairs has, however, its dangers, and they spring from the 'digest' nature of most informative television. For we live at a time when more people than ever before know a little about everything but not very much about anything. It is too easy to sit before a television screen in one's own living-room and to believe (out of laziness rather than conscious conviction) that a short series of pro- grammes, however well produced, can say all that needs be said about either ancient Greece or contemporary chronic illnesses. To watch Sir Kenneth Clark or Sir Gerald Kelly discussing the masterpieces of painting (and moreover in black-and-white) is no substitute for a visit to an art gallery, and the job of tele- vision in the field of information should surely be less the satis- faction of our needs than the provision of the sort of stimulus which leads us to pursue each subject further and deeper in our time.

I am not arguing here out of pessimism, for happily there is evidence to suggest that this is precisely what is happening. We know, for example, that a television outside broadcast from an exhibition in Burlington House is immediately followed by a dramatic increase in attendance at the exhibition itself. We also know that the emphasis which British television showed for many years in archaeology was directly reflected in the buying and borrowing of books on the same subject. And is it, one wonders, purely coincidental that more people are attending evening classes than ever before?

The programmes which I am discussing in this chapter have a single purpose, to convey knowledge interestingly. They are not, with rare exceptions, didactic programmes, or programmes of debate, nor do they pretend to present a personal vision of the world. They rarely make claims to be works of art. The techniques they employ are harnessed to this single purpose, and the function of the producer and director is of a nature to demand the utmost self-denial. Here is no place for smart gimmicks or personal flourishes. Each programme must, of course, entertain as well as inform, or the audience will gradually drift away into other and more stimulating pastures, but they will fail at the moment when the entertainment gains the upper hand, or the information seems to be dull or unimportant. What is needed, clearly, is subdued shownmanship, and what James McCloy has written about programmes of science is true of all the subject-matter within this very broad field:

"In all exposition of science, showmanship is as important as it is elsewhere in television. The creation of suspense may however take a quite different form in which intellectual tension substitutes for emotional tension as in many detective stories. This engagement of the curiosity of the audience so that they are led step by step through the unravelling of a scientific argument adopts a kind of detective-story technique. Controversy is unfortunately rarely possible as a component to involve the attention of the large audience. For one thing there is little of it in the scientific knowledge at the level of the audience. Where it is present is usually at the frontier of knowledge, and scientists arguing it out in a natural manner in front of cameras would be unintelligible to an audience with no background of science. To take an admittedly extreme case, it is difficult to imagine Hoyle and Royle arguing out the rival merits of their theories of cosmology for the entertainment of a peak-hour audience."[1]

[1] *The Journal of the Society of Film and Television Arts*, Winter 1963-4.

Precisely; and the first duty of the producer in this field is to decide at what 'level', whether of intelligence or interest, he should aim. If he is making programmes about archaeology he is not presumably making them for professional students. For such people there are specialised programmes which are transmitted during those hours labelled For Schools or Adult Education. What he wants is the largest audience he can get without lowering his standards. All the pitfalls of the professional populariser lie before him, and he has done his work well if he holds the attention of a big audience without forfeiting the respect of those who work in whatever science or art he has chosen to handle. This is a thin tightrope, and many have fallen off it during the public performance. For it is as disastrous to be cheap and superficial as it is to be pedantic and obscure.

This basic challenge confronts the producer of science as well as the producer of history, and the producer of programmes on gardening as much as the producer of programmes about the customs of remote tribes. It is against the background of this challenge that any survey of information programmes must be made.

Aspects of History

History, as a subject, lends itself very readily to treatment by television, for so much of the past is still available in visual form: ancient monuments, paintings, household objects, photographs and, for the past three-quarters of a century, moving-film and the existence of eye-witnesses. Television's essays into the past have assumed a wide variety of forms, from an archaeological parlour-game like *Animal, Vegetable, Mineral* to the imaginative use of still photographs to recreate *The Real West*, from a straight lecture without illustration of any kind, to such highly sophisticated compilation films as *The Thirties* and *The Jazz Age*, and from acted reconstructions to programmes in which eminent Generals relive their victories and distinguished politicians record their deepest thoughts for the benefit of future generations.

To generalise; the producer of programmes of history has the choice of using costumed actors, genuine eye-witnesses, or professional historians; he can bring ancient objects to the studio, or he can take his cameras to the ancient objects; he can show paintings or still photographs, and he can raid the film libraries for the wealth of original film which has been shot at any time between the beginning of the century and the present day. He may recreate the past by means of models. He may use these devices separately or he may choose to combine them within a single programme or series of programmes, and they are by now so much a part of the routine stock-in-trade of contemporary television that it is perhaps wise to treat them in turn.

Costumed Actors

This is the least used and probably the least successful of all those devices. To have actors play Napoleon or Henry VIII or George Washington or Oliver Cromwell may be an obvious way of presenting the past, and indeed a series called *You are There* ran for some time both in the United States and in Britain, but it is ultimately both restrictive and artificial, and can too easily degenerate into the worst form of village-pump mummery.

You are There had at least the advantage of an imaginative gimmick, for each programme was presented as though it were a live outside broadcast or a filmed current affairs report. In this way the audience was involved more intimately than usual in the proceedings. Yet this was essentially an artificial device, and *You are There* remained an artificial series, a charade of only moderate conviction, poised uneasily between routine costume drama and an intellectual exercise. Not only did it tend to lack authority (being largely the work of dramatists rather than of historians) but its very nature made it superficial, a series about incidents and people rather than the deeper significances of history.

As Patrick Hazard wrote:[1] "*It tends to over-personalise history: great men (they can be seen in dramatic close-up) overshadow great trends. . . . It tends to over-simplify causation and motivation: a half-hour is no time for historiographical quibbling. It tends to focus on surface exotica at the expense of significant explanation; the strange clothing, the odd custom, the telegenic detail—all these come to the surface of a television screen more easily than human motivation, social tension. Finally, violent action fills a screen more arrestingly than below-the-surface transformation.*" Or, in James McCloy's admirable phrase, 'intellectual tension' had not taken the place of emotional tension, and the merits of *You are There* were those

[1] In the issue of *Contrast* for Winter 1962.

of the drama, with each sequence written and played for its dramatic interest rather than its historical relevance. It was an easy way out of the problems of presenting serious history seriously, and like most easy ways it proved in the end to be a path through a barren landscape.

A far more successful experiment in the same field was Peter Watkins's *Culloden* (BBC), which reconstructed this rather ignoble moment of British history by a film that was shot on, or near to the scenes of the actual occasion, and which used non-professional actors, many of them the descendants of the Highlanders who fought there. *Culloden* also employed the familiar devices of the current affairs report, so that those who supposedly lived through the battle and its aftermath faced the camera and related their experience. *Culloden* certainly succeeded despite the artificiality of its central device. The reason for its success, I suspect, lay in its sense of mission, for this was much less of an objective piece of history (indeed as history it was somewhat tendentious) than a personal essay on war and cruelty. As such it had a tremendous power. Its emotive content was so great, and its sincerity so transparent, that the viewer hardly ever found himself conscious of its essential trickery.

Genuine Eyewitnesses

Old men forget, so we are told. Fortunately, however, this is by no means always so, and television, like sound-radio before it, has done a considerable service to itself and to posterity by recording the views and the experiences of those who have observed great events. When *CBS Reports* persuaded General Eisenhower to return with a film unit to the Normandy bridgehead—the programme was shown simultaneously in several countries on the twentieth anniversary of D-Day—they must have known that their completed programme would in the course of time become a document of greatest historical value. A few years previously Field-Marshal Montgomery had accepted an invitation from the BBC to discuss with the aid of film and maps his own campaigns during the second world war.[1]

When the American Broadcasting Company produced their series, *The Valiant Years*, based on the memoirs of Sir Winston

[1] Also, on the twentieth anniversary of VE Day the BBC and CBS combined, by satellite, to present a live programme in which Eisenhower and Montgomery took part on opposite sides of the Atlantic.

Churchill, they sensibly included statements by people, great and small, who had been present on occasions of significance. Both *The Twentieth Century* and *European Journal*, in items which reconstructed the attempt on Hitler's life in 1944, chose to look at the past through the eyes of those men who themselves either took part in the plot or were witness of it. In *The Life and Times of Marshal Tito* (written for the BBC by Sir Fitzroy Maclean and produced by Stephen Hearst) sequences of archival film were punctuated, and indeed illuminated, by carefully spaced extracts from an interview which Tito had recorded for the programme. The film thus became a dialogue on his life, seen partly through the eyes of Maclean and partly through those of Tito himself.

It has become almost a tradition for American Presidents and British Prime Ministers to submit to lengthy and frank interviews in depth, in which they are given the time to discuss fully their own policies, the personalities of their time, and their views on world affairs and political systems. Ex-President Truman has already committed himself in this way, as have Earl Attlee and Harold Macmillan, and it has sometimes been a condition of such interviews that certain sections of them shall not be made public until either special permission is given or else a suitable period of time has elapsed. In this way it has been possible to achieve complete frankness (essential for the historians of the future) without overstepping the barriers of tact and discretion.

It is clear from this random catalogue that television's eye-witnesses have been of two kinds; the men who 'do' (politicians, generals, scientists, writers) and those who merely 'watch' (soldiers, spectators, and friends of the famous). Often, of course, the same programme will include both kinds—the set of profiles which *Panorama* has produced, for instance, has included both Cabinet Ministers and those less exalted persons who knew the Cabinet Ministers when they were at school, or in industry, or perhaps selling furs in a large store. In programmes about war, the memories of the private soldier are often as valuable as those of the Field-Marshal, and many television programmes have found room for both.

By definition, of course, the eye-witness, even in these days of human longevity, is limited to the subject-matter of the past three-quarters of a century, but the point is worth making here

134

that most television programmes are recorded in permanent form, either on film or on tape, and there seems no technical reason why those of them which deal with contemporary history should not be preserved for the benefit of future generations. To appreciate the true value of what is being shown in our own time, one has merely to imagine the impact of a television series, in which we ourselves could see and hear Napoleon, Washington, Gladstone, or Disraeli. The duty of the makers of historical programmes is not entirely, or perhaps even primarily, to the audiences of their own age.

Professional Historians

It has always been one of the merits of television that it can obtain the services of 'the man who knows' and persuade him to pass on his knowledge to the public as it sits comfortably before several million little screens. In this sense the historian is the equivalent of the scientist, the doctor, the artist, or the gardener. He is the professional, and as such he commands respect.

The most surprisingly successful example of television's exploitation (I use the word in the nicest possible way) of the historian was the series of lectures given in Britain by the Oxford don, A. J. P. Taylor. I have written 'surprisingly' not out of any disrespect for Mr. Taylor, but because the very idea of asking a gentleman from academic life to stand before a single camera and speak for the greater part of an hour, without either notes or visual aids, would once have produced hollow laughter among those theorists who used to protest most loudly that television is a visual medium (and I know, because I myself was one of them).

The success of the experiment (the producer was John Irwin) lay largely in Mr. Taylor's impish personality and genius as a lecturer (if he chose to talk about a blade of grass he could keep his audience spellbound), but also in the very obvious enjoyment which so many of us share about the past. History is interesting, and we are prepared to accept it as such. Of course Mr. Taylor and his producer chose subjects (and often these subjects were people) which contained drama and excitement, nor did they ever wander too far into those paths and alleys which are a delight only to the professionals. But the point was well and truly made; a historian can stand up in front of a television camera and hold a large audience for an hour or so without rushing for sanctuary to the customary visual aids. Yet, of course, it is not quite as simple as that, for Mr. Taylor is also a television performer of considerable experience who has also written and narrated compilation programmes of contemporary history. The professional historian who hopes to succeed in television must also take his television as seriously as he takes his history.

It also helps if he is something of a personality—what in a friendly way we would call a 'character'. A. J. P. Taylor is such a person. So is Sir Mortimer Wheeler, the archaeologist, who became a television star in the most popular sense, after his appearance in that intellectual parlour-game, *Animal, Vegetable, Mineral*. Since then he has appeared in many more ambitious programmes, never failing to transfer to the audience his own infectious enthusiasm for ancient civilisations, and for the detective story that is called archaeology. In *Hellenic Cruise* he took us by boat to ancient Greece, and later, in *The Grandeur that was Rome*, he steered us across the Roman Empire from Britain to North Africa and from Gaul to the Near East. He, like A. J. P. Taylor, is not only respected in those erudite places where academics meet over bottles of claret, but is also a man who has worked hard at television, has studied it carefully, and does not despise the need to popularise. Moreover he can do it without either slipping into inaccuracy (the very idea is indeed absurd) or losing dignity.

Ancient Objects in the Studio

Or not, perhaps, so ancient. *Animal, Vegetable, Mineral* was a parlour game in which, in each edition, a museum produced some of its choicest specimens, mainly archaeological, and defied a panel of experts to recognise and describe them. On other occasions and in other programmes our television studios have contained objects whose size has varied from a tiny coin to a stage-coach, and the merits of being able to bring into people's homes something of the value and flavour of a museum is too obvious to need labouring.

Taking the Cameras to the Objects

An 'object', in this sense, can be a museum or a castle or a battlefield. Many years ago John Read produced a series of

136

programmes about Britain's country houses and their splendid contents. He filmed the houses and the gardens, and he brought some of their most exciting treasures to the studio. This was at a time when the outside broadcast was in its infancy : today the whole of each programme would almost certainly have come from within the houses themselves.

In the summer of 1964, in a series called *Brush off the Dust*, Fyfe Robertson visited a series of British museums, taking in each case a theme or a story as the shape of the programme; the materials from the Admiral Blake Museum in Bridgwater served to illustrate the Battle of Sedgemoor, and some remnants in the National Maritime Museum at Greenwich—a bit of fur, some gold braid, a few spoons and forks—were used as the pathetic evidence of that sad voyage in 1845 when two naval ships, commanded by Sir John Franklin, set off in search of the North-West Passage and were last seen moored hopefully to an iceberg near Lancaster Sound. History, drama, heroism, and mystery were all intermingled. To take outside-broadcast cameras to a museum and merely to show some of the exhibits in their glass cases is obviously not enough. It is just as important to relate them to their social background, to the human beings to whom they were familiar daily objects, and to the true incidents of which they remain the only visible evidence.

Thus, in *The Glory that was Greece* and *The Grandeur that was Rome*, film cameras visited the surviving monuments of those classical civilisations; but the successive themes of each series were the epic that was Greece and the epic that was Rome. One of the purposes of such programmes must be to give life to evidence that is inanimate and apparently dead, to recapture its memories, to use it as a starting point in an imaginative evocation of the past. One of the most effective programmes in this field was the BBC's film on the Battle of Agincourt (written and narrated by Robert Hardy and directed by Peter Newington) which attempted to express the true feeling and meaning of that battle, and which used the available evidence in the way that the hero of a detective novel will use whatever clues happen to come his way. In this case the clues included armour and weapons, the weather (the mud of north-eastern France was a vivid reference for those who remembered Flanders from 1914 to 1918), and the precise location where the battle was fought.

Similarly, on the hundredth anniversary of the outbreak of

137

the American Civil War, *CBS Reports* persuaded Carl Sandburg to make a pilgrimage to the battleground of Gettysburg.

Paintings and Still Photographs

When Sir Brian Horrocks presented a series of popular biographies called *Great Captains* (produced by Thérèse Denny) he made use of contemporary portraits. Sir Basil Spence in his film on Sir Christopher Wren (produced by John Read) referred to plans and prints of the day. Hogarth's London, like Canaletto's Venice, has proved a reliable stand-by for the television producer who seeks something more than the contents of a museum or the visible ruins of the past, and the imaginative use of stills, whether they be paintings or prints or photographs, has inspired some of the most exciting moments in television's treatment of history. In NBC's *Project XX*, Donald B. Hyatt has used 'action stills', specially composed music, and narration, in a way which prompted many television organisations elsewhere to wonder why they themselves had never thought of doing it, and to set off in search of rare stills of all kinds.

Hyatt's subject-matter has been specifically American. It is American history that he has presented, and the nostalgia of Americans for their not-so-distant past on which he has relied for his emotional impact. In *Meet Mr. Lincoln, Mark Twain's America,* and *The Real West* he gave a new edge to traditional themes, so that his audiences seemed to be seeing their childhood legends for the first time. He was not afraid of exploiting familiar music, and he was not shy of an occasional trick—for example, he used the late Gary Cooper, an actor who had appeared in many Western film, to introduce and to narrate *The Real West*.

Inspired by Hyatt's activities, and slightly envious of his initiative in being the first to enter the field (or apparently so, but the National Film Board of Canada had showed the way even earlier with a quite superb film made from still photographs of a gold rush), British television has since made a few sporadic sallies into the same field. John Read's film on Scott's expedition to the South Pole used, among other means, the magnificent still photographs which were taken on the expedition itself, and Paul Bonner has ventured into less familiar territory in his *Strange Excellency*, a portrait of Sir John Pope-Hennessy, the nineteenth-century Colonial servant. Still

138

photographs have become one of the regular ingredients of television biography, whether in short pieces like the *Panorama* profiles (the distinguished national leader seen in the middle of the back row of the school group) or in more ambitious works like the BBC's life of T. E. Lawrence, a subject on which there is very little material in the form of moving-film.

There are also those occasions when the only way of treating an essential moment of history is by the use of stills. Such a moment was the assassination of the Archduke Ferdinand at Sarajevo in 1914. This was an occasion which could scarcely be omitted in any television treatment of the events of that year, yet the event was not in fact covered by any film which is known to exist.

A still picture need not be a dead picture. By isolating parts of it, by moving a camera across it, by zooming into it or out of it, by taking angled shots of it, by cutting it dramatically, by using it with an imaginatively composed track of sound-effects or music, its essential stillness can be successfully camouflaged. I myself once met an enthusiastic viewer of *The Real West* who never realised that what he was watching was a set of still photographs. He thought he had witnessed a carefully composed 'compilation' film.

The Use of Library Film

The use of historical film is perhaps the most effective way of presenting the history of our own century. The method is not new—some splendid 'compilation' films had been made for the cinema—but television has used it more consistently and more effectively than the cinema has ever done. In 1954 the BBC began a series called *First Hand* (produced by Paul Johnstone and Nancy Thomas) which included among its subjects the *Titanic* disaster, the first transatlantic flight, the first tanks and the first airships, and the Suffragettes. Each programme consisted in roughly equal proportions of statements in the studio by those who had themselves experienced the events, and historic film—a formula which has since become a routine. In the USA the pioneer was Henry Salomon, who worked for NBC and died, sadly young, in 1957. He was responsible for *Victory at Sea*, a naval history of the second world war, and in 1954 he launched *Project XX*, with *Three, Two, One, Zero*, followed by *Nightmare in Red* (a history of Communism), *The Twisted Cross* (the story of Nazism), *The Great War*, and films about American life in the 1920s and 1930s.

Much of the success of a historical compilation depends on the imagination and technical skill of its film editor, and it was Salomon's own editor, Isaac Kleinerman, who joined CBS in 1957 to become associate producer, with Burton Benjamin, of *The Twentieth Century*, a series which has regularly presented twenty-six programmes a year since then (not all of them have been compilation films, but most of them have). *Victory at Sea* was followed in Britain by *War in the Air*, an almost exactly parallel series, made by the BBC under the direction of Philip Dorté, and produced by John Elliot, and six years later the American Broadcasting Company presented a series based on the Churchill memoirs, *The Valiant Years*.

Having thus disposed at considerable length of the second world war—or one would hope so, though in such matters nothing is ever certain—television organisations have more recently turned their minds to its predecessor, realising in their endless search for topicality that it began fifty years ago. The BBC were the first in the field this time, offering twenty-six films, each of forty minutes, with the exact title of *The Great War*, and produced by Tony Essex (a distinguished film editor who had worked for several years on *Tonight*) and Gordon Watkins. CBS began their own Great War series a few months later, and the name of Isaac Kleinerman figured prominently and almost inevitably in the credits.

If the Americans have tended to concentrate on the broad sweep of contemporary history, the British have specialised in biography. On the eve of the American Presidential Election of 1960, Anthony de Lotbinière made a composite biography of the two candidates, Kennedy and Nixon, in which he used historical film, statements by those who had known them at various stages of their lives, still photographs, film that was specially shot in places with which they had particular associations and, in the case of Kennedy, a personal interview. The same method was used in a double portrait of Konrad Adenauer and Willy Brandt (produced this time by Malcom Brown) on the occasion of the West German Election of 1961.

Malcom Brown also collaborated with Philip Donnellan (a producer whose name had previously been associated with highly personal documentaries) in a series of ambitious bio-
140

graphies which included among its subjects T. E. Lawrence, Nehru, and Nkrumah. All of these films were made by the BBC, but Independent Television entered the field when Granada mounted two series of *Men of Our Time*, produced by Patricia Lagone.

On broader non-biographical lines, Malcolm Muggeridge has written and narrated for the BBC several compilation films, of which the most distinguished were *The Thirties* (produced by Andrew Miller Jones) and two films on the USA and Soviet Russia respectively, and called *The Titans* (produced by Thérèse Denny). Granada has for three years produced a regular series, *All Our Yesterdays* which draws on period film as well as still photographs, for a weekly picture of life twenty-five years ago.

In theory there must be an end to the amount of historical film which is available and still untapped, and indeed many of the same shots have appeared on several occasions in films with different titles and made by different producers. The most obvious example of this kind of cliché is the sequence at London Airport in 1938 when Neville Chamberlain returned from Munich and displayed the 'piece of paper' which carried his signature alongside that of Adolf Hitler. Both world wars have produced dramatic shots which have cropped up with a some-times tedious regularity. There was overlapping between *Victory at Sea*, *War in the Air*, and *The Valiant Years*, and much of the same material from the war of 1914 18 appeared in both the BBC and CBS series—no doubt inevitably, for there is expectedly less film from 1914–18 than from 1939–45.

Sequences of Britain in the depression of the 1930s, of the 'gay' 1920s in America, of the Russian revolution of 1917, of the Spanish Civil War, of the Wall Street crash, of the abdication of Edward VIII, of Hitler's rallies, of Roosevelt's New Deal, all these have become the familiar quotations of the television his-torian. For each successive producer the task of finding original film becomes slightly more difficult—and, incidentally, con-siderably more expensive, for those who possess rare film of this sort have long since realised its market value. It was not perhaps the fault of the producers that *The Valiant Years* seemed less exciting than *Victory at Sea*, or that the film of Hitler in *Men of Our Time* appeared to add little to what we had already seen.

The making of a successful compilation film, involving as it does an assembly of shots which were originally taken on a score of separate occasions, without any thought of their ultimate relationship, demands the imposing of a shape and a style on material which otherwise would seem to be random and haphazard. This can be done partly in the editing—the flavour of trench warfare can be suggested by the skilful use of shots that were taken on many occasions by cameramen of several nationalities—but it depends also on the quality of the spoken commentary, on the imaginative use of sound effects, and on whatever music may be chosen or written. It is hardly a coincidence that some of the richest commentaries in British television have been written for compilation films; by Malcolm Muggeridge for *The Thirties*, *The Titans* and *Stanley Baldwin*; by James Cameron for *Lenin*; by Patrick O'Donovan for *Nehru* and *Nkrumah*; by A. J. P. Taylor for *King George V*, and by John Morgan and Robert Kee for the *Panorama* profiles.

A writer of quality, working with a producer and an editor of high technical skill, can create the impression that he himself has chosen the pictures with the same care that he has devoted to the words. The relationship between words and images is both precise and subtle. So it should be with music: a section of music can bind together a sequence of images, so that what might otherwise appear to be a careless selection of pictures, each apparently having the slenderest connection with the next, becomes a pointed comment.

In this way a set of original variations on the popular music of the 1920s can do rather more than merely bind together a collection of shots of that time, and in his film on *Elgar* Ken Russell made an effective comment on illusion and reality by placing the first Pomp and Circumstance March (whose main theme still means Land of Hope and Glory) behind shots of the horror and carnage of the first world war.

Effects, often without either words or music, can also have a similarly 'binding' quality. All the shots taken during the Soviet Revolution were inevitably silent, but there were effective and realistic revolution sequences in *The Titans*, *Lenin* and *The Life and Times of Marshal Tito*. It never, apparently, occurs to the viewer that what he is witnessing is a fake, that the pictures are authentic but the sounds are fabricated in a dubbing theatre. For him it is enough that the film is persuasive and fluent.

142

Maps, Diagrams, and Models

When those wartime generals, Eisenhower, Montgomery, and Horrocks, discussed their campaigns on television, they all made good and necessary use of maps and diagrams. When Sir Brian Horrocks considered the Duke of Marlborough's achievement at Blenheim, he used a model of the countryside surrounding the battlefield. Television has used models of warships, Roman villas and Greek temples, old railway engines, and chariots. It could hardly be expected to ignore the facilities which have been the schoolmaster's stock-in-trade for so long, but the problem of the television producer is an artistic one—how to make use of something which is essentially artificial within a programme which contains much that is real.

Combination Methods

I have listed these 'devices' in this way purely for convenience, nor am I suggesting that they are mutually exclusive. Indeed the success of the producer of programmes of history will depend upon the extent to which he can blend them without losing either style or integrity. It is, for example, difficult to mix historical film or still photographs (which are genuine) with actors (who are artificial). This mistake was made, with very unhappy results, in one or two of the earlier films in the series *The Valiant Years*, when familiar character actors appeared as officers of the armed forces or as blitzed Londoners. The moment they entered the screen was also the moment when the film lost conviction and integrity. Nor is it as easy as it might seem to contain within the same programme the outside 'expert' and the genuine eye-witness, or the model of a battlefield and film shots of the battle itself, or still photographs intercut with moving pictures.

The most effective programme of history tends to fit into one of two opposite patterns; either it is extremely simple (a straight lecture with or without exhibits, or a compilation film in which all other devices are excluded), or else it uses several of those devices and succeeds because the producer has managed to fuse them so successfully that the fact of their being different in kind has been altogether concealed. In his film on the Scott expedition of 1912 John Read moved smoothly from stills to film, and then back to stills again. Peter Newington's essay on

143

Agincourt, more ambitiously, used museum exhibits, film of the battlefield, contemporary illustrations, and recreated impressions of the time and the weather, and yet each separate device seemed to be absolutely correct, necessary, and in its proper place.

The function of the producer or director in programmes of history, as indeed in information programmes of every kind, is to translate the known and available facts into acceptable sequences of images and sounds. To some extent his work is a compromise, for he is (whether he likes it or not) a professional populariser. He knows his audience better than does the historian on whose knowledge he has to rely, and he knows rather more history than his audience. He is thus a middle-man, with all the frustrations and anxieties of the middle-man. His historians and his eye-witnesses will almost certainly ask for more detail than the mass audience can take, and the audience itself can be too easily satisfied with the half-truth or the academically slipshod. Yet he has one very considerable asset on his side; he knows that the public are interested in the past, and in the people of the past. It is not difficult therefore to 'sell' history to a big audience, as long as it is lively and full of feeling, and as long as it avoids what is dusty and dull.

Presenting Science

When Sir Cyril Hinshelwood was the President of the Royal Society he wrote these words of science in general:

"It is very difficult for any but experts to understand what is going on, not as so many non-scientific people are fond of asserting, because men of science are incapable of expressing themselves clearly, or are unwilling to try, but for the simple reason that many aspects of the subject are of very great inherent difficulty. They are based upon unfamiliar conceptions, often developed by advanced mathematical reasoning and sometimes expressed in a complex and abstract symbolism."[1]

Science is much more complicated than history, partly for the reasons given in that quotation and partly because so much of it is less directly related to our ordinary daily lives. The problems which confronted those who lived in the past, whether

[1] Quoted by James McCloy in the *Journal of the Society of Film and Television Arts*, Winter 1963-4, page 11.

in ancient Rome or in the America of the 1920s, are recognisably the familiar problems of men and women in any period. Only the techniques of living are different. On the other hand, there are many aspects of science which seem to affect our daily lives only remotely, and which, because they are concerned with ideas and with objects instead of with people require a conscious intellectual effort before they begin to have any meaning. A shop-girl who can easily become interested in what women were wearing in the eighteenth century is likely to take fright at the prospect of a television programme on relativity.

Of course it is absurd to suggest at a time when man is striving to reach the moon, and when more and more bizarre machines are taking over his daily tasks, that science must always be boring or academic. The truth is that some science is both of those things, and that ideas in the world of science are often highly complicated and sometimes obscure. Scientists, moreover, are accustomed to address their remarks to other scientists, in a language which is familiar to them but is often difficult for the rest of us.

I believe therefore that the producer of programmes of science has a more delicate task than the producer of history in making his basic decisions about the size, background knowledge, and initial interest of his potential audience, and for this reason there are always likely to be more minority science programmes than minority history programmes.

The producer of a series about aspects of health can probably assume a large and responsive audience, for health is something which we all share, and mankind has constantly displayed a curious and sentimental interest in the sick. If however his assignment is in the field of physics or mathematics he can assume neither initial concern nor potential curiosity, and he is faced with a language and mode of thought which are unusually complicated. He may therefore decide that to popularise means to distort, and that he must reconcile himself to a small but highly discerning audience. Although, for instance, Professor Bondi's BBC programmes on relativity broke new ground merely by communicating to a television audience a series of ideas and principles which had hitherto been the preserve of a tiny group of those who were professionally interested, it nevertheless was transmitted out of peak viewing hours and was advertised as adult education.

K

At the other extreme there have been series of programmes like *Eye on Research* (which took live outside broadcast cameras to British research establishments) and *Your Life in Their Hands* (which took similar equipment to leading hospitals) which have collected and retained huge audiences, partly because their subject-matter seemed more immediately relevant to everyday life, and partly because it was never difficult to understand. The amount of intellectual effort which the average television viewer is prepared to give at the end of a tired working day is strictly limited, and as soon as he is pressed beyond his normal limits of co-operation he will either switch off or change to another Channel.

It is possible, however, to show what scientists are doing, without going too deeply into the arguments and principles which lie behind their activities. It is also possible to show what scientists *are*. Television has effectively achieved both these ends in recent years and without much difficulty. There was, for example, the hour-long BBC programme about the virus, *Smaller than Life*, which admittedly started with the advantage of a subject which concerns every human being whose nose has ever run, but which explained in considerable detail the structure of various types of virus, what is known about their behaviour, and how far science has reached in its fight to conquer them. The BBC has also mounted several programmes designed to show scientists as human beings, instead of as machines which can think but can rarely feel: *The Prize-winners* (about the British biologists who were awarded the Nobel Prize), *The Surgeons, The Cosmologists*.

Technique of the Science Programme

In terms of developed techniques television is admirably suited for the communication of science, for the translation of science into terms which a non-scientist can understand is made much easier by the use of visible apparatus (which sound-radio cannot supply) and of animated diagrams (which are beyond the scope of either radio or the printed page). The television studio can easily be converted into the scientist's laboratory; the viewer seems to be there, with the scientist, a guest in a peculiarly fascinating workshop, someone who is personally being shown the inner mysteries, and who therefore enjoys a spontaneous feeling of privilege. It is perhaps for this reason

146

that at a time when factual programmes have increasingly preferred the use of edited film to the comparative slowness of the
studio, science alone has frequently remained where it was, and
for a reason which is admirably stated by James McCloy:

*"Electronic studio cameras have one special quality in pre-
senting science in comparison with film technique. A scientist
talking about his subject naturally wants, and for effective communication needs to show, various bits and pieces—the materials he works on, his apparatus, models, and so on. These
demonstrations in fact should be closely woven into the exposition. To present this on film involves a long series of indi-
vidually prepared and separately taken shots which are later
edited to give the illusion of continuous action. In contrast,
using three or more television cameras, we have continuous
action and the programme can be recorded without any interference to the flow of the argument. With an amateur speaker
the gain in naturalness and sense of communication achieved
by this technique adds almost another dimension."*[1]

James McCloy writes there of a programme which can be
recorded on tape, but it can also be argued strongly that programmes of science, and especially those which involve the
performing of an experiment of some sort, should ideally be
transmitted live. For an experiment that is carried out in a
television studio, or on location by means of an outside broadcast, has something of the natural drama of a sporting event in
which something unexpected might happen at any moment.
The experiment might fail, or it might run into problems which
are themselves a heightening of the dramatic tension, or it
might produce a different result from the one expected.

The fact that such excitements hardly ever occur does not
destroy the atmosphere of expectant anticipation. The viewer
is watching something which is truly taking place at the very
moment of transmission, and no one really knows what will
happen. The tension which such a situation produces in the
audience is something which was once regarded as one of television's greatest assets, and to pre-record a programme (and
thereby eliminate anything which departs from an arranged
plan) is to throw this enormous advantage through the window.

[1] *The Journal of the Society of Film and Television Arts*, Winter 1963-4,
page 11.

Television cameras, for instance, have frequently visited the operating theatres of hospitals, and audiences have been privileged to watch surgeons at work, performing a real operation on a genuine patient.

To transmit such a sequence live is infinitely more effective than to pre-record it, for there is always an added sense of occasion in being present when something so dramatic is actually happening. To be allowed to watch something which took place yesterday or last week is a poor substitute.

The Expert Approach

The best programmes of science, I believe, are those which are live, which either rely upon a distinguished scientist for their entire exposition or else can call upon a series of such experts to explain various facets of the subject as they arise, and which either use the studio as a laboratory, filling it with models or moving diagrams or pieces of practical equipment, or else go themselves to the laboratory.

Science, more than any other subject-matter, needs the personal communication of the expert, making use of equipment and devices which are familiar to him in his professional life. The function of the producer is to translate the arguments and the information into the technical language of television. It is not his job to impose a view of his own, though he will often find himself saying bluntly to Professor This or Doctor That, "I'm very sorry, but no one who isn't a scientist can possibly be expected to understand this particular section. We'll really have to expand it, or else simplify it in some other way."

The producer will therefore make suggestions, but they will be suggestions of presentation rather than of essential content. He may, for example, realise that a point which is obscure when presented in the form of spoken words becomes perfectly clear when helped along by an animated diagram. What is important is that the completed programme should seem to be the work of the scientists themselves, and this is the main reason why programmes about science rarely use script-writers in the conventional sense. *Smaller Than Life*, for example, was given a shape and an over-all argument by Gordon Rattray Taylor, who is a scientist, a journalist, and a man with considerable experience of the resources of television. But the programme itself succeeded less because of Mr. Taylor's admirable activities

148

than through the authority of the scientists who in turn 'conducted' each section of the programme and the clarity with which they expressed their (sometimes) complicated information and ideas. This clarity was not of course achieved by the scientists alone, but was the result of the combined expertise of the scientists, the writer (Gordon Rattray Taylor), the producer (Philip Daly), the director (Bill Wright), the designer of the studio sets, the makers of models, and so on. These television practitioners existed to help the scientists in their task of popularisation with integrity, but as far as the audience is concerned it is the scientists themselves who must seem to be in control of the programme.

It is, I hope, generally accepted that television has an obligation towards science and the scientist which should be as compelling as its more familiar wooing of politics and politicians. In modern society's attempt to bridge the 'two cultures', television has an essential part to play, and the fact that many of the more significant of scientific ideas and arguments are highly complex and apparently obscure is really no excuse for dismissing them as irrelevant.

On the other hand it is a fact that the audience for programmes which are concerned with scientific principles is likely, for the time being at any rate, to be a small one—but so at one time was the audience for serious programmes devoted to current affairs.

The BBC by means of its second channel, has given itself both an excuse and an opportunity to dig more deeply into current scientific wisdom than a single service, with more than half an eye on the size of its audience, could ever hope to do. Moreover both the BBC and some of the independent contractors have deliberately experimented in adult education, offering serious programmes of information at times of day when the audience is limited to a few eager enthusiasts—in the mornings and afternoons of Saturdays and Sundays, or before breakfast. Education at dawn has for some years been a familiar part of American television, and it may yet spread to the continent of Europe. The bridgehead, at any rate, has already been made.

Popular Science

Despite these admirable activities, there must always be a place for science programmes of a less erudite kind, presented at

149

peak hours and aimed at a mass audience. The subject-matter of popular science is already considerable, from astronomy (the BBC has for several years run a series called *The Sky at Night*) to electronic machines, and from patterns of disease to cosmology. Society is increasingly calling upon its scientists to help it in fields of economic and social development, and science is constantly in the news; the contraceptive pill, the route to the moon, an outbreak of typhoid, the design of a supersonic aircraft, the arguments for or against the fluoridation of water, the connection between smoking and lung cancer—all these are occasions when the frontier between science and current affairs is blurred and uncertain.

Although many areas of science will for a long time remain obscure to the layman, and especially those which are concerned with what science *is* rather than with what it does, it is reasonable to suppose that in an age of technology more and more scientific information will become not only interesting but necessary. The audience for programmes of the more general kind will increase, and so, significantly, will the willingness of that audience to accept information which only a few years ago would have baffled and bored it. When, in the spring of 1964, the BBC presented a programme called *From Strength to Strength*, which had as its subject the search for new materials (for defence, for industry, for housing, and so on), it received so many letters and enjoyed such an enthusiastic public response that the programme was repeated several weeks later. Yet the subject, on the face of it, was scarcely a box-office one.

The future development of programmes of science, in the strategic sense, will presumably show a widening of the audience both for the popular subjects (what science is doing in the modern world and what scientists *are*) and for the minority subjects which at present are always transmitted at off peak hours and frequently at those times of day which are consciously devoted to adult education. Let us hope that the popular programmes will stimulate an interest in science that is serious enough to tempt at least a few non-scientists to try the more erudite minority programmes. In this way the barrier between popular science and academic science might gradually disappear, and so, ultimately, will that profounder and more depressing barrier which in the public mind still separates the 'two cultures'.

150

Travel, Natural History and Anthropology

These are three branches of popular science. They are also a field of television where depth of intellectual content does not necessarily imply a loss of audience. Travel, of a chocolate-box sort, can slip delicately into anthropology, and natural history is a subject which can exploit man's fascination for animal life and lead the passive viewer into byways whose profundity becomes deeper without becoming obscure or tedious. Every showman knows that human beings are always willing to be interested in animals, foreign countries, and other human beings.

Television's treatment of natural history began with programmes in which an expert (usually the curator of a zoo) brought a few animals to the studio. If the expert was an attractive personality, as George Cansdale certainly was in the early 1950s, this was a simple and effective way of introducing a large audience to a subject whose appeal is immediate but whose true significance, like that of an iceberg, lies concealed.

To be given the chance of studying animals in close-up, and to have their behaviour patterns explained so simply and effectively, was a compulsive experience for millions of people whose knowledge of natural history had hitherto been confined to whatever could be gleaned from a Sunday afternoon visit to the local zoo. Yet although it served admirably as an introduction to its vast subject, this studio-bound method of presentation was certain to give way sooner or later to something more expensive and ambitious. For animals do not naturally live in zoos—still less do they live in television studios—and before long it became clear that the next step was to show them in their true environment.

The next stage in television's technical treatment of natural history was therefore to send out a film unit with the expert, and to photograph wild life as it really is. Thus both Peter Scott's programme, *Look*, and David Attenborough's *Zoo Quest*, included film sequences of animals living their natural lives, as well as sequences in which the animals were seen in the studio. *Zoo Quest*, indeed, was very accurately titled. It was a series in which David Attenborough travelled far and wide in search of the animals for the London Zoo. We saw the search for the animals, we saw their capture, and we saw them under the controlled conditions of the television studio. In *Look*, Peter

Scott frequently invited naturalists to come to the studio and show us both their own films and some of the birds and animals which were the subject-matter of those films.

The usual ingredients of a natural history programme were therefore (a) the expert, who was also an accomplished television personality, (b) film sequences shot on location and often in far-away places, and (c) the use of the live studio both for closer shots of captive animals and for interviews with other experts. More recently, programmes in this field have increasingly been made entirely as films. The studio sequences in *Zoo Quest* decreased in size and scope, and there seemed to be an insatiable demand for the popular zoological travelogue.

The BBC has for a long time had its own full-scale Natural History Unit, and Granada responded by setting up a unit of its own at the London Zoo. Its series, *People Like Us*, made a splendid attempt to inject into what had hitherto been a very personal and almost sedate form of television something of the techniques of urgency which have characterised *World in Action*. It used a highly professional narration, background (and sometimes foreground) music, and an editing style which had more in common with a current affairs series than with quiet films about bees and ants. Perhaps it went a little too far (like being drunk in church), but in many ways it was a logical 'next step' on the journey which had begun before the war when a charming enthusiast had first walked into a television studio with a monkey on his shoulder.

Need for the Expert

Many natural history programmes have added the appeal of travel to the appeal of animals, and films of travel and adventure, with or without the animals, have long been a staple part of the average viewer's diet. Often they have been the work of professional film-makers, and television has proved a consistent supporter of that recent phenomenon, the traveller-film director. But sometimes they have been the work of men who are professional travellers but only amateur film-makers, and occasionally, and most notably in the BBC series *Adventure* (edited successively by David Attenborough and Brian Branston), the man who is an amateur traveller as well as an amateur cameraman, has managed to sell his wares to television.

The snag about programmes of travel is the danger of repetition. It was possible until relatively recently to avoid this particular hazard by going slightly farther afield than anyone had ever been before, at least in a television programme, but today there are few areas of the world which have not been visited at some time or other by television film cameras. The tribal dance, however bizarre, has become a familiar cliché. We are the victims of a surfeit of riches, and the only cure is to substitute depth for breadth. When almost everywhere in the world has become familiar, the next step must be to look more profoundly at the same old places; to have less 'travel' and more 'anthropology'. It is at this point that the amateur must take his bow and leave us, for this is a field where the cameraman who is not an anthropologist cannot be sure that he is taking the right pictures, and the anthropologist who is not a film-maker has no idea how to take the shots he needs. David Attenborough has written about this particular dilemma :

"The film we need can only be produced by someone with an insight into the findings of anthropology. There are, however, several reasons why it is difficult for a practising anthropologist to provide such a film, particularly if he is expected to do so in the process of his own research. Merely using a camera may hamper him. As an anthropologist he should be an inconspicuous observer whose presence does not disrupt or interfere in any way with the activities he is witnessing. But if he is make a competent film of, for example, some ritual, he must obtain close-ups and wide-angle shots from several different viewpoints, and to do so may well disturb the participants in the activity he is recording. Worse, his value as a scientific observer may be considerably reduced, for instead of noting every action—and many may be going on simultaneously in widely separated places—his attention has to be distracted by the technicalities of handling his camera, and at crucial moments his eye, instead of being wide-ranging and alert for every detail, must be glued to his viewfinder.

"To produce the film we require an anthropologist must devote himself to the project for some considerable time, and allow no other consideration to deflect him. He must be as expert in cinematic techniques and requirements as he is in his own discipline. He must already be familiar with the people he is studying and know precisely what he wishes his film to say

153

before he begins filming. Few anthropologists would regard such work as being the most valuable way of spending their all too limited time in the field.

"One or two workers, however, have done so. Jean Rouch has produced vivid and profoundly revealing records of ceremonials in West Africa, and John and Elizabeth Marshall of the Peabody Museum, Harvard University, have filmed many aspects of the life of a nomadic band of bushmen in the Kalahari Desert. These brilliant films are pointers to what can be achieved."[1]

David Attenborough is no doubt too modest to mention his own name, but in Britain at any rate it is largely due to his own work for the BBC that the lay public has been guided gently from simple programmes about animals to complex and sometimes quite profound essays on primitive societies and the nature of human co-operation.

It is inevitable that until videotape is a more mobile device than it is at present such essays should be made on film, and because a ciné-camera is for many societies in the world a strange and intrusive machine, the equipment must be as portable and as inconspicuous as possible. So, indeed, must be the human beings who operate it. An anthropologist might succeed alone in conquering the hazards which David Attenborough has described, and he might return with a film of quality which he has shot himself. But at the other extreme, it is highly doubtful whether a film crew of normal size, with all the equipment and vehicles which they usually employ, could hope to catch a primitive society off its guard. The photographing of wild life, or of traditional and self-conscious communities, is a specialised activity, and if the anthropologist-director cannot use a camera himself he will be wise to join forces with someone who is not only a professional cameraman but who is interested enough in his subject-matter to take the necessary pains and to suffer the necessary inconveniences and hardships. Men like Hugh Gibb, Jean Rouch, Heinz Sielmann, and Eugen Schuhmacher have operated their own cameras; on the other hand David Attenborough worked for several years with one of two cameramen (Charles Lagus and Geoffrey Mulligan) who became highly praised experts in this field.

[1] In *The Journal of the Society of Film and Television Arts*, Winter 1963–4, page 15.

There is, of course, a significant social aspect to all this, and it is well expressed, once again, by David Attenborough:

"What is to be gained from such difficult work? It would certainly be possible to impart an understanding of societies organised on a totally different basis from our own. This is a need which is becoming increasingly urgent as the world contracts and as we sadly realise that racial misunderstanding— and its inevitable product, intolerance—remains more widespread and deeply rooted than we often care to admit. In addition, by the comparative use of film shot in several areas among dissimilar people, we can begin to recognise the factors and compulsions, the necessities and inevitabilities, which operate within all societies of human beings. Thus we may be able to look back at ourselves with a degree of objectivity that can be achieved in no other way. By understanding other societies, we may at last begin to understand the tangled and mystifying working of our own."[1]

When that happens, television will have travelled far from those early programmes when captive animals were first introduced to television studios.

Problems of the Arts

The presentation of the arts confronts the television producer with two basic problems, that of the audience (which is small and to some extent even hostile), and that of the subject-matter (which is only occasionally suited for the domestic screen).

We know statistically that the audience for such programmes is a small one. The BBC's fortnightly magazine programme, *Monitor*, had an audience one-third the size of that of *Panorama* and one-fifth that of *Coronation Street*. Inevitably, and as an immediate consequence, there have been comparatively few programmes on the arts, and those few have usually been relegated to off-peak viewing hours.[2] It is extremely difficult, moreover, for the producer to decide at what 'level' he should aim. Should he accept the smallness of his audience as an unalterable fact, and therefore limit his activities to making programmes

[1] *Journal of the Society of Film and Television Arts*, Winter 1963–4, page 15.

[2] In 1965 the BBC set up a new department, under Humphrey Burton, to handle programmes of a generally cultural kind, but at the time of writing it is too soon to assess its impact, though some splendid programmes of music have already been seen on BBC-2; which, sadly, is still a minority Channel.

for the few who are known to be interested, or should he try to attract an increasingly larger audience with programmes which are designed as incentives to conversion? Do his employers, come to that, give him the choice?

The problems presented by the subject-matter are equally disturbing, for television is often an unsatisfactory medium for expressing the arts, even those which are happily described as visual. Visual they may be, but black-and-white and two-dimensional they are certainly not.

Television is better—or perhaps I should write 'less wretched' —at presenting the merits of some painters than others, better at Delacroix and Canaletto than at Van Gogh or Turner; better when faced with pictures whose appeal comes from line and pattern rather than colour or texture. Sculpture is equally frustrating because, like architecture, it, too, is robbed of a dimension, and to track the camera round a sculpture is a poor substitute for the human being's ability in a gallery to look at it in his own time from whatever angles he chooses.

Two-dimensional television flattens everything out, and destroys perspective. I have myself yet to see a satisfactory television presentation of architecture, presumably because architecture presents the same problems as sculpture.

As for the non-visual arts, they have baffled television from the beginning. How does it present poetry, for instance? By letting us look at a man reading? By suggesting patterns and images which might conceivably reflect the mood of the poem? Or, because one of the most satisfactory ways of enjoying a poetry reading is to sit with one's eyes shut, by presenting us with a totally blank screen (a device which was once used experimentally by Cecil Day Lewis and Michael Redington)?

What about fiction? How does television discuss a novel? By having someone read from it, by having a group of critics discuss it (with or without the author), or by dramatising part of it? For the truth is that a work of fiction, like a poem, conjures up its own images in the reader's mind, and no two readers will ever see the same images.

How should television handle music? By showing us the musicians in the act of performance, or by attempting to illustrate the music in some way, as Disney did with eccentric results in *Fantasia*?

I am not concerned in this chapter with such television occasions as a concert, or an opera, or a ballet, for these are scarcely factual television. What does concern me is how television should behave when it assumes the role of the intellectual feature article or magazine—and, even more importantly, whether it assumes this role as often as it could or should.

The Audience

Let us consider, first of all, the problem of the audience. Of course to say somewhat sadly that programmes about the arts are minority programmes, watched by a small audience, is to use words which are extremely relative. The audiences of *Monitor* and *Tempo* (ITV's regular magazine of the arts, produced by ABC–TV) are no doubt small when compared with those of a popular light entertainment show, or a drama series, but they are nevertheless larger than the sales of almost any mass-circulation daily newspaper. To persuade up to five million people to spend fifty minutes or so watching and listening to an intelligent treatment of the fruits of the human creative imagination is a feat unique in British history, and should hardly be despised.

The point is worth making, because there is sometimes—indeed frequently—a tendency in this audience-conscious medium for programme executives to express worry and concern because certain programmes are less popular than others, regardless of the proven fact that they could never, at least at this moment of history, be popular in television's meaning of that word. To place them at ten or eleven o'clock at night, or perhaps in the barren wastes of a British Sunday afternoon, is merely to ensure a continuation of the very state of affairs which is supposed to cause so much concern. The circle is vicious; a programme has a small audience, therefore it is placed in severely off-peak hours, and therefore it has a small audience.

The producers of arts programmes are aware of this dilemma, and their awareness often determinies the way in which they make and present their programmes. The pressures, their own as well as their employers', are always in the direction of a search for larger and larger audiences. How therefore, in programmes about the arts, to get them? The first way is the traditional one of hitching your programme to a man who is an attractive personality in his own right; Sir Gerald Kelly, for instance, or Sir Kenneth Clark. Here are two men, one of them a painter (a traditional one, which helps) and a former President of the Royal Academy, and the other a distinguished critic, collector, and former Director of the National Gallery. These two distinguished men became television personalities in the best sense, popularisers who never lost their integrity. Sir Kenneth Clark's early series for ATV (much of it produced by Michael Redington) is still probably the most effective concentrated attempt by television to treat art seriously and at the same time hold as large an audience as possible. They were illustrated lectures of great charm and subtlety.

The Human Approach

Art, of whatever kind, is an intensely human activity, and it has been one of the consistent merits of television's approach to it that the human beings who conceive it are never forgotten. Whether because of the ease with which the small screen can capture the essential merits of a personality, or because of its comparative failure to reproduce effectively some of the finest of the arts, it has always been characteristic of television to concern itself as much with the artist as with his work, and to ask why a particular person has produced work of a particular sort.

John Read made an admirable series of films with precisely this intention, showing us the artist at work, letting us see what manner of person he is, showing us his paintings or sculptures, and persuading him to tell us himself just how he approaches his work, chooses his subject-matter, and develops his personal style. Although a narration was used in a few of these films, the aim was to try to look at the art through the eyes and with the mind of the artist himself, and among those who co-operated in the venture were Graham Sutherland, Henry Moore,[1] the late Sir Stanley Spencer, L. S. Lowry, Barbara Hepworth, Josef Herman and Anthony Gross.

For *Monitor* Peter Newington made a film with and about Sidney Nolan, and John Schlesinger made one about four young and relatively unknown artists in London. Each of these films was as much a portrait of the artist as an assessment of his art, and each was a work of considerable intrinsic merit.

To be introduced in one's own living room to some of the

[1] *CBS Reports* made, in 1965, an hour-long film of Henry Moore, the work and the man, produced by William K. McClure.

158

most important of living painters is a privilege which television is particularly well-equipped to provide. It is also something which will no doubt be welcomed by future generations, just as we ourselves would have welcomed a television programme in which Leonardo was seen painting the Mona Lisa and telling us just what he had in his mind when he did so. This is, moreover, a useful way of breaking down some of the public resistance to the arts, for although there are those among us who still sneer at painting and sculpture there are very few human beings who cannot be made interested in other human beings. They will admit that although the art may be a bore, the artist might himself be interesting in a lunatic sort of way. When they discover that he is not really a lunatic but a charming, sincere, and even amusing person, they are already half-way to accepting that such a being might also create works of art which ought not to be rejected out of hand. In this way television not only provides valuable documents both for the present and the future, but gently increases the number of those who are prepared to open a corner of their closed minds.

I have written that such portraits of the artist are usually made as films. This is because of the flexibility of film cameras, which can take us to the artist's studio, follow him to wherever he may be painting, show the gradual creation of a picture (a film can suggest this in a couple of minutes, whereas in reality it took several hours or even days), watch him in his daily domestic life, and catch him off guard both in action and in speech. The value of such films will inevitably increase even further when colour transmissions are the normal form of television; and when this happens we will no doubt regret that so far they have been shot almost entirely in black-and-white. This is an area of television where the spending of money on colour photography in the 1950s and early 1960s would have reaped a considerable reward in the 1970s.

Not only painters and sculptors but the practitioners of all the arts seem increasingly willing to parade themselves and their work before television cameras. Novelists discuss their novels (and those of others), dramatists defend their plays, composers try to express in words the inner workings of their minds. Programmes like *Monitor* and *Tempo* became the *Panorama* or the *This Week* of the arts, current affairs programmes in their own right, presenting us with news and comment on plays, books, exhibitions, architecture, music, and such fascinating by-ways as the world of Sophie Tucker or the creation by Johnny Dankworth of a jazz composition based on the characters of Charles Dickens.

Also, like those other 'topical' programmes, the arts magazines have developed their own patterns, so that familiar techniques recur month by month; the extracts from a new play, followed by a conversation with its author and/or producer; the art critic discussing the subject of a current exhibition, reading his well-written words behind a sequence of still reproductions; the short film which shows us the fashionable novelist at home; the biography, also on film, which, with the use of authentic locations and personal objects, together with some discreet impersonation, attempts to suggest the essence of a particular writer or poet or artist. Ken Russell's film on *Elgar* was arguably the best of these, though there was much merit in David Storey's essay on D. H. Lawrence.

The danger of these attempts at biography is the one which I suggested when I discussed *You are There*; it is possible to evoke an appropriate mood by imaginative use of whatever authentic material may still exist, but the mood itself is too easily smashed by the introduction of a costumed actor. I recall being very impressed by an item in the old BBC series *Bookstand*, in which the novelist Muriel Spark visited the home of the Brontës, and I admired the way in which Miss Spark and her director (Christopher Burstall) had used the Yorkshire landscape, the bleak little village of Haworth, and the almost sinister churchyard. But I am absolutely sure that my appreciation would have been utterly destroyed if a trio of actresses, impersonating the Brontë sisters, had entered the scene. I was mildly uneasy at the dialogue scenes in David Storey's film about Lawrence, and I was amused altogether the wrong way when I watched, in another *Monitor*, a tall actor, disguised as Lord Tennyson, parading the countryside of East Anglia.

The Artistic Approach

It is not perhaps the function of programmes about the arts that they should create works of art themselves, though it is scarcely a coincidence that *Monitor*, especially in the years when it was edited by Huw Wheldon, was responsible for some of the most exciting documentary films ever made for television, whether in Britain or anywhere else. The very first *Monitor* included John Schlesinger's remarkable portrait of a circus, and the same director made several other films of equal distinction which still remain in the memory several years later —*The Innocent Eye* (about the child's approach to art), *Hi-Fi*, *The Class*.

Elgar was possibly the best of a set of equally distinguished films made for the same programme by Ken Russell, but one also recalls with pleasure his *Prokofiev*, *Bartok*,[1] an amusing piece about Brass Bands, and a few essays into the field of Victoriana. There was Humphrey Burton's portrait on film of *The Allegro Quartet*, which must have gone far to persuade the sceptical not only that musicians are human but that they also have to face the mundane irritations that accompany any attempt to organise one's professional life.

All these films, presented for the most part as separate items in a fortnightly magazine programme, deserve to be described as personal works of art in their own right (and for this reason I shall mention some of them again in my chapter on The Personal Documentary). I make the point here because it seems appropriate that a television programme which takes the arts as its subject-matter should itself possess a high level of distinction in its technique and its presentation. From the beginning, Huw Wheldon made of *Monitor* a programme which gave pleasure of a high order to the eye and to the ear, which from time to time offered some of the most exciting pieces to be seen anywhere, and which was never afraid to risk the dropping of heavy bricks in the case of new and imaginative television.

Still Not Enough

The sad thing is that so little of television's millions of hours of programme time is devoted to the arts, as though they were merely of minor moment in the life of mankind. When so much time, money, and talent is devoted to political matters, it seems almost an abandonment of television's responsibilities that it can spare so little for the works of the human spirit. Until the BBC began its second service in the early spring of 1964 the position in Britain was very sorry indeed. *Monitor* and *Tempo*

[1] I recall with less pleasure his 1965 film on Debussy, which for me was a thing to admire rather than to enjoy. I was constantly aware of Mr. Russell, but not always of Debussy.

had become the only regular series on the arts in the whole of our networked television.

Certainly the position has improved since the opening of BBC-2. Its magazine programme *Time Out*, whose theme was leisure, found time now and then for the arts. There was an ambitious series called *The Artist in Society* whose professed aim was nothing less than "to examine different aspects of the role played by the artist in society during a thousand years of European civilisation". We have been offered a series of programmes about the French *New Wave* in the cinema. There have been admirable programmes in which the 'cellist, Paul Tortelier, and the violinist, Yehudi Menuhin, played, taught, and spoke about music, and there have been several occasions when writers have been given a chance to speak and argue intelligently and at length about their craft. But BBC-2 still reaches only a small audience, and with two channels at its disposal the BBC can presumably afford to take new risks.

It remains generally true that if you are a person who enjoys reading good books, looking at fine pictures, or listening to great music, you will still get sadly little assistance from British television. Now and then you may catch an artist in an unannounced appearance here and there—*Tonight*, for example, has consistently sought out the authors of new books, and has kept a wary eye open for original efforts in the visual arts, and *Face to Face*, *The Young Tigers*, and *After Dinner* have included creative people among their victims—but it remains genuinely true that after nearly thirty years of life, British television is apparently frightened of this tremendous area of human experience.

We already know, on the evidence of the films and programmes which I have mentioned by name in this chapter, that television can be an excellent guide and companion to those of us who cannot accept that the arts are less significant than politics, science, or even religion (which in Britain get a great deal more time on the air than the arts have ever done). It may well be that the BBC's second service will ultimately fill the gap, but at present its audience is so small, both geographically and in numbers, that any realistic assessment of the position must still confine itself to the networked programmes of the ITA and to the BBC's first channel.[1] There, alas, the position is

[1] Since these words were written, the position on BBC-1 has been improved

162

both incredible and slightly shameful, unless one accepts that the importance of a subject can be accurately determined by its public popularity, or else dismisses the arts as a minor and perhaps unworthy waste of time.

---

by the introduction of a weekly series "on artists and the arts", called *Sunday Night*, with Stephen Hearst as executive producer.

R OGER MANVELL has this to say on television in the educational field.

"It has sometimes happened in the past that new opportunities for communication have developed at precisely the time they were needed for the practical application of new thinking. The most obvious example has been the indispensable part played by printing in the development of European thought and education during and since the Renaissance. . . .

". . . The new opportunity in the twentieth century is broadcasting in sound and vision, combined with recording on film and tape. This form of communication has arrived at a time when the whole pattern of civilisation is changing, and when the thinking that goes with this needs the widest possible dissemination. The twentieth century represents a new educational era in human history."[1]

Education is one of those puzzling words with large meanings, like culture or love or science, whose mere mention produces a hundred ripples in the human mind. Because most of television is 'education' of a kind, from *Z Cars* to *Bibliothèque Européenne*, from *Cinq Colonnes* to *Dr. Kildare*, what precisely is meant by 'educational television'? If we just mean television for schools then we must be careful to avoid confusing it with the merely didactic, for schools television has also included productions of Shakespeare and Ibsen, and documentaries about current affairs and modern art. But why merely for schools? What about the BBC's programmes of adult education, covering a splendidly varied collection of themes, from *The Painter and His World* to *Human Biology*, and from *Einstein's Principle of Relativity* to *Home Dressmaking*?

[1] *Journal of the Society of Film and Television Arts*, No. 12, Summer 1963, page 2.

Television audiences in the West Indies have seen a film of social education about pre-natal care, and in Kenya a local housewife recently supplied her own commentary to a Walt Disney film that was originally designed to teach hygiene to Americans. In the USA there are more than a hundred colleges which concede diplomas or degrees to students who graduate through TV correspondence courses. In Italy a television series taught 40,000 illiterate adults to read and write, and the United Arab Republic has recently begun a similar experiment, providing three lessons a week to classes of up to one hundred students.

An imaginative proposal of a different sort has been made by a group of enthusiasts in the United Kingdom :

"Television for Industry Ltd. has been formed as a result of the increasing realisation that an effective communication system for keeping the whole of industry and other sections of the economy aware of rapidly changing technical developments is urgently needed. . . . Technical advances in methods of production, management, and marketing which would, if applied, effect vast improvements in productivity, product quality, and export trading, are largely unknown to those who could apply them; a situation due mainly to the lack of an effective means of communication. . . . Television for Industry Ltd. seeks authorisation to provide such a service. . . . Programme policy will be guided by advisory boards drawn from industry, agriculture, scientific and professional bodies, institutions of technological education, trade unions, and Government Departments and agencies."

If that is not a proposal for a form of educational television, then what is it ?

In the Classroom

To begin with, however, let us consider the children.

Television in the classroom, so it seems to me, has three particular uses. First, it can introduce to the pupils leading experts in a wide range of subject-matter : scientists on science, geographers on geography, poets on poetry.

Secondly, it can add to the teacher's equipment; his limited possibilities for scientific demonstration are augmented by television's ability to go to any laboratory in the land, or for

165

that matter, in the world; his wall-map is brought to life by a camera that can wander from one continent to another; his comments on drama can be underlined by a professional performance of whatever text may be the official choice for the year.

Thirdly, and if necessary, television can actually replace the teacher.

"In its extreme form a television teacher simply takes over the class teacher's role completely", writes Kenneth Fawdry, Head of the BBC's Schools Television Service. *"This is exceptional, but we recently had four transmissions weekly which exemplified it. They were part of a series of 96 twenty-minute programmes spread over two years and designed to help the mathematician on his way from 'O' level to 'A' level. The incentive to provide the series was, of course, the known shortage of good, even competent, maths teachers at this level."*[1]

Fourthly, television can widen the aesthetic and emotional experience of the child at school by guiding him through the confused and complex world in which he finds himself in a way that is altogether wider and deeper than anything that the teacher alone can do. Kenneth Fawdry calls programmes of this sort "memorable interruptions of schools routine", and the phrase seems an admirable one. These interruptions may vary from films on abstract art to a series on careers, and they are arguably as important in educational television as the more didactic programmes that form its expected bread and butter.

In Britain we have been curiously slow in appreciating the value of television in schools. Or rather, as is so often our way when we are confronted by a novel notion, much lip-service has been paid but rather less practical action has been taken. Although British TV reopened after the war in 1946 the first regular transmission to schools—actually by a commercial company, Rediffusion—began as late as May 1957, and when the Pilkington Committee reported to the Government on the state of British television five years later it gave the number of schools equipped with television sets as "rather fewer than 4,500".

In the USA and Canada television was by that time universal.

[1] *Journal of the Society of Film and Television Arts*, No. 12, Summer 1963, page 11.

Japan had some 28,000 sets, but France and Italy had approximately the same numbers as the United Kingdom. The present British estimate is that some 6,000 schools now have TV sets; or, to put it another way, in 1964 only one British school-child in every six had the advantages of classroom television. Britain is still without a national Educational Television Service, though such a service was recommended by the Independent Television Authority in 1961. In the USA not only is television universal in schools, with a wide mixture of programmes by wire, closed-circuit, and even, in the Middle West, by airborne transmitter, but at present

"Fifty-five non-commercial educational stations are on the air, most of them thriving. Some are built around single schools or educational institutions; others are 'community stations' operated jointly by educational and public service groups; while still others are run by state educational agencies. Their money comes directly and indirectly from tax sources, national and local foundations, local industries, wealthy private donors, public fund drives, and the organisations which provide the programme. Although in a few instances commercial broadcasters have opposed such stations, in most cases they have helped them through gifts of funds and equipment."[1]

Those are the words of Mr. Burton Paulu, Director of Radio and TV Broadcasting in the University of Minnesota, and there is something admirably American in his description. For whenever the Americans embrace anything they hug it vigorously, and it is a long time since they first embraced education. If the day ever comes when all teaching is carried out by automatic machines it will surely be a citizen of the United States who presses the button.

To each nation its own merits. The British, who have sometimes been caught in attitudes of doubt at the American "Twenty-one-Inch Teacher" have nevertheless managed to provide some very fine programmes for their one-child-in-six, and have trained a team of producers and directors who are among the most accomplished in the world in their own field. Moreover, the producer of programmes for schools is a specialist whose craft imposes a self-discipline that might well frighten

[1] Quoted in the *Journal of the Society of Film and Television Arts*, No. 12, Summer 1963, page 7.

his more sophisticated colleagues in the wider world of general programmes. Not only does he have to consider the size of his audience (groups of thirty or more instead of families of three or four) and the physical conditions of the classroom (whose acoustics are frequently highly dubious), but he also works within the laid-down conditions of a teaching syllabus that has been conceived by professional educationalists as much as, and sometimes more than, by television executives.

Educational Activity in Britain

It follows that the most exciting examples of educational television are likely to occur in those places where the subtle relationship between the television makers and the education authorities is creative as well as administrative; and in Britain we are particularly lucky here, for the organisation of our educational television is sufficiently elastic to combine the merits of a central organisation (or to be precise, two central organisations, the BBC and the ITA) with the maximum of local flexibility, thereby reflecting our educational system itself. It is indeed in Britain that some of the most adventurous examples of creative liaison between those responsible for television programmes and those concerned with education in the conventional sense have occurred.

Much of it is in fields outside of the schools themselves, in areas where experiments in learning and in teaching would be taking place today even if TV had never been invented, and some of the most interesting examples are listed here by Mr. Joseph Weltman, Education Officer of the Independent Television Authority:

"We have in this country a decentralised educational system which has created a favourable setting for experiment. Independent Television is also decentralised, and the regional companies are very much in touch with their areas. They know the people, the local authorities, and are able to keep aware of current trends and feelings in their region. In particular they are in touch with the sort of people who serve on local education committees. If these educationists have an idea they think television would help to materialise, they can go to their regional company and put forward their scheme. They can, and do. There have been examples of this recently particularly in adult

168

education. Ulster Television, with the co-operation of Queen's University, Belfast, transmitted a series called Midnight Oil, an adult education programme on about the same level as WEA classes. This was highly successful. It proved that a substantial local audience existed. It was followed up with a similar series called The Inquiring Mind.

"Scottish Television, in co-operation with the Glasgow Post-Graduate Medical School, are transmitting a more specialised series for general practitioners and doctors in hospitals, helping them to keep up to date with the latest advances in medical research. This is a new field for educational television, but obviously one of great importance.

"In the south-west, Westward Television and the University of Exeter Institute of Education are co-operating in a similar venture for the 'in service' training of teachers.

"Another specially interesting experiment arising from regional initiative is Dawn University, a series of six early morning lectures given by Cambridge dons like Professor Fred Hoyle on The Mathematics of Violence, Nobel prizewinner Dr. J. C. Kendrew on The Molecules of Life, and Raymond Williams on The Changing Vision of the Future. These programmes have been made possible through the co-operation of Anglia Television, Cambridge University, and the ITA.

"A closed-circuit two-way television link is being set up between Cambridge University and Imperial College in London for an interchange of information and ideas between postgraduate researchers, a sort of research colloquim. A link is also being set up between Norwich University and Cambridge University, so that undergraduates at both, in their respective lecture rooms, can share the same lectures.

"Another example of local experiment comes from North East Scotland, in primary education this time. The Chief Education Officer of Aberdeen hopes to be able to stimulate improvement in the primary school curriculum. He approached Grampian Television and asked them if it would be possible to put out a new series of programmes for primary schools. The company have co-operated, and the series is being transmitted as an addition to the nationally networked schools programmes on Independent Television. The education authorities are providing the scripts, the teachers, and the sets, and there will be periodic conferences of teachers to discuss how the series is going. Over a

169

hundred schools in the area are already lined up to take part in the experiment."[1]

I have quoted Mr. Weltman at length, not because the activity he describes is unique (for it is not), but because it is typical of the enormous flurry of activity that at present exists in most of the countries where intelligent men and women have realised the forceful part that television can play in an age of educational revolution, when old teaching techniques are almost daily being thrown out of the window.

The form which this activity takes must depend upon the immediate needs of each country. In Britain it may concern itself with undergraduate, post-graduate, and adult education in subjects that lean towards the very advanced, the highly specialised, and sometimes the downright esoteric. In the United States it may concentrate on the practical work of granting degrees and diplomas to the new 'undergraduates of the air'. In the developing nations of Africa, Asia, and Latin America the emphasis may be on the most elementary education for children and on social training for adults. In Egypt, at this particular moment, the main need may appear to be a literacy course for villagers.

Avoiding Outside Pressures

From year to year the patterns change, as the social needs themselves change, and educational television, more than television of the general sort, is an accurate barometer of a nation's social and cultural climate at any particular time. Also, of the many manifestations of TV, educational programmes are perhaps the most consistently cheering, because it is in their nature to resist an easy compromise with state propaganda on the one hand, and commercial pressures on the other.

Inevitably this resistance is not always easy, nor is it everywhere successful. Programmes of modern history or current affairs are not in all countries entirely guiltless of subtle attempts at political brain-washing, and in the newly independent nations the departure of the colonial master has too frequently been followed, in a matter of days, by the arrival of the commercial television salesman, hawking studios and programmes like refrigerators, and only doubtfully concerned with tele-

[1] *Journal of the Society of Film and Television Arts*, No. 12, Summer 1963, pages 14–15.

vision's social benefits. There are other problems too; a correspondent of the *Times Educational Supplement* noticed last year that in Southern Rhodesia "the programmes were mainly directed to the educational needs and capacities of the Europeans. . . . Education is regarded as too frightening for Africans."

"On a continent", the same writer continued, *"where both the need for education and the urge to acquire it are overwhelming, such an assumption is crippling. Fortunately commercial television does not have the last word. In Northern Rhodesia both the Government and the education departments of the copper companies are embarking on the training of television teachers, and the systematic development of television techniques for the exclusive service of education. Wisely these preparations are centring on closed-circuit work, at a tiny fraction of the intimidating cost of a commercial service. In Ghana the Government, deaf so far to the advertisers' sales talk, is building a nationwide public service system with education as its main concern. In Uganda television opened with a public service committted to some advertising, but determined to eschew undue dependence on commercial interests, to make locally produced material predominant, and to devote at least half its output to education. . . .*

". . . These latecomers to television seem to be recognising that education, like medicine, is inadequately served when it takes second place to commercial interest."

It remains true, I believe, that educational television is at its best when its divorce from commercial interests is complete. This is clearly the case already in the new television countries of Africa, Asia, and Latin America, and it has so far proved true in continental Europe. In the United Kingdom several of the commercial programme contractors run admirable educational broadcasts and have initiated some splendid experiments; but they are more closely supervised by the Independent Television Authority in their educational transmissions than in any other form of programme. Moreover, it is in this specialised field of educational television that the only really effective co-ordination exists between the ITA and the BBC. I myself have never been persuaded of the logic or value of dividing Britain's schools TV broadcasting between two organisations who are normally in competition and one of which is concerned for nine-tenths of its life with making a profit. In the USA, educational TV is virtually removed from the commercial networks, and like so many American achievements is the result of local enthusiasm, boundless energy, an apparently endless supply of technical talent, and a queue of rich benefactors. It is fundamentally non-profit-making, it is decentralised, it allows room for re-markable individual experiment, it is usually wonderful and frequently chaotic. What educational television needs, I suggest, is a monopoly organisation to ensure consistent direction and purpose, and the neatest liaison with the educational authorities, together with the maximum of decentralisation within this single organisation. Learning, like peace, is indivisible; it is not a commodity to be bargained for, like corn-flakes.

Future Possibilities

Are there any valid generalisations to be made about the likely development of educational television in a world that despite its many more frightening characteristics is at least showing an admirable thirst for knowledge? I believe it may be possible to hazard a few safe guesses:

First, that television in the classroom is a sufficiently well-established device for us to assume its future acceptance in countries that are so far without it. Indeed it may well be the main channel of teaching in those developing nations where the supply of trained teachers is likely to be sadly inadequate for many years to come. In Western Europe its main curiosity is the odd reluctance of so many professional educationalists, especially in Britain, France, and Italy, to accept it. The fact that in Britain less than 7,000 schools had television sets in 1964, although 29,000 were equipped with sound-radio re-ceivers, is nothing to boast of; and has it, one wonders, anything to do with the familiar attitude of those intellectuals who per-sist in regarding television as something incurably philistine?

Secondly, we can assume that many of the most valuable experiments in educational TV will be by closed-circuit, if only because the basic educational unit will always be a school or college, or a group of schools or colleges. The conflict between a national educational TV service, which must presuppose that every teacher will accept it and every student will understand it, and a purely local service aimed at a single group and directed by those who teach that group and know it intimately can never be resolved except by an acceptance of them both. It is expectedly in the USA that the most numerous and stimulating essays in closed-circuit educational television have so far taken place, but it is a fair guess that schools and colleges in Europe will soon realise its possibilities, and that within a decade at the most we shall regard television teachers and tutors, as well as television technicians, as an accepted part of the normal academic staff. At a time when the needs of students exceed the supply of qualified teachers it is the merit of closed-circuit TV that it can convert a class of twenty into a class of hundreds. Many of the disadvantages levelled against TV as 'packaged education' disappear when an audience of millions becomes one of dozens, and when the TV syllabus is a part of a particular curriculum in a particular institution at a particular time.

Thirdly, we can assume that television in the western world will for some time to come be seen as a partial solution to the chronic problem posed in societies which have far more potential undergraduates than they have universities to put them in. In *The Placing of Education in Relation to Economic Growth* the Organisation for Economic Co-operation and Development prophesies that by 1970 its European members will have to educate thirteen million extra students between the ages of five and twenty-four; in the USA and Canada facilities will be needed for an additional sixteen million students. It is because of this grim challenge that we have lately been hearing so much about a 'University of the Air', an imaginative conscription of television's resources during an emergency period for the specific purpose of teaching those undergraduates who would otherwise stand little chance of admittance to the universities. Although successful experiments along similar lines have been carried out in the USA, the idea of a University of the Air was scarcely canvassed in Britain until Harold Wilson made it the main theme of a speech in Glasgow in September 1963, when he outlined a plan that would also include courses by radio and correspondence—what he then described as "a dynamic programme providing facilities for home study and higher technical standards on the basis of a university of the air and nationally organised correspondence courses".

At a time of national educational crisis—and certainly we are living in such a time at present—it may be true that one of the few practical ways of teaching the 'bulge' of potential university students, especially in the field of science and technology, is by the use of sound-radio and television. Yet it would be a pity to assume that students can be taught as effectively in this way as by the more traditional methods. That television can take over the function of a college is a belief that too readily ignores the essential environment without which a student is not truly a student at all. To be completely effective a University of the Air surely needs to organise its students into disciplined groups, needs to provide opportunities when each programme is over for the normal exchange of ideas between student and tutor, and needs the social comradeship which is part of the meaning of a university. In other words, the University of the Air needs these very facilities whose absence has called it into being. To claim—as some do, though certainly not Mr. Wilson—that a University of the Air is an electronic conjuring trick which produces a form of instant education that is in every way the equal of university teaching of the more familiar sort, is the kind of exaggeration which only appeals to those with a taste for gimmickry.

Fourthly, and lastly; I believe we can assume in Britain that a full educational channel is sooner or later sure to happen. It is also a fair assumption that it will either be controlled by a national organisation free of commercial interests, or by the BBC. Mr. Wilson, in the speech from which I have just quoted, envisaged "a new educational trust, representative of the universities and other educational organisations, associations of teachers and broadcasting authorities, publishers and producers capable of producing television and other educational material". Britain's fourth channel could be used for this purpose; or, by waiting for the development of further UHF channels, the technical problems would vanish altogether. If this happens, the new service is bound to pay considerable attention to those who are outside the normal educational system but are eager to learn.

"The field of potential subject matter", Kenneth Fawdry writes, *"is vast. More people want to enlarge their appreciation of art than those who have the kind of background which a programme like* Monitor *tacitly assumes. More people want to acquire the elements of a foreign language, perhaps because*
174

they are going abroad for the first time. More people would like to understand more about money than their daily life has hitherto required them to—it may be because they have never used a bank before, or because they are considering making small investments or because they are tired of hearing phrases like 'the balance of payments' or 'the bank rate' bandied about in the news, without really understanding them.

"More people, better educated than they were ten or twenty years ago, are working in jobs which do not fully stretch them; and they have more leisure time which they could, and would with encouragement, use more creatively—perhaps to master the skills of dressmaking, perhaps to acquire a new interest in archaeology. This kind of programming requires of the producers a sensitivity to audience needs, involving continuous consultation with those working in the adult educational field, just as we have with the schools; a belief that people want to learn; and a recognition that learning is bound up with feeling, that programmes for learners must therefore be as imaginative as any others, and that this is likely to call for the full resources of television."[1]

[1] Journal of the Society of Film and Television Arts, No. 12, Summer 1963, page 13.

THE PERSONAL DOCUMENTARY

B Y personal documentary I mean a programme, usually made on film, which is very much the individual work of its producer and/or director and which, through its imaginative handling of reality, expresses his own attitude not only to the programme's immediate subject-matter but to the whole of the world in which he lives. It is in programmes of this sort that factual television has come closest to making works of art. Indeed there is a very vocal body of opinion which claims that in the work of a small handful of documentary producers television—and especially British television—has enjoyed its finest creative moments.

It may well be that the television of our own time will not be remembered for its new dramatists, its rediscovery of satire, or its presentation of controversy, but for the programmes of a small group of men who have used the television documentary as a means of expressing their own vision of our age : in Britain, Denis Mitchell, Ken Russell, John Schlesinger, Philip Donnellan, Don Haworth, John Ormond, Richard Marquand, Peter Morley, John Boorman, Peter Watkins; in the USA, Richard Leacock and Albert and David Maysles; in Canada, Ronald Kelly.

These are men who rarely present objective reports, preferring to express a highly subjective view. They may occasionally use spoken narration (and if so, it will usually be of their own writing), but they never use a reporter in the conventional current-affairs manner. They will throw away anybody or anything which comes between themselves and their subject-matter. They are concerned with people rather than things, with the 'why' of life rather than the 'how' of it.

Many of their programmes have titles which are simple descriptions of persons or groups : *The Entertainers* (Denis Mitchell), *The Crystal Makers* (Philip Donnellan), *Citizen '63* (John Boorman), *Showman* (Albert and David Maysles), *The Tear-*

aways (Ronald Kelly); or, more precisely, *Ed and Frank* (Denis Mitchell), or *Elgar* (Ken Russell). These are also intimate documentaries, commenting obliquely on the whole of life by exposing a tiny corner of it. *Chicago* (Denis Mitchell) is less a portrait of the American city than a personal essay on the violence and pathos of urban society in an age of confusion. *Borrowed Pasture* (John Ormond) is superficially about two elderly Polish refugees who bought a piece of barren Welsh landscape and made it fruitful, but at a deeper level it is concerned with man's struggle for survival, not only against the forces of nature but also against his persistent inhumanity towards himself. It is about courage and about human dignity. *Elgar* is much more than a biography of the English composer : it is a study both of the creative process, and of the essence of religious faith.

Citizen '63 was not just a series about half a dozen haphazardly selected people, but was a deeper analysis of British society in the 1960s. *Culloden* (Peter Watkins) was arguably less of an historical reconstruction than a personal essay on the madness of war.

Above all, these are programmes whose appeal, unlike that of the more routine forms of television journalism, is as much to the heart as to the mind. They are for the most part programmes of sensations rather than of thoughts, and this is why they are so personal and, when successful, so moving.

The Personal Viewpoint

Men whose natural medium is one which combines sounds and visual images are not necessarily the best people to describe their aims in terms of the written word, and to ask a poet (in whatever medium) why and how he creates as he does is to pose an unfair and unanswerable question. Here, however, is Denis Mitchell's comment on what he is attempting to do :

"I don't believe it is possible to do serious work unless one has something to say, some vision of the world which one wants to express. I find I can express my own vision more readily in the form of television films about people than in any other way. I believe it is possible to express the essence of the human situation in our own time more effectively, because more truthfully, through the documentary than, say, through a fictitious drama.

M

The audience, when it watches this sort of film, recognises itself in the people who are appearing in the film, and does so in a much closer way than is possible, so I think, through the creation of characters that are fictitious. 'That boy', they say, 'is just like my own son'; or, 'That's exactly like what So-and-so said in the market yesterday'; or, 'That's just how I feel about it myself'.

"The producer of this kind of film tries to show people as they truly are, expressing themselves in their own words, and doing the things they normally do. They are real people living in a real world. But what the producer has also done—and this is why such films are more than journalism—is to give a harmony to the people in his films by means of his own vision of them and of the world they live in. He himself has something to say about them—must have something to say, otherwise he wouldn't have become interested in them in the first place. His task is to imply his own view of life (he can never openly state it by any form of editorialising) without distorting the truth that is the lives of the people he has chosen. What he manages to say, or rather what he and his selected people say together—for this is in a profound way a piece of mutual co-operation—is in my opinion much more significant than what is said in a current affairs programme with a spoken pseudo-objective comment."

These 'personal' producers are essentially artists who use ordinary people as the symbols with which to express their view of life, as the dramatist creates his own characters and as a painter mixes his own paints. They are constantly attempting two things which on the face of it seem contradictory : they are trying to get continually closer to the people who are their heroes and heroines (and to this end they are always forging new techniques and stimulating the creating of new technical equipment), but they are also trying to impose (to risk a word that is perhaps a shade too provocative) on those same people their own attitudes and their own vision. They are concerned to fill their programmes with men and women behaving naturally, living their true lives before the camera, speaking their deepest thoughts without the prompting of an interviewer. Thus Denis Mitchell began (in a *Special Enquiry* on teenagers in 1955) by using the 'wildtrack' voices—or as some prefer to call them, 'think-tapes'—of his selected people to add an extra depth to the words of his narrator (who then and later was invariably himself).

By 1959 (*Morning in the Streets*) he had dropped narration altogether, and carried his narrative by a combination of wild-track and synchronised speech; finally, in *The Entertainers* in 1964 (which he devised and produced, but which was directed by John McGrath) he removed the wildtrack completely and relied entirely on improvised dialogue. Denis Mitchell's development, which has stretched across a decade, has been echoed by others whose experience is not so long. In the personal documentary, narration has largely vanished, subjective wildtrack is used only occasionally, and the job of the synchronised sound-camera is to eavesdrop on those who live in whatever corner of the world the director/producer has chosen.

Thus Peter Morley writes of *Black Marries White—The Last Barrier*, a film about mixed marriages in Britain:

"I dispensed with the narrator and the interviewer, even the prepared script. All three might have imposed a different and irrelevant set of attitudes which could have come between the viewer and the people in the film, and it might have blurred the fundamental issue."

Complete naturalism is the aim, and whenever (as in the *cinema-verité* activities of Richard Leacock and the Maysles) it can only be achieved at the expense of clarity in picture and sound, then it is always the technical quality that must give way.

Retaining Technical Quality

Of course these technical imperfections, though always a possibility, are by no means inevitable, and the techniques of *cinema verité* are not shared by all of the makers of personal documentaries. Indeed one of the most successful examples of the 'reporting of reality without comment' was *The Class*, made by John Schlesinger for the BBC. This, in technical terms, was a highly professional film indeed, glossy, well photographed, brilliantly edited, and finely recorded. Yet it had throughout the ring of unrehearsed truth. How was it conceived and made? John Schlesinger himself writes:

"The idea of The Class came to us by accident. Monitor had commissioned me to make a film about a drama school, and

179

together with Michell Raper I had spent a week at the headquarters of the Central School of Speech and Drama in London.

"We started with the idea of making a film about the school
in all its aspects, when we happened to sit in one morning on an
acting class taken by Harold Lang in a chilly church hall. It was
quite unlike anything else we had seen. After five minutes we
had discarded notebook and pencil as we became involved and
fascinated with what was going on. . . . Over lunch we decided
to abandon our original idea and concentrate on what we considered would result in a more compelling and valuable film.
Our problem was to catch spontaneously the essence of what
we had seen, allowing for the technicalities of film-making. . . .
We allowed ourselves five days in which to make the film,
working with a single blimped Arriflex and a midget tape
recorder in a bare classroom at the top of the Embassy Theatre.
For two of the days a second camera unit was brought in.

"The unit responded wonderfully to this period of improvised
shooting. Everyone realised that mobility was essential, that
little could be rehearsed and something unexpected would
almost certainly happen in each set-up.

"Lang, himself an experienced film and TV actor, was the
pivot on which everything turned. We would agree together
what we wanted to achieve in each sequence and, with him
conducting the class from behind the camera, shot the reactions
to each exercise first.

"The Class is in no way spectacular. We shot it simply, using
as many close-ups as possible, indulging directorial fancy only
at rare moments. At all times we aimed to preserve the immediacy of what was happening under Lang's unique personality.
The fact that many of our audience assumed that the film was
made during one session is the highest compliment that could
be paid to it."[1]

Capturing Spontaneity

The key phrase there is John Schlesinger's statement of his
aim : "to catch spontaneously the essence of what we had seen,
allowing for the technicalities of film-making". This is precisely
what the makers of the personal documentary would claim to be
doing, and indeed it is sometimes what they appear to achieve
exactly, no more and no less. Richard Leacock's Quint City is

[1] Journal of the Society of Film and Television Arts, Summer 1961, page 9.

superficially an unedited account of the daily round of a mother who had given birth to quintuplets, authentically and therefore erratically photographed, and sometimes poorly recorded. Precisely the same point could be made of *Showman*, the film by Albert and David Maysles, which appears merely to follow the hectic professional life of the cinema impressario, Joseph E. Levine, and to present it as accurately as possible without any comment whatever, stated or implied. In place of the traditional documentary, well organised and fully scripted, with its well-lit interiors, the careful phrases of its well-spoken commentator, and the rehearsed spontaneity of those who take part in it has come something that seems to be infinitely closer to the chaos of real life. Nor is there any doubt that *Showman* gains immeasurably in conviction by being so clearly unrehearsed. Even its technical weaknesses, the woolly sound and now and then the picture that is poorly exposed or soft in focus, seem to add to its essential reality.

"To catch spontaneously" as John Schlesinger puts it. Thus Richard Leacock in *The Chair* caught the defence lawyer, in an emotional moment, genuinely weeping as he sat alone in his office. Thus Albert and David Maysles filmed the immediate reaction of a man who had just been fired by Joe Levine. In *Chicago* Denis Mitchell took his camera with the city police on a murder call, and Ronald Kelly made a complete film about what actually happened during one night in one hospital. Similarly NBC made *Police Emergency, Fire Rescue*, and *Emergency Ward*. In *The Entertainers* (Mitchell and McGrath) a young pop singer had an audition in Manchester for a potential assignment in one of London's more fashionable night-clubs. The whole of the (perfectly genuine) audition was recorded, and so was the singer's immediate reaction to the result of it. Neither the singer, nor the manager who auditioned him, nor the makers of the programme knew what would happen. The programme reflected absolutely authentically, and quite without rehearsal, what in fact took place.

Whether such attempts to catch illuminating moments of truth will suceed or fail depends of course on a wide variety of factors. They are more likely to succeed, for instance, if the subjects themselves are involved in a personal situation which is so vital to them that the presence of cameras and technicians is of relatively minor importance. To take an extreme case, a dying man is not likely to be very alarmed by the activities of a film crew, because he has more significant matters on his mind. Neither was the lawyer in Leacock's film, and neither—though at a much lower level of emotional temperature—was the young singer in that Manchester audition.

There is a sense in which this sort of film-making is a direct application of news techniques to longer and larger themes. Those who appear in documentaries of this kind are in the position of those leaders of revolutions, or conductors of political campaigns, or winners of motor races, who are either unaware of the cameras during their moments of personal drama or else are able to relegate them to a tiny corner of their consciousness. It is, I think, one of the weaknesses of the *verité* method that it is most effective on such supercharged occasions, as those who have made their names by it are only too willing to admit.

Richard Leacock, for example, once said that

"I tried to write down a definition of what we know we can make a film of relatively easily: 'A film about a person who is interesting, who is involved in a situation which he cares about deeply, which comes to a conclusion within a limited period of time, where we have access to what goes on. We can be there, in other words.' "

It is interesting that Leacock used the phrase 'relatively easily'; he seems unwilling to admit that these are perhaps the only situations in which a good *verité* film can be made, and to support himself he has quoted his own film about Nehru:

"He wasn't involved in anything that came to a conclusion. He was just doing what he does day after day. I guess our feeling is that at the moment we're young. We do need high-pressure situations. As we get smarter and as our equipment gets better, as we learn more about this kind of film-making, we will be able to go into situations that are less and less pressure situations."[1]

But this has yet to be proved; and, after all, it is even arguable that a Prime Minister going about his daily business is by definition a 'pressure situation'.

A great deal has been written and spoken about *cinema verité* in recent years, and it is surely necessary to get it into perspec-

[1] In *Movie*, April 1963, page 18.

tive. It is *not* true, for example, that cameras are now so small and recording equipment so insignificant (and cameramen and recordists smaller in size too, one wonders?) that ordinary people can be filmed going about their normal lives without knowing that the equipment and the technicians are there. It is palpably and provably false that the latest equipment, needing only a tiny crew (say two men), and working without extra light, can produce pictures and sounds that are technically as good as those achieved by traditional equipment, methods, and crews. Nor, on an artistic level, does it follow that the best way of capturing a man's essential personality is to trail him for a couple of weeks in the hope of catching him off-guard long enough for the necessary moments of illuminating self-exposure. Nor is it necessarily true—though it occasionally is—that a technical crew of two will do a more truthful job than a crew of eight or nine.

Dispensing with the Script

Assuming that one of the principal aims of the maker of the personal documentary is to present people as they really are, then it follows almost by definition that they must dispense with a formal script. For a script would impose both actions and attitudes on men and women whose lives are lived from moment to moment, whose conversations with one another are unprepared, and whose feelings sometimes bubble to the surface at random. A programme which asks 'how' can be scripted accurately in advance, but a programme which asks 'why' must very largely be made from shot to shot, and its most significant sequences will often only emerge in the cutting-room. This is one of the essential differences between a documentary on, say, how a computer works, and one that concerns itself with human relationships and human aspirations. The first can be prepared in advance, but the second cannot—or, if it is, then it is unlikely to succeed. Ask the director of the personal documentary to produce a shooting script, and he will either show you a few scribbled notes or else a very general treatment. To accept the unexpected, to realise its significance in a pattern which is still unformed—these are necessary qualities in those who make programmes of this kind. Flexibility, both technical and artistic, is essential. The mood of the director/producer at the moment when he is about to begin shooting a film of this sort has been typically suggested by John Ormond, who writes of the eve of shooting *Borrowed Pasture*.

"By then random quotations and ideas had appeared in my notebooks—sketches of possible sequences and individual shots: thorns, decaying blackberries, cows' eyes; the water-wheel which had been broken when the two refugees arrived at the farm and which now, when there was a big enough flood of water, drove a dynamo that powered a milking machine, gave light and electrified fences to keep the cows from straying.

"I had no script other than the notes and sketches, and some music jottings of Polish folk-tunes that I had recorded at another farm and which were later to form the basis for Arwel Hughes's film music. On paper I had nothing but promptings to myself."[1]

Of *Black Marries White*, Peter Morley says:

"In most of my previous work I had approached the subject with my own preconceived ideas, and with some sort of shooting script. This time I deliberately banished any personal attitudes that I might have had. The last thing I wanted to do was to impose my own views on the people who had agreed to appear in the film, or to concoct any incidents or sequences that had been born in my own mind rather than in their lives. What I wanted to do was to record accurately how they thought and how they felt—feeling being perhaps more important than thinking in a film of this sort. Also, of course, this was one of those occasions when those who appeared in the film—the married couples—felt sufficiently strongly about the subject-matter of the film itself to be able to forget me or the technicians or the equipment. What they had to say to one another about the problems of a mixed marriage was so important that after a time all the paraphernalia of film-making simply did not exist to them. They said things that could never have been prepared or scripted in advance, and the most effective parts of the film were, as always, the most sincere parts of it, and as nearly always, the least rehearsed parts of it. The final shape, the cross-references between this sequence and that, the counter-pointing of images and ideas and feelings—all these came later still."

[1] *Journal of the Society of Film and Television Arts*, No. 5, Summer 1961, page 7.

Similarly, and if I may be forgiven for quoting from my own experience, I found myself attempting, for the first time, a personal documentary in the summer and autumn of 1963. My theme was to suggest the changes, economically, socially, and in personal attitudes, that had occurred in a working-class area of Britain in the previous thirty-odd years. Because on this particular occasion I had deliberately decided to avoid the more routine treatment of the current affairs documentary I found myself face to face with all the problems, opportunities, and techniques which I have already mentioned.

I had made up my mind to avoid a general and statistical approach, and to look at my theme through the eyes of a particular community and a particular group of people. Very well then, where was this community, and who were these people? I had decided—for precisely the reasons given by Peter Morley —to dispense with formal narration and to avoid the use of a conventional interviewer. I wanted nobody and nothing to come between the viewer and the people who had lived through all, or part, for the past 30 years. I chose my community—a group of coal-mining villages in South Yorkshire. This choice was in a sense quite arbitrary, and I might just as well have chosen any one of a hundred other areas and any one of a score of other industries.

Having chosen my community I spent the greater part of three months among its members—for it is one of the characteristics of this form of factual television that the initial research and preparation must take a long time. The producer/ director, if he is to express the essential character and feelings of those whom he has chosen, must live among them for at least several weeks. He must do this for two reasons: first, because he has chosen to discover their true characters and their genuine (though often superficially concealed) attitudes, and this is a form of research that cannot be tossed off in a week or two; and secondly because it is an essential part of his job that, by the time he begins to shoot his programme, he must be accepted by the community, as a whole as well as a set of individuals, as a friend who can be trusted. For men and women do not express their deepest thoughts to a stranger, and they are less likely to be distracted by the paraphernalia of television if someone whom they have come to regard as a friend can act as their guide and support.

In the course of my stay in the coal-mining villages I met hundreds of people, and of these hundreds I selected less than twenty to appear in the programme. Because I had decided to build the programme round a (real) wedding—as an occasion which naturally prompts reminiscence and homespun philosophy, and when people are less likely than usual to conceal their deepest feelings—most of those who took part were either the relations or the friends of the bride or bridegroom. It is relevant to the points I am making in this chapter that although I had selected them all before shooting began, their numbers were actually increased during the actual period of shooting by the addition of others who came along by chance; and some of these 'additions' proved to be even more valuable than some of those chosen as a result of three months' concentrated selection.

I did not have a script, but before I began shooting the programme I had prepared a list of sequences and an order in which I assumed they would eventually be assembled—extracts from the wedding service, a Bingo session, a debate in the local youth club, the annual pit Gala, the bridegroom's eve-of-wedding party, and groups of conversations between those who by this time had been asked to take part. I organised these sequences— there were 26 of them in all—into a shooting schedule, so that even though we had no precise script we at least knew where we were going and what we were hoping to achieve day by day.

However—and this is the core of the matter—the programme as finally edited resembled only slightly that prepared treatment of sequences. The order had been entirely changed. Several sequences were omitted completely. Conversations were broken up, so that Mr. X, who in reality had spoken to Mr. Y, was shown as though he were speaking to Mr. Z. Suggestions and ideas which had been raised by this man or that, quite independently and on different occasions, were placed side by side, either because they illuminated the same theme (poverty, courage, colour prejudice, money) or because together they made an effective counterpoint. Indeed, when I was working on the final version I did not even refer to the original treatment at all; I worked at home every evening, creating a new shape altogether, presenting the editor each morning with the equivalent of five minutes of the programme, and when I sat down at my typewriter each night I had no idea how I would place the visuals, or the words, or the sequences.

There were, of course, scores of ways in which that same material might have been edited and it is a fair bet that no two directors would in the end have assembled it in precisely the same way. The way I finally chose for myself was a reflection of what *I* thought about those Yorkshire miners and their families, and was in this sense as much my own view of life as theirs.

The Film-makers' Bias

I referred earlier to the apparent contradiction in all this; that the maker of the programme is at the same time trying to get as close as he can to the real lives and real feelings of his chosen people, and yet insisting on imposing on those lives his own vision and his own point of view. In making his selection of shots, of actions, of words, of gestures and expressions, he chooses those which seem *to him* to be the truest and the most relevant. They would not necessarily seem so to someone else and would probably not seem so to the people whose lives are being 'edited' in this way.

As Peter Morley has said,

"How can you get at the pure, uncontaminated truth when, right at the beginning there is a subjective selection, not only of the scene being filmed, but also in the composition of the shot, let alone the final selection and juxtaposition of the material in the cutting room? The personal attitude of the team concerned is bound to influence the final result."

Richard Leacock makes the same point:

"Obviously we have our own bias and selection, obviously we're not presenting the whole truth. I'm not being pretentious and ridiculous: we're presenting the film-maker's perception of an aspect of what happened."

A good and simple example of the way in which a personal documentary can make a comment is the end of Denis Mitchell's *Chicago*. The camera shows the floor-numbers of 'the fastest elevator in the world' flashing in succession as the car rides rapidly upwards; the sound track is the words of an anonymous citizen of Chicago, a man who by the sound of him has been

187

neither too prosperous nor too successful in his life so far. He says: "I'd like my children to live in a world where if I had shortcomings and I couldn't quite keep up, the world would come and take me by the hand and say 'All right, you're going to show us up a little bit but you've got to come along too; you're a human being, you're a human being.' "

That particular statement, over that particular visual image, seems to sum up *Chicago*—not the whole of that city, nor anyone else's view of it, but what Denis Mitchell felt was an essential way in which cities of that sort and size tend to treat (or perhaps not to treat) their citizens in the mid-twentieth century. Those words are less an observation on Chicago than on the human condition, and so for that matter is the whole of that very personal film.

Similarly, in *Borrowed Pasture*, John Ormond ended his film with the words of one of his two refugee farmers, spoken over a long-shot of the farm's landscape, with the farmer himself a tiny retreating figure in the distance:

"What is life? You know, it is trouble. Without trouble, you know, life is nothing. It is too easy, but it is not life. You know, without the farm I am nothing. I am the farm, and, you know, the farm it is me."

There is a frankly emotional appeal about those statements, which seem to express the essence of the films in which they were uttered. They grow out of each film, naturally and almost inevitably, so that the viewer is tempted to say to himself when he hears them 'Yes, yes, of course.' They are the expressions of attitudes to life, the conclusions reached by individual men who have reflected on the human condition and formed their conclusions out of their own hard personal experience.

These are therefore subjective films, the very opposite of the objective approach which typifies the more familiar current affairs programme, and whose final conclusion is nearly always a carefully phrased and balanced assessment of opposing arguments. The words spoken in the personal documentary are rarely phrased with care, for they are the spontaneous speech of ordinary men and women. Nor, usually, are they an argument in the conventional sense. They are frank, and biased, and heartfelt, and brave, and cowardly, and funny, and sad, and angry, and generous, and malicious—all in turn. As they come
188

from the heart, so their appeal is to the heart also, and this is one of the main differences between these two complementary kinds of factual television. The current affairs programme obeys the rule of unbiased objectivity, whereas the personal documentary is subjective and therefore the expression of a personal point of view (or a series of such points of view).

The Need for Subjective Programmes

I have just written that these different types of programme are complementary, and indeed I believe that any responsible television service must go out of its way to include both of them. For each of them helps to correct the weakness of the other. The objective documentary runs the risk of confusing people with statistics, rarely makes an appeal to the emotions (for the human heart is a notoriously biased organ), and has a habit of implying the kind of generalisation which ignores the fact that people cannot accurately be lumped together as though they were identical pieces of machinery.

Conversely, the personal documentary, by choosing a tiny corner of the world and by concentrating on a small number of people, runs the risk of seeming to imply that this small segment of life is really the whole of it. By limiting itself to human feelings it might seem to be stating a faith in the behaviour of men and women which is scarcely justified by the known statistics. The world consists of facts as well as people, and people have minds as well as hearts. This is why I believe the objective report and the subjective documentary to be complementary in an essential sense. A television service which accepted the value of only one of them would be unable to present an adequate picture of the age we live in.

The many *Panorama* reports from South Africa were thus part of a pattern which included Denis Mitchell's three subjective pieces called *The Wind of Change*. The numerous objective analyses of British industry were made more relevant by the series of films made by Philip Donnellan, which were highly subjective portraits of industrial workers in steel, in shipbuilding, in pottery, in the manufacture of motor cars. *Black Marries White* was just as necessary as the several unbiased enquiries into British colour prejudice, and *Borrowed Pasture* was as essential as any or all of the perfectly fair examinations of the refugee problem. The many hours of television that are devoted

189

to reflecting the activities of Americans during an election year needed as a counterpoise the very human, and within its terms of reference equally 'true' film by Richard Leacock called *Primary*.

If I am right in regarding these two forms of documentary, the objective and the subjective, as being complementary (and therefore of equal value), then we should all regret that there are so very few of the latter and literally hundreds of the former. I think there are many reasons for this unhappy state of affairs, and a few of them deserve rather more than a casual mention.

The basic factor, I suspect, is the essential unpredictability of the personal programme. The more individual and courageous a work of art is in any medium, the less certain is its success. The current affairs documentary is made to a formula, is usually predictable, and often appears less to be the work of one producer/director than of a highly professional committee. Granted the normal amount of competence in its making, and granted also that its subject-matter is of some concern to the millions who watch it, its success is assured in advance. Not so, however, the personal documentary. Created to a large extent by one man in isolation, forged and modified minute by minute, depending entirely on his own skill in extracting what is finest and most relevant from the corner of life which he has chosen, this is a form of television which is full of surprises, and no one can tell in advance (least of all the creator himself) whether the surprises will be pleasant or horrible.

We know, moreover, that many of the most exciting personal documentaries have either failed to communicate to the audience, or else have been completely misunderstood. Some of the best of them have been total disasters in terms of audience ratings, and many more have been received with indifference. *A House in Bayswater* by Ken Russell, and *The Tearaways* by Ronald Kelly—admirable films, both of them—were viewed with apparent hostility by a small audience. *Borrowed Pasture* was received with enthusiasm. *Black Marries White* had a vast audience (next to *Coronation Street* it was in these terms the most successful programme of the week) but many people seem to have been prevented by their inborn attitudes to its theme from understanding it. *Chicago* was regarded by almost all the serious critics as being by any standards a major work, and it had a large audience; but it was apparently too violent for many

190

people, and its audience was more conspicuous in size than in enthusiasm.

There has also been a danger that the subjective programme might be confused with the objective one. *Chicago* was condemned out of hand by numerous individuals and pressure groups in that city, including the Mayor, as being a totally unfair portrait of the place—though one's respect for their views would have been greater had more of them seen the film before so vigorously expressing them. Philip Donnellan's *Coventry Kids* received equally rough treatment from the official spokesmen, and for similar reasons—though this time they had at least seen the programme. *A Wedding on Saturday* was followed by righteously indignant letters from several local councils who complained that it omitted such splendid amenities as parks, swimming baths, maternity hospitals, and the like.

The sad aspect of all this is not that the complaints were unjustified—for most of them were factually accurate—but that they totally misunderstood what the programmes were about. *Chicago* was not an objective portrait of the place; *Coventry Kids* was not made as an objective report on the city of Coventry; *A Wedding on Saturday* was about a group of people concerned directly or indirectly with a wedding, and was never meant as an accurate travelogue about a particular area.

The fact remains that on each of these occasions a genuine misunderstanding occurred, and to this extent the makers of the programmes had failed to make their intentions clear. No doubt the fault is partly theirs, and partly that of the local audience which had decided in advance (and quite erroneously as it happened) what each programme was trying to do. It is this element of advance doubt, this danger that the producer who is let loose to combine his own attitude and vision with actual people in actual places might cause havoc and confusion of all kinds, which I believe lies behind the comparative failure of the personal documentary to establish itself as a regular part of our television schedules. Is it unfair to say that certain television executives openly prefer the more objective form, partly because it is more predictably successful, but also because it is less likely to involve them in post-mortems that are concerned with those horribly fundamental matters of taste, fairness, and impartiality? For how can a subjective programme be impartial without also destroying itself?

I am not suggesting, however, that television organisations should be willing to give complete freedom of the air to every young man who comes along and asks to make a personal film. Everything depends on the known abilities (or very carefully assessed potentialities) of the young man and on the probable effectiveness of his idea. Cyril Bennett, executive producer in charge of Features and Children's Programmes for Rediffusion (London),[1] tells how he was once asked by a director if he could have permission to make a programme in the West Indies. "All right," Bennett asked, "and what's the story?" He received no satisfactory answer, for the young director's mind was empty of either story or point of view. "Oh, I'll just go and shoot it *cinema verité*," he said. Bennett's tart comment on that anecdote is: "We're in for a load of junk if this is to be the attitude of programme-makers." Of course the young man might conceivably have made a magnificent film. He might have had a great deal of luck to help along his growing talent. But it was impossible to assume that he would do so. Such an assumption is far too big a risk for a programme executive to take. For, as Peter Morley once put it, there is all the difference in the world between *cinema verité* and *cinema de bonne-chance*.

The Handicaps of Unsuitable Equipment

Purpose determines technique, and each technique demands its own precise technical resources. "To catch spontaneously the essence of what we see" is John Schlesinger's description of the purpose. "The film-maker's perception of an aspect of what happened" is what Richard Leacock, perhaps over-modestly, claims to be seeking. Let us combine those two statements and suggest that the maker of personal documentaries is trying to capture what to him seems to be the essence of something that is genuinely happening and of human beings who are genuinely living. This search for the 'essence' is what has determined the technique, and through the technique has influenced the physical equipment with which this type of programme is made.

It is, above all, a type of programme which, almost by definition, cannot be presented live and if there have ever been any live documentaries of this highly personal sort, then I myself do not know of them. The reason is clear enough. To capture that desired essence of a person or a situation, and at the same time

---

[1] Cyril Bennett was appointed Director of Programmes in 1965.

to impose on the programme one's own vision of the world—these are achievements which demand a great deal of shooting and many weeks of editing. It is clearly not enough merely to stick a set of electronic cameras in front of the subject-matter and then transmit it live—even assuming enough cameras to cover all the chosen locations and people. The personal documentary, therefore, depends for its success upon the ability to record the images and sounds, and to edit them thereafter. It can be made either on ciné-film or on video-tape.

In technical terms, the makers of this kind of programme have been pressing down the years for film (or tape) equipment which would be sufficiently unobtrusive to meet two essential conditions; to record pictures and sounds at a moment's notice, without the traditional time-wasting that was always involved in setting up cameras, sound equipment, and lights; and to be either small enough, or otherwise inconspicuous enough, to be easily forgotten by those quite ordinary men and women who are appearing in the programme, and the authenticity of whose performance depends to a great extent upon their ability to forget that it is being recorded. The relationship between technique and equipment is a two-way traffic. The desired technique creates the demand for more modified equipment, and the invention of new equipment encourages the programme-maker to devise techniques which will make the fullest use of it.

It is a fact that in British television the personal documentary was unknown until the invention of the portable tape-recorder in the early 1950s. Until then the word documentary had meant either the reconstruction of reality in the studio, using built sets, rehearsed actors, and written dialogue (we used to call it dramatised documentary), or else the familiar kind of documentary film which television had copied from the (often distinguished) work of British film makers before and after the second world war, and which was always objective and usually relied upon a carefully written narrative to tell its tale.

The most famous and as I think the finest example of the dramatised documentary was *The Course of Justice* (written for the BBC by Duncan Ross and produced by Ian Atkins), which portrayed the procedures of justice in Britain by means of a series of reconstructed court cases. Examples of television documentary which continued the style of the 1930s and '40s were *War in the Air* (a compilation series) and *The World Is Ours* (a

N

series on the work of the United Nations and its agencies which was inspired by Paul Rotha, himself one of the most distinguished of the pre-war documentary makers).

What was missing from our television documentaries before the mid 1950s was, quite simply, *people*. Our programmes were either global or national surveys of one sort or another, and the men and women who appeared in them were used merely as statistical evidence. *The World Is Ours*, for example, was full of humanity—refugees, nurses, teachers, scientists, farmers, children of all nationalities—but never once did we try to discover what these people were really like. They were merely symbols of a general condition, wearing nearly-visible labels, 'doctor', 'sick child', 'stateless person', and so on.[1] The only occasions when people appeared 'in the round', with recognisable personalities and emotions and hopes, were ironically in dramatised documentaries and then they were not real people at all, but the creations—based on fact, no doubt—of a scriptwriter, a producer, and a group of actors.

The main cause of this state of affairs was, I suggest, the absence of the necessary technical equipment. Videotape did not exist, and the available film resources were still those of 20 years earlier. Ciné-cameras, always 35 mm, were heavy and ponderous, optical sound recordings involved a huge vehicle the size of a furniture van, and the quantity of lighting equipment, as well as the time taken to assemble it, was substantially that of a full-scale feature film. To try to get the essence of either a person or a flexible situation with equipment of this sort, and within the shooting-time normally allocated to television productions, was almost impossible. I would have written absolutely impossible, but some of the remarkable results achieved by directors of imagination who pushed the equipment as far and as fast as it would go (for instance Anthony de Lotbinière in the *Special Enquiry* programmes on the slums and the colour bar) made one wonder if the apparently impossible might have been achieved.

The Influence of the Tape Recorder

Eventually the technical break-through came with sound and not with pictures, in the form of the portable quarter-inch tape-recorder, a light machine which had been developed at the

[1] The fault was mine. I was the producer of *The World Is Ours*.

BBC's request for its sound-radio programmes. Similarly, it was a radio producer, Denis Mitchell, whose use of this new equipment for his own personal essays in *radio-verité* had already generated much excitement in broadcasting circles, who now brought it into television. To catch the spontaneity of human speech and behaviour might still be difficult in film terms, but a tape recorder at least made such things possible on the sound track.

Ordinary men and women—and some extraordinary ones also—would speak frankly and openly to a sympathetic interviewer whose only equipment was a small green box and a microphone. An essential intimacy was achieved which had hitherto been prevented by the size and paraphernalia of a film unit. Moreover tape could very easily be edited; an hour's conversation became a set of essential statements and attitudes which lasted two or three minutes.

It was Denis Mitchell's first contribution to television that he realised the possibilities of combining these sound-tapes with silent pictures, using one as a counterpoint to the other. His first film was a report on British teenagers in the *Special Enquiry* series, and what might in other hands have been a routine job became a piece of television history. Not that, in retrospect, this was a particularly admirable film. Its significance lay in what it was trying to do rather than in its actual achievement, and the detailed combination of images and taped words were often naïve and obvious. But at least we seemed to be closer to the real hearts and minds of those teenagers than to any other people in any previous television programme.

Although there was a certain amount of synchronised sound (there were statements, carefully set and rehearsed, by some of the teenagers' parents) the main impact of the programme came from the words of the youngsters themselves, originally spoken into a tape recorder, and laid against silent pictures in the cutting room. By concentrating on a silent camera, which even in those days, and even using 35 mm film, was fairly portable, and demanded a much smaller crew than a full synchronised-sound unit, a considerable amount of spontaneous action was also possible.

The lessons of this *Special Enquiry* were applied with increasing success in the films that followed it, and which Mitchell made for the BBC's North Region in Manchester: *In Prison* (in which the tape recordings of the prisoners were evocatively used against silent shots within the prison itself), *Night in the City*, and *Morning in the Streets* (in which Roy Harris was co-director). In each of these later films the combination of sounds and images was often extremely subtle and moving; I remember the voice of an old man on the sound-track of *Night in the City*, saying:

> *"The only enjoyment I ever had in life was studying very deep literature, and I made it my business to wade through economics, mathematics, political economy, psycho-analysis, philosophy and psychology. I studied the great works of Aristotle, Plato, Marcus Aurelius, Tolstoy, Rousseau, Voltaire, Einstein, Nietzsche, Kropotkin,* The Decline and Fall of the Roman Empire *by Gibbon. I studied Buckle's* Civilisation In England, The Martyrdom of Man *by Wynward Reid, and then I went on to Oriental studies. . . . All I've got to say now that I'm seventy-two years of age is 'thanks for the memories'."*

Those words were heard against a picture of an old man, tatty and sad, strolling slowly across the dark open spaces of a Northern city. The words alone were moving; the pictures alone were interesting; the two together gave to each other qualities of drama and of emotion that separately had evaded them.

The danger of being a pioneer is that everyone copies you. Some do it well, but others do it with only moderate success, and the general effect is to deflate the currency. The least desirable effect of Denis Mitchell's experiments with a tape recorder was a long list of films made in the same manner but with only a quarter of the skill and a tenth of the feeling. Young men, and even a few young women, became obsessed by the deceitfully simple technique, and mistakenly assumed that with a small 16 mm silent camera and a portable tape-recorder they could make their own little masterpieces.

There were always a few television executives—and blushingly I admit that I was once one of them—who encouraged this activity in the hope of finding now and then a tiny nugget of gold. Many films were made, but few of them were shown outside of such cinéastic circles as the British Film Institute (which was generous enough to sponsor some of them) and the film societies. Their subject-matter was depressingly repetitive.

196

There were films about markets, about the East End of London, about days at the seaside, about down-and-outs and eccentrics of all kinds. These were places where facilities were free, where most of the shooting could take place out of doors, and where 'characters' (in the conventional sense) are commonly supposed to congregate.

The young makers of these films made many mistakes, but the worst of them were to assume that it is an easy matter to discover the 'essence' of a personality by means of a few tape-recordings, and that this particular technique was an end in itself. Tape recording is certainly an easy matter technically, but so for that matter is the use of pen and ink. To operate a tape recorder does not make a technician into a creative director, just as the ability to write words on paper does not make a poet. Moreover, and this is especially important, those who used this technique most effectively were always the first to concede its limitations and to admit that it was at best a compromise. What they ultimately wanted, and were constantly pressing designers and engineers to give them, was the equipment which would allow them to record, on film or anything else, the essentials of a human being's everyday life, both in picture and in sound. The use of wildtrack tapes was merely a means of catching the spontaneous thoughts of people at a time when syncronised sound was so ponderous a process that spontaneity was altogether out of the question.

It remained a ponderous process for several years, though during that time (1955 to 1960) several personal documentaries of great merit were made in Britain, and today I find myself looking back on them with remembered pleasure. There was Philip Donnellan's *Joe the Chainsmith*, a portrait of a craftsman in the English Midlands. Donnellan used more synchronised speech than Mitchell had done so far, with obvious advantages. But the cumbersome equipment which he was forced to use, although giving him a surface reality, robbed him of true spontaneity, and forced him into coaxing 'performances' from the men and women of the Black Country. In fact he achieved admirable performances from them, but they inevitably failed to give him as much of their true selves as might have been coaxed from them with a tape-recorder. Even so *Joe the Chainsmith* still stands as a landmark in the British TV Documentary.

A personal film of a rather different type was *The Man at*

Dover (directed by Richard Cawston and Pamela Wilcox Bower), which looked at Britain through the eyes of a refugee, and which was chiefly memorable for its visual wit—a merit that has always been curiously rare in factual television. John Schlesinger made several short films for the BBC's programme *Monitor*. In *Circus* he used the tape-recorder to evoke sounds rather than to record human speech, and by combining them with the pictures of a silent camera managed to suggest the mood of a circus in a way that would probably have escaped him had he chosen to shoot his film with a fully synchronised camera. In *The Innocent Eye* he tackled, with equal success, the relationship between children and art.

The Development of 16 mm Equipment

The next technical development was a double one; the substitution of 16 mm for 35 mm as the normal gauge for television film-making, and a modification of the tape-recorder which allowed it to operate as a synchronised sound recorder with the film-camera. At once the equipment became more portable, and the cost of production was reduced. *Morning in the Streets* was shot in this way, and since then Denis Mitchell has never out of preference made a film on 35 mm. Philip Donnellan moved to 16 mm for a series of industrial portraits. It was at last almost possible to approach the *real* lives of people, and to film any part of those lives without making compromises because of technical deficiencies rather than artistic needs.

A tiny film which in retrospect seems to have been a signpost for the future was *The Outing*, made for the BBC by Jack Gold, and which was quite simply the record of a coach trip to the seaside by the workers of an East London factory. With 16 mm cameras and $\frac{1}{4}$ in tape recorders he was able to record as much of an uninhibited day as he wished, from the quiet sober start in the morning, to the singing on the journey, the gaiety of the funfare, and the somewhat inebriated road back. This little film, made as an experiment, would a few years later have been called *cinema verité*. In fact, and strangely, it passed almost unnoticed.

The available technical equipment had still one serious disadvantage. When the 16 mm camera (of whatever manufacture) was sound-proofed, or blimped, it was far too heavy for rapid mobility, and when it was unblimped it was much too noisy for

198

normal operation within the rooms of a building. It was not yet possible, therefore, for a cameraman to hold his camera by hand in any situation which needed synchronised sound, unless he was out of doors and in a normally noisy location. The director was still confined to a combination of mobile silent shots and very static—or else very carefully prepared and rehearsed—sound shots. Moreover the problem of lighting still remained. Admittedly lights became more portable, and year by year it became increasingly possible to use fewer of them; but the day had not yet come when an adventurous cameraman could shoot an interior either with no extra light at all, or else with the substitution of photo-floods for the normal domestic light bulbs. Neither the film stock nor the laboratories had yet accepted the implications of this particular challenge.

The situation has changed very dramatically in the last two or three years. Faster film stock has been made available, and the laboratories have been willing to push it much farther than before. Tape recorders have become both more sturdy and more portable, and the use of striped sound (a small strip of magnetic tape running down one side of the 16 mm film stock) has made the process of recording synchronised sound much more mobile. The problems of camera-weight and camera-noise have been largely resolved by new developments in the production of light-weight cameras, notably the camera designed in France by M. Coutant and now marketed by the Eclair Company; this is sufficiently silent for the recording of speech in an interior close-up, and sufficiently light for a cameraman to hold it either by hand or by a simple harness for the duration of a ten-minute take.

In the USA the team of Robert Drew and Richard Leacock has also experimented successfully in the field of synchronisation. Realising that one of the reasons why the shooting of synchronised sound has tended to be too stationary an occupation is the fact that the film camera and the sound-recorder have had to be connected together by a cable, they developed a method of separating them physically without destroying their inter-relationship. The link between camera and tape-recorder is by means of a radio signal, passed from a transmitter on the camera to a receiver built into the recorder.

This set of technical developments, mainly in France and the USA, has at long last provided the director with all the facilities which he has been seeking for over a decade. It is now possible to shoot sound-film with a hand-held camera, using a recorder that is physically disconnected from it, and to do so without extra light.

The Verité Technique

These technical developments have profoundly affected the traditional theories of film-making. It had hitherto been assumed, for example, that the choice of a particular shot should be determined by the director with the advice of the cameraman. But by the philosophy of *cinema verité* (or *tele-verité*) this decision is determined by the subject-matter. If the camera's function is to record, as literally and unobtrusively as possible, what is actually going on, then it must follow the action as best it can. When Mr. X, the central figure in the film, rises from his desk and crosses the room it must follow him—and so must the microphone. If it is eavesdropping on a business conference then it must try to shoot whoever is speaking at any given moment— and again the microphone must be able to catch the words of each speaker in turn.

In this kind of film-making the director would seem to be unnecessary, for each decision must be taken by the cameraman. There can be no discussion about each shot, and there is no time to consider the artistic merits of each camera angle, or each movement of the camera. What we see and hear is entirely determined by what is happening, and by the agility of the cameraman and the recordist to keep pace with it. For this reason several of the practitioners of *cinema verité* have abolished the word 'director' altogether, and substituted 'film maker', though it is quite obvious that the cameraman is in fact the most important person in the unit.

The technique of *cinema verité* also raises questions about the role of the film editor. For if the purpose of the film is quite simply to record what is literally being done and said, then the mere process of film editing is philosophically unjustified as an amendment of the literal truth. The most that should be permitted, one imagines, is the joining together of complete scenes. To select in the cutting room one shot as against another, to place shots in a new order, to lengthen or shorten them, to alter the sound-track—all these sinister but usual activities are in the same category as the deliberate selection by a director of the
200

actual shots in the camera. If the role of the cameraman is to follow the action, and the role of the recordist to record the existing sounds, then the job of the editor should be reduced to stringing together the shots that he receives. In fact, and expectedly, this is a purist view which has never been sustained in practice, but Ronald Kelly, who has made some very effective *verité* films for the Canadian Broadcasting Corporation, puts the problem in practical terms.

"I made a film about life in a big hospital during the night, and I set out to film exactly what was happening, as it happened. As I had no idea—nor did the hospital—what was going to take place, I therefore had no notion in advance of the content of the film. I shot the film in long takes, trying to capture the action and the speech and the various hospital sounds as they happened, using a hand-held camera and adding only photofloods to the normal lighting of the hospital. The biggest problem, artistically, came in the cutting room. All my instincts were to edit the film in the usual, traditional way, building up each sequence by carefully selecting the shots, and deciding the precise length of each of them. But in fact this didn't work. I had shot the film one way, and now I was trying to edit it in quite another. I had made a series of long continuous takes (which is how life is lived) and now I was thinking of breaking up these lengths of reality and thereby destroying the truth of them. In the end I abandoned this traditional method of editing. A new way of shooting needs a new way of editing—in this case involving far fewer cuts, and far fewer short shots."

In *cinema verité*, therefore, we are faced with a new way of making films; and despite the word 'cinema' these are in fact films which have so far been made more frequently for a television audience than for the audiences of the commercial cinema (where in any case their technical deficiencies are magnified on the large screen). The equipment now exists which makes it possible for the director, or the film-maker, to record in images and sounds virtually everything which is being done or being spoken.

The first consequence has been a set of films which have followed a person (or persons) during a chosen period of time: a politician, an actress, a pop group, a fashion model, a mother of quintuplets, a condemned man and his lawyers, an impresario. I have suggested earlier in this chapter that these films have two serious limitations of content, apart from their technical imperfections. They have been concerned with unusual people, and they have reported unusual situations. It has yet to be proved that the method can be used outside of the unusual and the dramatic, and one suspects that a *cinema verité* film about a rather dull day in the life of an apparently dull office clerk would not exactly make compulsive television. The more exciting the central figure and the more dramatic his life, the more successful is the film.

As in a news programme, the interest of the film is in direct proportion to the interest of what is actually happening in front of the camera. There was a time—and we are only just emerging from it—when *cinema verité* became as much of a craze as the wild tape recorder had been ten years previously. It was too frequently assumed that a good film could be made merely by taking a light synchronised camera and recording almost anything and virtually anybody. Cyril Bennett has indicated the essential fallacy behind this:

"We are in danger of losing certain of the good features of traditional presentation. You might add up to say that we're in danger of losing certain traditional forms of self-discipline. 'Don't bother about a story-line. Don't bother about discussion. Don't bother about the traditional disciplines in film-making.' There's a tendency now to think that all you need to do is shoot film, without pre-thought, and edit the results without any regard for structure. Picture for its own sake is being replaced by a new danger—technique for its own sake."

This is a serious danger indeed, a very grave instance of the tail wagging the dog. For life, as we know, is usually shapeless, and it is one of the merits of dramatic art—in which I would include the documentary film—to impose a shape on it. This shape, as I have suggested in these pages, is partly the personal vision of the director. Remove the shape, abandon the vision, and all that remains is a newsreel which has been extended beyond the point of human endurance.

It is no coincidence that some of the most satisfactory examples of *cinema verité* have indeed been straight news reports, and no account of this sort would be fair that did not include a reference to the pioneering work of Erik Durchmeidt for

Panorama. By hand-holding his camera, and by carrying his own tape-recorder over his shoulder, he both filmed and recorded quite remarkable material in Algiers (with Robert Kee and David J. Webster) and in the Yemen (with James Mossman), and in East Pakistan (with David Dimbleby). If these films were not *cinema verité* then the phrase is quite meaningless.

The Development of Videotape

So far in this discussion of the personal documentary I have referred almost entirely to those programmes made on film, and the technical developments I have described have all been in the field of film-making. Yet although this form of television is always likely to be pre-recorded, it by no means follows that this recording must inevitably be in the form of ciné-film. It could be—and in the future is increasingly likely to be—on video-tape. For video-tape, recording both images and sounds on the same piece of material, has several advantages, either actual or potential, over film.

The main reason why video-tape came so late into this particular field was the difficulty in editing it, for unless and until it could be edited with something like the precision of film, it was never likely to satisfy the director whose effects depended so largely upon his creative work in the cutting room. In Britain it was not until 1963 that one of the commercial programme companies, Granada, had made a modification to the normal tape equipment which made it possible for recorded tape to be edited with accuracy to within a tenth of a second. The first producer to exploit this new development was Denis Mitchell, whose programme *The Entertainers* was shot and edited entirely on video-tape. A few weeks later I myself made the second British video-tape documentary, *A Wedding on Saturday*.

The merits of tape seem to be six in number :

The first advantage is that of being able to shoot for up to an hour without stopping. This avoids the necessity of having to change the magazine just when a speaker is getting into his stride. To obtain a usable minute or two of a man or woman talking, 60 minutes can be recorded, if necessary, without disturbing the flow of talk or without worrying about the cost of it. For videotape, like ordinary sound tape, can be wiped and used again. When someone is trying to express their own feelings

203

and their own view of life in their own words, it is obviously a big advantage that they should be able to go on for so long without interruption. The longer they go on, the less conscious they become of the camera.

The second advantage is that the rushes can be seen immediately after the scene is shot. The tape is recorded on location, and it can be played back at once. If the result is not satisfactory, the scene can be shot again, eliminating the suspense of waiting until the next morning, after the film has been processed, before knowing what it is like. This also means, of course, that those who took part in particular sequences can see what they did, and therefore see their own mistakes. An incidental advantage is that the second take can automatically wipe the first one.

The third advantage is that much less light is needed, because electronic cameras are more sensitive than ciné-cameras.

The fourth advantage is that excellent night shots are possible. This can be done genuinely, taking shots in the middle of the night and under conditions which in film would be totally impossible, or a realistic night effect during daylight can be created by electronic means, and without any delay whatsoever.

The fifth advantage is that, if necessary, more than one camera can be used. There were sequences in Manchester clubs in *The Entertainers* which were shot on three cameras, all linked to the same tape, and John McGrath cut from camera to camera in the normal manner of a television studio. This is a big advantage in set pieces of this sort, when a great deal of action is going on in a big area. The extra cameras can also be used to save time in setting up the next scene. In *The Entertainers* most of the shooting was done on one camera, in various rooms of a boarding house. Because there were three cameras available, and therefore the crews of three cameras, it was always possible to set up one scene ahead of whatever was being shot—'leap-frogging' about the house, in fact. This is an obvious saving of time.

The sixth advantage is that all the sound is automatically synchronised on the same physical tape as the pictures.

The disadvantages, at this moment, in the development of video-tape, are entirely concerned with its relative lack of mobility. The cameras must be connected physically with their control vehicle; the process of recording the tape needs the space of approximately half a vehicle; holding the cameras by hand is out of the question; the crew is a large one (normally over twenty men) and both the crew and their equipment are extremely conspicuous. To 'snatch' shots is normally impossible. Indeed, as far as the technical equipment is concerned, video-tape is as cumbersome as film used to be some fifteen years ago. The fluidity of shooting which the latest ciné-cameras have made possible is quite out of the question. To the director who insists on shooting life as it goes on about him, without technical restrictions, video-tape seems to be a form of self-imposed paralysis. Work of the *verité* kind is impossible. Everything has to be planned beforehand.

There are two further points to be made about video-tape; the first is technical and the second is artistic. The technical point is the simple one that use of video-tape in this way (shot on location as a film is shot, and edited afterwards with almost equal precision) is in its infancy. The equipment being used for it is still basically the equipment used for the routine outside broadcasts of sporting events, church services, and public functions. The development of the highly mobile film camera followed years of pressure by television producers who complained that the existing equipment was inadequate for their needs. A similar process, one assumes, will take place in video-tape, until the day will be reached when the fluidity of the portable film camera will be combined with the advantages of recording on tape. When that day comes, it is more than likely that film, at least in television, will die.

The second point is an artistic one. Even with video-tape recording as cumbersome as it is at present, it is still arguable that it allows the director to get closer to that elusive 'essence' of a situation or of a person than is possible even with all the advanced resources of *cinema verité*. To give precise examples: I myself felt that I knew much more about the club artistes in *The Entertainers* (on tape) than I learned about Joe Levine in *Showman* or about the mother in *Quint City* (both on film).

To follow a man, without restrictions, for a week or two, and to see him going about his business and saying whatever he would normally be saying, does not necessarily present us with the whole of that man. Indeed it is possible that it merely presents us with his public image, the exterior personality which he wears like a suit whenever he goes about his daily life.

The reality of the man, his deepest feelings and thoughts, might perhaps be obtained more readily as the result of a long conversation or set of conversations, as in *Face to Face*.

The facility given by video-tape to record a human being for a continuous hour might be a greater advantage to the documentary maker than the fluidity of shooting which is the most obvious asset of the latest film equipment. Certainly programmes made on tape must still be very carefully planned and shot, and there can be no pretence that the cameras are inconspicuous. But planning is not necessarily a disadvantage, except to those who are incapable of it. Discipline, as every creative person knows, is one of the springboards of success.

The Merging of Drama and Documentary

Those of us who believe that people are as important and as exciting as opinions and statistics will always be prepared to defend the personal documentary and to resist any attempts to push it aside. The genuine maker of the personal documentary is an artist, no less, and this means that like artists elsewhere he is liable now and then to fall flat on his face, to provoke the hostility of those who misunderstand him, and even to misfire altogether and produce a work that is interminably boring.

All this has happened in the past, and it will happen again. But what has already been achieved is infinitely more significant than those occasional calamities, and this is a field in which, by any standards, much of the finest in television has flowered and flourished. I myself regard works like *Morning in the Streets*, *Joe the Chainsmith*, *Elgar*, *The Chair*, *Culloden*, *Chicago*, *The Innocent Eye*, and *Borrowed Pasture* as among my most moving memories as a spectator in any medium. They have affected me as all works of art affect me, by moving me profoundly and by giving me a deeper insight into the human condition, thereby altering me slightly, though on each occasion perhaps only infinitesimally, for the better. This is surely the effect on us of the most genuine forms of music, drama, the novel, and the visual arts. It is not, however, the effect upon us of a light entertainment programme, however brilliant, or a news programme, or (except on the rarest occasions) a current affairs documentary.

Drama, of course, can affect us in the same way, and it seems to me that the personal documentary has much in common with
206

the more serious forms of television drama. It too can tell a story, can examine human beings in depth, can indulge in verbal and visual wit, can move us on several levels. Whether it can ever hope to cover as broad a field as drama is an issue on which I prefer to suspend judgment. But there are those—Denis Mitchell is one of them—who have deliberately moved from drama to documentary and who believe that the personal documentary can defeat drama at its own game. It is an important part of his belief that the spontaneous dialogue of ordinary men and women is truer, more moving, and more full of poetry than the words written by a dramatist. 'Realistic' drama is a contradiction in terms.

I accept that the true documentary artist can sometimes handle his 'real' people in such a way that the impact is as great as that of a play—and possibly greater, for what he shows us is true and not entirely the creation of his own mind. Certainly a very good documentary is far more powerful and moving than a competent play, and the impact of *Morning in the Streets* is arguably greater than that of, say, *Love on the Dole*. Yet there are certain areas of human experience which, so it seems to me, the documentary maker, however skilful, will enter at his peril.

There are facets of the human condition which cannot be expressed in terms of actual, living persons. Men and women will expose themselves thus far and no farther, and even if they crossed this invisible frontier, there are the laws of libel and slander to be considered. Sexual relations are obviously matters which are best and more honestly discussed in fictional terms, and so are those of professional relationships whose truthful public exposure would do more harm than good to the people concerned. To claim that television documentary can do everything that drama can do, and then do it better, is something yet to be proved. That it can be as moving and at least as true as drama over the increasingly large area where the two overlap is, I believe, already certain.

The cross-fertilisation of drama and documentary is a particularly interesting phenomenon, and has recently been evident on several levels. Much of contemporary dramatic dialogue carries echoes of the spontaneous speech of the tape-recorder. The work of Harold Pinter, for instance, is full of the pauses, *non-sequiturs*, sudden and oblique illuminations of personality,

207

and bizarre wit that one finds in the most authentic television documentaries.

Conversely, the documentary has itself been creeping closer and closer to drama. Many documentaries have adopted a conventional dramatic plot, with a beginning, middle, and end, and with appropriate minor climaxes along the way. *The Entertainers* actually *looks* like a play—indeed *is* a play as well as being a documentary, but a play in which not only the dialogue but also the developing relationships are improvised and spontaneous. Ronald Kelly's extremely interesting Canadian film, *The Open Grave*, is a piece of symbolic fiction (the symbolism relating to the Resurrection of Christ) made with the techniques of *cinema verité* and even containing such deliberate mistakes as jump-cuts, wobbly hand-held shots, and flaring.

Novelists and dramatists have also, however tentatively, been turning to television documentary. David Storey, author of *This Sporting Life*, has directed films for the BBC's *Monitor* programme—one of them an essay on D. H. Lawrence which was sufficiently personal to tell us as much about Mr. Storey as about his subject. Robert Bolt both wrote and narrated, also for the BBC, a portrait of Bertrand Russell.

It may well be that the boundary between drama and documentary, between fact and fiction, is being slowly erased, and that in having separate departments called drama and documentary our television organisations are keeping them apart for reasons of administrative tradition and convenience long after their separation has ceased to be artistically desirable. For the man who writes a personal documentary and the man who writes a true play have much in common, and the man who wants to create television programmes which tell the truth, as he sees it, about our world and its people, is as likely to choose the documentary as the play. It may even be that drama and documentary are dead words which television has inherited from the theatre and the cinema respectively. What we are really discussing are programmes, and in this chapter I have been considering programmes which are both personal and true, and which are the individual work of a creative mind. What name we choose to give to them is of relatively minor importance.

TELEVISION AND PEOPLE

P EOPLE—and I hope this is clear from what I have written
so far—are the very stuff of television. Yet I now find that
what I had planned as one of the longest chapters in this
book has become the shortest. For although the presentation of
people on television has occupied the minds of executives and
producers for nearly 30 years, there is very little to say about it.
There are, in fact, precisely two things to be said. The first is
that people make good television, and the second is that they
should be presented simply and without fuss.

I remember the days when complicated sets were built as a
background to this person or that, a mock library for the professor or a suggestion of a lush office for the industrial magnate,
and alas it never occurred to us that we really needed no background at all. The most impressive interview programme yet
presented, *Face to Face*, owed part of its success to the fact that
its producer, Hugh Burnett, realised from the start that what
mattered was the face of the person being interviewed. It was
not necessary to have a set (what in fact he had was almost an
'anti-set'), nor was it necessary to see the interviewer.

Sets are a Distraction

What was needed was a sequence of shots, of portraits even,
of whomsoever was the subject of each programme. The human
face, caught in moments of emotion or reflection or repose, is
one of the most consistently powerful of all the images presented on the television screen, and any attempt to distract
from it by carefully considered sets, or props, or backgrounds, is
both unnecessary and mistaken. The technique of presenting a
living person is therefore very simple indeed: let us see that
person in as carefully-lit and well-composed a shot as possible.
That is all.

This effect can, of course, be achieved best in a studio, where

o   209 all the necessary lighting facilities are so readily available. But it can also be achieved from an outside broadcast point, or on film. A coal-miner can speak from his cottage, a Prime Minister from his official residence, a housewife from the shopping pavement where the film camera has accidentally captured her. It makes no essential difference. Let us see the face and hear the voice.

This, of course, is to describe a technique in terms which are strictly technical. There is also the human technique, the initial choice of people, the selection of those who will be most effective in an unrehearsed discussion, the search for someone who can be relied upon to explain a complex scientific subject in terms that are comprehensible to the layman and who will at the same time prove to be himself an attractive personality. Let me suggest a few general principles:

First, people are better when they are unscripted. Very few people (and this is as true of public figures as of 'men in the street') can either learn a part convincingly or read naturally. It follows that television's biggest successes with people have been either in interview programmes or in unrehearsed discussions, as in *Face to Face* or in *Let Me Speak*, for instance.

Secondly, if a person is really interesting, then he can be interesting for a long time. I make the point because it was assumed for many years that a human face and a human voice could never be held for more than a very few minutes without some other form of visible or aural distraction. Four people could argue for half an hour (as they did very successfully in *In the News*) but one person could only speak for two or three minutes at the very most. In fact this was proved to be nonsense as long ago as 1951, when in a series called *Speaking Personally* several distinguished persons (among them were Sir Tyrone Guthrie, Margaret Mead, Lord James, and Nigel Balchin) sat in front of a single television camera and spoke impromptu for a quarter of an hour. Since then there have been several series of interviews in depth, conducted by John Freeman, Malcolm Muggeridge, John Berger, and Jack Hargreaves, each of them running for about half an hour, in which the person interviewed could express himself at leisure in the perfectly normal situation of two-way conversation.

Thirdly, unless they are by profession in the public eye, most people are more likely to be effective in their homes than in the
210

highly artificial and frequently terrifying atmosphere of a television studio.

Fourthly, the technique of choosing ordinary people (meaning housewives, steel-workers, teachers, and so on, rather than politicians or other public figures) is one which cannot be written down. The extroverts are not always the best, and some of the liveliest characters have been known to relapse into a complete silence when it comes to the actual performance. Moreover people's moods change, and we all have our off days; a man who would have been superb on Monday might be merely adequate on Tuesday. There is luck in all this, and the only advice I would myself dare to give is that necessary virtues are sincerity, calmness, and a sense of humour. Even more important, without any doubt, is the personality of the producer himself. I have known many men and women who have been destroyed—in programme terms—by a producer or a director who was aggressive, or superior, or shy, or an intellectual snob.

Finally, the easiest way to express the views of ordinary people is by the filmed *vox pop*, which was brought to perfection by *Tonight*. The technique is the simple one of filming a dozen or so ordinary people in the street, and seeking their opinions on any subject which seems topical or interesting. The resulting statements are then broken down in the cutting room, and a sentence or so of Mr. A placed next to one of Mrs. B (who says the exact opposite), and so on. In this way a controversy can be created in human terms, and only the best sections of each statement will be used. The fact that this is an artificial way of generating a debate is perhaps a moral question to which insufficient attention has been paid. The impression is created of a genuine conflict of public opinion, but the people themselves are selected by means which are purely arbitrary and unscientific.

CONCLUSION

TELEVISION differs from the other media of communication in three significant respects: it can transmit both pictures and sounds live, at the moment they are taking place, it has a much larger audience, and it is usually seen by small groups of people, often threes or fours, in the privacy of their homes. Of these characteristics the first is by far the most significant, and it therefore grieves me that in writing this book I have devoted such small space to the discussion of live programmes.

Dearth of Live Programmes

The reason, of course, is that nowadays there are so few of them, and this is very odd when one considers how many of the truly memorable moments of factual television have been transmissions of live events: the Coronation of Queen Elizabeth II, the funeral of Sir Winston Churchill, the arrival of the first Soviet astronaut in Moscow, the funeral of President Kennedy, the international relays from the Olympic Games in Tokio, the coverage of national Elections, some of John Freeman's frank and subtle interviews in *Face to Face*, the BBC's first 'Teach-In' in July 1965, clashes between opposing politicians, the bizarre activities of the Committee into Un-American Activities, a baseball game or a Cup Final.

It is significant that very few of such programmes were created for television, and even those of them which took place in a television studio achieved their impact through the unexpected—the effect of an astute unrehearsed question by John Freeman, or the spectacle of two national leaders in spontaneous discussion on a subject about which they were in profound disagreement.

Otherwise the big moments of factual television have tended to be the transmission of films; *Morning in the Streets, Elgar,*
212

Death in the Morning, Television and the World, Capital Punishment, The Great War, Culloden, Black Marries White, several of the *CBS Reports*, Robert Kee in Algeria, James Mossman in Viet-Nam. Certainly all of these films were made by television organisations, but that is perhaps merely to say that at another time they might have been sponsored by other organisations working for the cinema. It is hard not to regret that in so many of its achievements television's role has been limited to that of a film-projector.

Originality is Rare

Also, and here I speak as a fairly regular viewer, very little of recent factual television has been particularly original in either style or technique.[1] News programmes, the magazines, discussions, personal documentaries—in each of these fields the pattern has scarcely changed for many years. There was a time when television constantly delighted us with new surprises, giving us *See it Now, Panorama, Tonight, Monitor, World in Action,* and developing more effective methods of presenting the news of the day. These surprises, as the years go by, occur far less frequently, either because television has already attempted everything (which on the face of it seems unlikely) or because the inspiration has sagged, or the mood has changed (or the encouragement to inspiration has vanished).

I can think of only three really original developments in the past three years—*That Was The Week That Was*, the experiments of *cinema-verité*, and the use of edited videotape in the making of documentaries. What we *have* enjoyed, however, has been a steadily increasing standard of excellence. Television productions have become increasingly efficient. One has only to compare the old *Special Enquiry* with *CBS Reports*, or *War in the Air* with *The Great War* to notice the difference.

Grace Wyndham Goldie believes —and she is usually right— that consistent excellence is as important as the creation of new programme ideas. She has argued, and clearly this is true, that although *The Great War* was not in itself a new form of television, it did create a new standard, so that compilation programmes can never be quite the same again. This is also true, for

[1] This is not so true of drama; witness *Diary of a Young Man* (BBC) by Troy Kennedy Martin and John McGrath, which broke into new territory altogether.

instance, of the series *Let Me Speak* (BBC-2) in which young people with strong and often rebellious convictions (Communists, Empire Loyalists, Anarchists) discussed their beliefs with Malcolm Muggeridge. On the face of it this was an ordinary studio discussion, a form of television as old as the medium itself, but because it was produced and directed with such force and wit, and because its basic *idea* was a new one, it must surely have prompted the producers of the more routine discussion programmes to go away and think again. In the same way the BBC's three-hour 'Teach-In' gave a new format to established techniques, and seemed boldly new.

The same is true of recent programmes of satire, *That Was The Week That Was*, *On the Braden Beat*, and *Not so much a Programme*. The techniques they employed were not new ones, but old ones deployed to a new purpose. *TW 3*, probably the best of them, drew freely on the methods of the television magazines, on the established devices of television light entertainment and television drama, and on the latest experiments in intimate revue and the *avant-garde* cinema. The content, at least in terms of television, was far more original than the method. That politicians (for example) should be satirised, and that the pompous should be punctured, openly and before an audience of several millions, was certainly a new development, and a risky one too, as it turned out. But it is surely salutary that a public corporation should once more take the lead, as it had done 15 years before in the area of public affairs, in trying to extend the boundaries of the permissible. These programmes, however, are barely on the fringe of factual television as I have understood it in this essay, and deserve consideration at greater length, but elsewhere.

The Next Development?

It may be that factual television itself has entered a period of consolidation, content to improve its standards within known areas, and no doubt this is an admirable phase as long as it is not accompanied by complacency and back-slapping. The next leap-forward is hard to predict, but it needs no particular gift of foresight to suggest that it will come when electronic cameras become more portable, and when the facilities to edit videotape become more mobile and more precise. The logical development of *cinema verité* is presumably live *verité*, in which hand-held

214

electronic cameras transmit what is happening in the life of a man or woman at the very moment when it happens. Moreover, as I have suggested earlier in these pages, it seems only a matter of time before news and topical current affairs programmes rely on electronic cameras and videotape instead of 16 mm ciné-equipment.

Otherwise, is it too much to hope that television might eventually remedy its most conspicuous deficiency—its failure to realise its full potentiality as an *international* medium of communication? It is sad to think that there are probably more international exchanges in the other media of the press, radio, and the cinema, than in television (the most powerful communicator of them all). It has become a commonplace of television criticism to complain that international relays have so far been used mainly for moments of pageantry, sporting events, and song contests. The enormous power for good which television could wield if it tried hard enough has scarcely been tapped. The reasons for this failure, which are those of politics and pride, are surely both inadequate and dangerous. The notion which many television men had nearly twenty years ago of a world which was completely covered by live television, and which therefore would use it as a constructive force in bringing together the people of all nations, has never yet come to pass; and for once it is the will, rather than the absence of technical resources, which has held us back.

Meanwhile, and despite television's failures and confusions, no book of this nature could end without a re-statement of what is gloriously obvious. That in television we have a means of communication which is more powerful and more immediately attractive than either print or the spoken word. Television matters because so many millions of people watch it. Therefore it also matters in whose hands television is controlled, and the hands which control factual television matter most of all.

The relationship between technique and purpose in any medium is always subtle and changing, but it is a safe generalisation that technique should be the best way of expressing whatever ideas or images a group of creative people wish to express. Technique for its own sake is either meaningless or sinister. In this tentative and somewhat personal book I have therefore considered technique as something which is inseparable from policy or content. "What are we trying to do?" is the

215

first question which producers must ask themselves, and the second is "What is the best way of doing it?" In writing this book I have always tried to remember that the second of those questions—which is the theme of the book—cannot be answered without constant reference to the first of them.

Executive Opinions

I would not wish the last words of this book to be my own. For the practising producer runs the risk of confusing the trees with the wood. He is too concerned with his own immediate area of activity to be able to step back and survey the whole scene. This, therefore, is where I stand down and, instead of drawing on the expressed opinions of other producers, must give way to the views of those who are more concerned with strategy than tactics, and who are in a better position to look at the past and the future of factual television as one continuous story—the Directors of Television organisations, the executives whose decisions operate over years rather than weeks. I have asked two of them for their opinions, Denis Forman of Granada, and Kenneth Adam of the BBC:

Denis Forman writes as follows:

"In the beginning there was the spoken word. And when Seen Pictures arrived, the whole of Current Affairs was divided in like manner into three parts: News, Talks, and Documentary. This was the BBC in 1955.

"Then came the age of the News Magazine. Panorama, This Week; *later* Tonight, Tempo, Monitor; *later still* World in Action *and* Gallery; *last of all* That Was The Week *and* Not so *much a Programme.* Panorama *for the good citizen;* TW 3 *and* Not so *for the readers of the posh Sundays;* World in Action *for the national newspaper reader; but all based on news—big news, quaint news, cultural news, and disgraceful news. This age of news is still with us, and is likely to remain until the quality of comment is better and the freedom to comment is greater. If John Wilkes and Sydney Smith were still with us, our libel-fearing society would relegate them exclusively to* Private Eye. *So we handle news like eunuchs. We present the raw materials but we cannot get involved. Alas for* TW 3; *weep for* Not so; *for they had opinion in them.*

"News is more interesting to see than to hear, and it is more

216

interesting to see the event than to see the Speaker of the Spoken Word speaking about the event. The Americans understood this some years ago, and their major news bulletins are a fast-moving parade of film clips, graphics, and still pictures, spun together by anchor men. Ours in Britain remain a recital by the high priests of news who let in, now and again, a bit of film from our cameramen on the spot. The major American news programmes run half an hour or more in peak time; the British, around twenty minutes. Perhaps this explains the phenomenon of the British television magazine programmes, which greatly out-number the news magazines in any other country, although America and Britain are about equal in the amount of time given to news in all its forms.

"The magazine programmes have shown a growing dissatis-faction with the studio interview with an 'expert'. This is always a poor second-best to the thing itself, or even a film background of the thing itself with a voice-over based, if you like, on the views of the expert. Experts are not always capable of speaking concise plain English, nor of evoking a picture that will strike the mind. They are seldom interesting unless they disagree emotionally. Intellectual disagreement is generally better expressed in the written word.

"Even the studio interview with, say, a resigning leader of a political party, is only a supplement to film coverage of the leader in the act of announcing his resignation to his followers. The event is the thing, and no doubt a major event can stand some consequential gossip in the studio; a minor event or a non-event can no longer stand any. Occasionally an event still takes place in the studio, as when Robert Mackenzie goaded Lord Hailsham (as he was then) into a posture of angry pom-posity. But politicians and their kind have become increasingly wary of unplanned happenings, and in Britain are not yet pre-pared to be a party to planned happenings, such as the Kennedy–Nixon confrontations.

"All of this drives the current affairs programme out of the studio into the arena, and this is expensive. Eight years ago Granada attempted to create an event in the studio each week with a confrontation programme called Under Fire. *The pro-gramme was successful, and it cost, say, £x per week. In 1965 Granada started a new programme with permanent bureaux to make film in five countries, including Japan and the USA. The*

217

weekly cost of The World Tonight *is £15x. And there is another penalty if you go into the arena.* Under Fire *could be given a dry-run and started or stopped at will. A programme like* The World Tonight *must be accepted as a commitment six months in advance, and it is not economically sane to run it for less than 39 weeks. So the equation runs:*

Under Fire : *4 weeks' notice, and £x a week* ad lib.
The World Tonight : *6 months' notice, and £15x a week for 39 weeks.*

"*Thus enormous sums of money are standing committed on the budgets of the BBC and of some ITV companies for current affairs series at a time when television economics contradict the journalistic logic of taking cameras into the arena. The bloated BBC is moving on to a rigorous diet. The ITV companies are bearing a major set-back in the form of the levy on advertising revenue. The next logical step is the use of satellites for the quick collection of news.*

"*The new satellites will not be nationally but privately operated, one for each major television organisation. Costs will be even greater than they are today, and what is going to happen then? Are NBC and CBS to be left to go it alone? Which would be the more intolerable, for the BBC to become a second-rate power, or to become a collaborationist with ITV? Could either party afford to go it alone? For independently-minded people this may be the dilemma of the decade, for no editor and no producer likes to work for a committee or for a consortium.*"

Kenneth Adam sees the situation this way :

"*Casting round, and back, for some peripheral claims to speak on this subject, I begin to realise that much of my life has had to do with the sources from which factual television has been derived. First, with radio journalism, as practised by Archie Harding in the Manchester studios in the very early thirties, when we were preoccupied with people, and by Laurence Gilliam in London nearly a decade later, where the concern was rather for themes, and by the six of us who started BBC News in four rooms with four teleprinters in 1934. (Two of the six are still working, and with distinction, in a vastly and unrecognisably expanded service, and one is an Ambassador.) Radio news, as it found its style, ran counter to much that was developing in*
218

popular daily journalism. It was a cliché of the London evening newsroom I served that there was always a good human interest story in the Zoo. But the BBC's best recruits were newspaper-trained. There was, and is, no unbridgable gap.

"Radio journalism came to a height of authority at the end of the war. Indeed, War Report was its finest hour. Today its unique contribution comes from a corps of specialist reporters and foreign correspondents, who nevertheless, are becoming increasingly ambidextrous. Not all of them switch so readily to the screen as Richard Dimbleby did, but in conciseness of presentation and intimacy of approach, radio fact has taught television fact a great deal.

"The second source, with which I was involved personally, and, for a time, as a critic, was the documentary cinema of the '30s, the great days of the Empire Marketing Board, and the GPO Film Unit, when you went to the Soho pubs just to listen to Grierson and Jennings and Elton and Watt, and to hear what they had to say about Flaherty and Lorentz and Riefenstahl. Nobody who did not share the excitement of those days will understand their sense of promise and of purpose. But the photographer had to go to war, and magnificently as he did, in the Crown Film Unit especially, there was nothing left afterwards but amiable and diffused sponsorships to which the survivors attached themselves. It was left to television to pick up the pieces, to assume the social responsibility, if that is not too pompous a way of putting it. There is, alas, very little worthwhile film documentary outside television today. But, at least, there was no gulf that could not be spanned here either.

"The third source was what I suppose one has to call photo-journalism, which had a heyday almost as short as the newsreel (and here may I tip a hat to The March of Time, on which, in a New York emergency, I once appeared as George Lansbury; four lines but oh, how telling!). Short over here in Britain, anyway. Life and Paris Match march on. But Picture Post, of whose declining years I ruefully saw much, and Illustrated, and the rest of the weekly fireworks have long ago fizzled out. Do not believe they had to go. The excuses were tidy, but the reasons were not. (That is another story.) Anyway, they made a double contribution to the 'graphic revolution'. They helped, more positively perhaps, to staff the newcomer. Tonight, without the men and women of Picture Post, would never have been what it *was. Again, there was little difficulty in changing over. Take Slim Hewitt, for instance. He jumped the ditch from still to film with an arrogant ease, and can still lead the field.*

"By now, I hope, you get my point. I do not acknowledge a mystique in factual television. I am suspicious of 'break-throughs' and 'revolutions'. To me it seems that what we are doing today, and will be doing tomorrow, in this area, is a clear and logical development of what went before. To read the Sunday paper briefers and insighters on televerité suggests the time has come for the National Film Theatre to revise Roquier's Farrebique. I will see what I can do about this; we might make a short season of old verité while we are about it.

"This note must end, because I have taken too long in looking backward, with some rather bald assertions on matters which are not obviously connected. Believing, as I do, in the organic relationship between the old journalism and the new, I am not prepared to see the reporter reduced to a cipher, sandwiched between the cameraman and the editor (any editor, and we have had several different kinds). Indeed, I want to see the reporter reaffirmed as the heart of the business and craft of factual television. He knows, or should, of what cameras are capable, and what editing means, and, on the spot, he is almost certainly the only man who can persuade the subject concerned of the need for his co-operation, which is, of course, something the old-time reporter seldom had to worry about. He knows, better than anyone, too, that such co-operation does not mean collaboration, in the wartime sense of that word, which is what politi-cians and industrialists alike expect. And, he knows that he does not, any longer, have to measure objectivity by the stopwatch. Give him his measure of independence, and he ceases to be the voice either of doom or of omniscience. Commitment will take the place of nonchalance, and that might be the next and most important development in television, bigger than the newest lightweight cameras and soundpacks, or even than a world ring of satellites.

"My next point is that, much as we in the BBC enjoy the opportunities a second channel gives us for serving many minorities, in this field of factual television, of news and near-news, and information, political, scientific and technological, success must be measured in terms of majorities. You cannot be committed to a mass medium and then spend your time dodging

220

its implications, running away from size, excusing it because it is broad and coarse and unsubtle. Either you believe in it, or you might as well become editor of one of the smaller political weeklies.

"Lastly, I want to say this. If this book helps in any way to correct the quite extraordinary illusion which our American friends and colleagues seem to hold about their pre-eminence in factual television, it will be a splendid victory. They are really unbearably complacent, especially and surprisingly, I regret to say, in academic circles, about a comparatively minor contribution to what old John Grierson called the 'enrichment of observation', minor in the sense that it is neither as consistent, nor as widespread, nor as deep, nor commanding anything like the regular proportion of the audience as what we do over here in our genuinely competitive situation, which with all its faults does give us the best television in the world. And I have been to see. And I am going again. If I think differently when I come back, I shall be in time to put this right for the second edition of this book."

I intended to end my final chapter with Kenneth Adam's words, but I will risk two or three further sentences of my own. Television is a medium which draws on a wide range of existing techniques—most of them from the cinema, which is the only other medium to combine moving images with co-ordinated sound—and many of these techniques seem to the new recruit or to the layman to be complicated and terrifying. In fact, as Kenneth Adam implies, they are not so, and many of the best practitioners of factual television, on both sides of the camera, have come from the other areas of journalism and very quickly found their feet in the new atmosphere. For what really count are the attitude and the subject-matter and the committed enthusiasm of those who move into television because they believe it to be both important and exciting. If they believe this, then they will find that the techniques will follow, and frankly without much difficulty. If they do not believe this then they are in the wrong place and should practise some other trade.

INDEX

222

226

227